Integrated Series in Information Systems

Volume 23

Series Editors

Ramesh Sharda
Oklahoma State University, Stillwater, OK, USA

Stefan Voß
University of Hamburg, Hamburg, Germany

For other titles published in this series go to,
http://www.springer.com/series/6157

Hans Lehmann

The Dynamics of International Information Systems

Anatomy of a Grounded Theory Investigation

Springer

Hans Lehmann
School of Information
Management
Victoria University of Wellington
Wellington 6140
New Zealand
hans.lehmann@vuw.ac.nz

ISSN 1571-0270
ISBN 978-1-4419-5749-8 e-ISBN 978-1-4419-5750-4
DOI 10.1007/978-1-4419-5750-4
Springer New York Dordrecht Heidelberg London

Library of Congress Control Number: 2010921283

Printed on acid-free paper

Springer is part of Springer Science+Business Media (www.springer.com)

Preface

The serious difficulties facing the developer of international information systems (i.e. supporting business functions in different countries) are widely known and their propensity to catastrophic failure has been acknowledged among practitioners for quite some time. Despite the often pivotal importance that such systems generally have scholarly research in this field has been surprisingly sparse. Information technology applications with a global range and reach are still largely unstudied and under-explored. Subsequently there is a distinct dearth of theoretical frameworks for dealing with them.

After a career in information technology line management I have been involved with multinational enterprises and their information systems for over a decade as a consultant, working in Africa, the UK, continental Europe, North America and Australasia. It was on joining a university in the early nineties that I discovered the near-vacuum in this field of research. When I decided to make international information systems my field of research it became clear that fairly fundamental work needed to be done.

I started the project described further on more than 10 years ago. It turned out a fairly difficult, necessarily broad based and, eventually, longitudinal research. The final research results presented here are now about half a decade old – and on the cusp of being revisited, extended and updated. This follow-on research needs to investigate if (and how) the sea changes in technology experienced over that time have influenced the content of the theories developed – although most of them deal with organization and management more than with technology per se.

On the other hand, the research method I had to assemble to deal with the specifics of large, very different and dispersed organizational cases has proved to be a lasting benefit from this demanding project. And not just for me: ever since I first published about it at the turn of the millennium I had requests for tutorial-type seminars about the methodology for academic researchers at a considerable number of universities internationally. And recently a number of people suggested that a detailed report would be useful that set out the way this research project had progressed and that puts a strong emphasis on the adaptations to the Grounded Theory methodology and the derived practical method. This volume attempts to do this. Interested readers could be among

- scholars embarking on the study of large and complex technology cases;
- researchers who are tackling Grounded Theory on a larger scale for the first time; and
- anybody who is interested in the description of a fundamental research undertaking in the Grounded Theory tradition; from its foundations in the philosophy of science paradigms to the adaptation of the classic method for organizational cases and the practical details of the method; together with a diary of the conceptual journey, including the many blind alleys; and in witnessing the evolution of theory as it slowly emerges from the data.

To keep the volume readable the case story, analysis and theory chapters are of necessity abridged to focus on the essential elements of both data and analysis. A more detailed record of the case and the analysis is, however, provided on a companion website. Please contact[1] the author for access.

This research project uses a case analysis method in the grounded theory tradition in order to establish the theoretical foundations for a better understanding of the factors that influence the design, creation and implementation of international information systems.

Establishing theoretical foundations requires theory building research methods. The paucity of research into the nature and dynamics of international information systems means that there is an insufficient base from which to derive hypotheses for use with verification research approaches. Grounded theory was chosen because it does not require pre-formulated postulates.

However, traditional grounded theory was developed for homocentric applications in the social sciences. In this form it was not applicable to the study of technology use in organizational cases. These cases are a hybrid, shaped by the interplay of individual, social, organizational and technological entities. For this reason, the grounded theory approach was adapted to work with cases. The resultant two-step method preserves the grounded theory principles of joint coding and collection, constant comparison and theoretical sampling for additional data.

This adaptation of a method, originally developed for sociology, turned out to be a useful tool for generating theory in information systems research. This, together with the acknowledged paucity of theory in this field,[2] were the reasons for setting out this book in a way that can provide a demonstration of the method.

---

[1] Best via email under Hans.Lehmann@vuw.ac.nz

[2] Already two decades ago (in 1989) Bob Zmud, then Editor-in-Chief of MISQ, issued a call for more 'theory building' contributions to the journal to counterbalance the predominantly empirical, theory-testing character of the submissions received. In 2003 Ron Weber had to re-iterate this plea because there still had been 'much more… written about theory testing than theory building.'

Three cases were used in the study. The data included some 120 hours of intensive interviews, transcribed onto 1,200 pages and a further 2,500 pages in the more than 150 notes, memos and documents of supporting internal and external information.

The first case, a large land based production co-operative with a widespread global subsidiary network, yielded 13 core 'categories'.[3] They were richly interrelated and fell into two interacting domains. The contrasting next case, a Danish shipping line, added another 4 core categories. In addition to these 'primary' categories, the comparison of the cases led to the formulation of two derivative categories. The third case, again in contrast to the first two in a number of attributes, is a large, Switzerland based corporation in the freight forwarding industry. More 'primary' categories were added and a number of cause-and-effect relationships were refined.

After every case, the relationships between categories were formally subsumed into theoretical frameworks. After three cases the 3rd framework contained 25 major theorems, supported by some 102 theses and explanatory postulates. In a process of 'densification',[4] a final, substantive theory of the factors influencing IIS was formulated, consisting of 10 theorems and 23 supporting theses.

The theory that the research eventually yielded about some of the dynamics of international information systems explains their specific nature and architecture; what affects the way in which they are built; and why their users will accept or reject them.

The theory defines a *generic architecture, specific* for international information systems, consisting of two parts, namely a 'Central' part, containing shared systems, and 'Local' systems that are unique for each site. The systems configuration at each individual site is a mixture of 'Central' and 'Local' technology elements. *Synchronicity,* the degree to which systems require online, same-time use of identical data and information, determines what should be the 'Central' applications – and what can be left 'Local'. It further governs the configuration and technical architecture of the IIS.

What is under 'Central' control and what remains within 'Local' discretion can become an adversarial, often acrimonious and predominantly political issue. These antagonistic politics are acted out in an ever-present 'Force Field'. The two related variables that influence the intensity of the Force Field interactions are:

Utility of the system's functionality lowers the conflict potential all around;

using the IIS to increase central *Control* intensifies local management's resistance against invasion of their 'turf'.

The probability of *Acceptance* or *Rejection* of an international information system then depends on the net-balance of these opposing forces.

At a more sophisticated level, *User/IT Consensus Processes* are shown as effective instruments for neutering damaging faction politics. Furthermore, by

[3] Grounded Theory terminology for the abstracted concepts that interpret and explain the data.

[4] Grounded Theory terminology for the delimitation process to reduce the 'conceptual redundancy' of the theory; also known as 'Occam's razor'.

assembling all stakeholders they marshal and maximize the knowledge about the global operation that the IIS supports. This deep knowledge maximizes the *Utility* of the resulting system, whilst the consensus processes substitute any *Control* conflict with rational dialogue or amicable persuasion.

Most of the theory can be directly translated into a practical methodology for designing, building and implementing international information systems. Many parts of the theory, however, are still in an 'approximate' state and point to several future research projects, concerned with refining concepts, constructs and their relationships as well as further adapting and improving the extended grounded theory methodology. Funding is being obtained and planning has progressed to an advanced stage to launch a project that will use the same methodology, but aims to update and extend the reach of the conceptual constructs into a more comprehensive theory of the dynamics of international information systems.

Many people, in many ways, have helped me to carry out this research and write this book.

Brent Gallupe, of Queen's University in Kingston, Ontario, deserves the first vote of thanks. He encouraged me to begin this project – and has helped me with positive, focused and wise advice to continue and not give in to easy compromise when the going became difficult and momentum and enthusiasm waned. And not least, a sincere 'thank you' for inviting me to Kingston where I could start writing in earnest.

This by no means detracts from all the pastoral care and practical help I enjoyed from Justo Diaz, my local boss at Auckland University, New Zealand at the time. He allowed me to structure my varsity work such that I could set aside good chunks of time for the research – I could never have done it without that kindness. Thank you very much, Justo.

Neither of these professional acknowledgements, however, compares with the gratitude that I have for my children, for whom this project had become an object of wry resignation, as they often subsisted, for the last few years, on the border of serious paternal neglect. I will make it up to you, Peter and Anna, I promise.

The whole research, of course, would not be there save for the close on half a hundred men and women all over the globe who invited me into their business and technology, explained it to me and were instrumental for my understanding of 'what's really going on' with the information technology support for their complex enterprises. I have thanked them personally and individually over the course of the project.

Finally, very many thanks indeed for the generous support I received from Neil Levine and Matt Amboy from the Springer office in New York – I really needed that!

All that remains to be said now is that I hope you enjoy the book.

Wellington
Spring 2009

Hans Lehmann

Contents

List of Figures

List of Tables

Chapter 1
Introduction

The global information systems challenge appears to be more complex than commonly suggested. There are no easy and straightforward prescriptions for practitioners involved with global information systems.
M. J. Earl, 1996

Managing multinational companies represents one of the most difficult intellectual and administrative challenges. The sheer complexity of businesses, the competitive dynamics and internal interdepencies of various kinds challenge the very best.
C. K. Prahalad, 1987

This research should have been done at least 20 years ago. The pivotal importance of information technology as the key driver of business has not been seriously questioned since the dawn of minicomputers some 40 years ago. Conversely, the notion that globalization is the only key to survival in a rapidly shrinking world has been a hackneyed cliché for many businesses since the early 1980s. Yet the obvious logical fusion of these two truisms, the application of information technology throughout global operations, is still widely ignored by academics and largely misunderstood by practitioners. As a result, international information systems[1] projects over the last 20 years have often been downright disastrous. Research into why these applications are difficult and how they could be mastered should be of high priority, but is not.

[1] These will also be referred to as **IIS** throughout this book. Similarly, **IS** will be used for information systems in a generic sense; and **IT** for information technology.

H. Lehmann, *The Dynamics of International Information Systems*,
Integrated Series in Information Systems 23, DOI 10.1007/978-1-4419-5750-4_1,

The most pressing job in such a research undertaking – and the overarching purpose of this particular project – is the building of a basic, substantive theory of international information systems. This can then serve as a guiding framework for first understanding and then mastering them. This research attempts to achieve this by establishing a theoretical foundation that provides:

1. A substantiation of the specific nature and architecture of International Information Systems that distinguishes them from other distributed information systems; and
2. An understanding of the factors – and their interactions – that determine an IIS's character, shape and acceptance (or otherwise) by its users.

Three principle reasons lead to this research: First, even the sparse research efforts by the academic community have been sporadic and dispersed over many and disjointed topics – leaving the field devoid of a firm theoretical base and framework from which to advise practitioners and direct further applied research;

Second, the author, over the course of more than a decade, has had in-depth personal, practical experience of consulting to multinational companies on the design and implementation of international information systems;

Finally, the inadequacy and scarcity of overarching conceptual frameworks in this field meant that qualitative and inductive theory creation methods seem intuitively a good approach and strategy. Theory building research requires a fundamentally inductive and method. The Grounded Theory method, an approach developed for domains where few prior theories exist, had been specifically designed to 'discover' social theory from empirical data. Traditionally used in human-centered research, it focused predominantly on individual interviews and observation data. Adapting this to work with large case histories and technical as well as sociological, organizational and political issues posed an interesting methodological challenge.

1.1 A Brief History of IIS

In the late 1970s a considerable number of multi-national companies began to extend their information systems across the globe. It soon became apparent that the traditional systems development approaches did not work well with systems for use in different countries. Another obvious reason was that by definition these 'global' systems were big projects.

Of these large projects as many as 80% (according to Jones, 1994, p. 29) fail because of 'creeping user requirements', which change at the rate of 1% a month (ibid.) in domestic systems. In a multinational company this rate of change can accelerate dramatically, depending on the number of subsidiaries involved and the degree of their autonomy. Unless they are fully independent from their home office, the rate of change will not be the full 1% per month, but they still all change at the same time. In this way a global information system with standard functionality for, say, ten semi-autonomous subsidiaries will obsolete 60%[2] of its functionality within a year. Barclays Bank learned this in the early 1980s when they tried to implement[3] a common account processing and financial accounting system for their small international subsidiaries. The Barclays International Account Systems (BIAS) never rose above an infinite series of re-specifications and modifications. The project was abandoned after 5 years of effort.[4]

Experiences like these lead to a first realization that international information systems are not just another class of 'large systems', but are different in essence. Buss (1982) established this basic fact in a seminal article in the Harvard Business Review. At the same time Keen et al. (1982), building on practical work, contributed to the discussion by floating the notion of 'common' (i.e. identical) versus 'local' (i.e. divergent) systems components in such global systems. This distinction proved to be a very useful construct for setting out the basic applications and technology architecture for developing international information systems during the 1980s.[5]

However, throughout the 1980s there was only a thin trickle of learned research into International Information Systems, concentrating in the main on the external influences acting on such global systems. By contrast, the accelerating globalization of business during the late 1970s and during the 1980s had sparked major waves of academic research in International Business. It was from this side that Deans (1994) at Thunderbird[6] started to look at the information technology issues associated with global business. It was also at Thunderbird, during a conference of the *Academy of International Business*, that the discussion of an exploratory paper (Lehmann, 1995) provided the final encouragement to undertake a major research project in this field.

KPMG (1993) had found that some 80% of a large sample of European international information systems projects were abandoned or remained uncompleted for reasons of inadequate management of the development process. Roche's (1992a) analysis that the crucial issues hampering global systems are firmly rooted within the organization, further emphasized the practical importance of the internal aspects of architecture, design and user-acceptance of these systems. This encouraged fixing the research focus on how and where the intrinsic 'nature' of such systems is different and what lessons that may hold for building them.

---

[2] If semi-autonomy translates into, say, 0.5% new requirements, then for 10 sites per month this results (×12) in 60% change at the end of a year – although some of the changed functionalities may well be similar.

[3] The author was involved in this project in South Africa and Zimbabwe in 1980–1982.

[4] Barclays nevertheless repeated this approach, resulting in the spectacular failure of their Barclays International merchant banking systems project, which contributed to their being forced to merge with de Zoete Wedd, a large Dutch merchant bank.

[5] Three such projects are described and analyzed in Lehmann (1994b).

[6] The American Graduate School of International Management, Phoenix, AZ.

1.2 Frameworks in the Literature

The literature was not much help in refining the research object. First attempts at establishing a framework (such as King et al., 1992 and Alavi et al., 1992a, b) were firstly predominantly focused on external factors such as government/firm interactions. Secondly, they were often too general (e.g. focusing on strategic congruence) to be of much use for addressing practical, internal development issues. To illustrate this, the focus of this research occupies only a very small part of a basic dimension of the King et al. (1992) framework. Their framework comprises two domains:

1. 'Primary' interactions occur between firms and their subsidiaries;
2. 'Secondary' domain transactions cover the interaction between them and their home and foreign governments, with other firms and finally between all of those and intergovernmental organizations.

The factors critical for the design of an international information system form, however, just a small subset of systems, involved predominantly in 'intra-corporate' applications. This is shown in Figure 1.1 below.

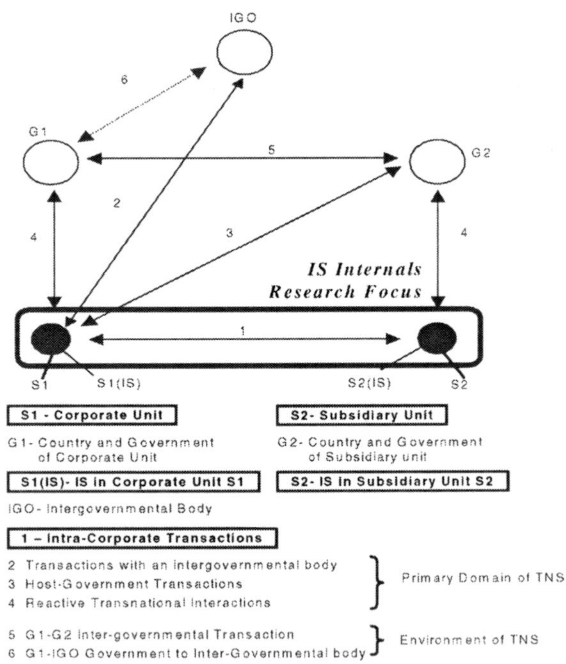

Figure 1.1. Focus of this research (shown in *bold*) within the King and Sethi (1992) framework

One main reason for the diffuse broadness of these first frameworks turned out to be the insufficient definition of these 'global' systems. The label of 'transnational' systems was attached to most systems in use by multinational companies or simply any system that was accessed and used across national borders. In this way, the definition included classes of systems which are logically not of a 'global' nature altogether – which, in turn contributed to the generality of the frameworks. They are:

- Information systems that are *accessed* globally, such as airline reservation systems, multi-country networks of automated teller machines, payment-clearing systems between financial institutions, and similar supra-national information technology applications. These are essentially centralized, 'domestic' information systems. Their local content varies with the scope of the access functionality but is usually contained in discrete front-end adaptations, the software equivalent of providing for various input/output devices.
- Information systems which support different business *activities*, e.g. in multi-divisional companies; the information systems of the banking division and the insurance division of a financial multinational will be different by definition. Where divisions are in different countries, but their operations do not cross borders, their information systems may be defined as 'multi-domestic systems', i.e. each self-contained in its own local market.
- Similarly, systems supporting different business *functions* (such as Sales, Manufacturing, etc.) are different for each function; and they, too, will be supported by 'multi-domestic' systems' unless the *function* straddles more than one country.

However, where divisions or functional units span more than one country, then their 'domestic' systems needs to adapt to the divergent requirements of multiple, different locations. Such systems are the 'International Information Systems' that form the object of this research. They are defined as

> distributed information systems which support similar *business activities* or *business functions* of *one firm* in highly diverse environments commonly found *across country boundaries*.

A classification of firm's international operations along the dimensions of 'business focus' (i.e. the degree of heterogeneity in its activities) and 'environmental diversity[7]' (of their operating locations) may help to sharpen the definition.

High 'Business Focus' characterizes firms that concentrate on single, or closely related, business activities. Examples are car rental firms, international banks, single product-line manufacturers and international franchises. Low business focus is present in diversified conglomerates with many activities. Examples are the large Japanese and American multinationals. Low 'Environmental Diversity' would typically be encountered within one country and high diversity across countries with different business cultures. Figure 1.2 below illustrates this classification.

[7] This includes differences such as business practices, cultural influences, political regimes, language(s), script and other diversity indicators.

The object of the research into 'International Information Systems' are thus the systems used by firms, divisions or other business units who fall into the class of 'International Operator', i.e. where a single set of related business activities is carried out in different countries – and where therefore the clearest manifestation of issues specific to international information systems can be expected.

There is no generally accepted term for the application of information systems and technology across borders in the literature. Often 'global' is used (e.g. by Ives et al., 1991), but 'transnational', first presented formally by Keohane et al. (1972) is also in general use (e.g. by King et al., 1992, 1993). Whilst 'global' invites associations of 'uniform everywhere', 'transnational' is open to confusion with the precise use of the term by Bartlett and Goshal (1989) for describing one specific style of a firm's operation in more than one country.

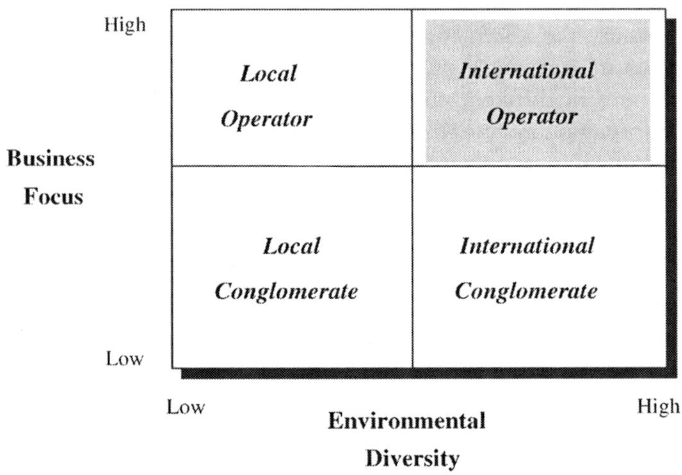

Figure 1.2. Classification of firms by business focus and diversity of their operating environment

It furthermore seems to be favored for describing single-site systems with global access (such as the cases reported by Cavaye et al., 1998). The term 'international' has also been used by Bartlett and Ghoshal, but in a more general sense, covering a wider variety of enterprises. For this reason, the term 'International Information System' (IIS) is used for the systems investigated in this research.

1.3 Choice of the Research Method

With a diffuse body of literature and frameworks too large to be of immediate operational use, qualitative research methodologies were the preferred choice from the outset. Moreover, the research would have to embrace organizational as well as technical issues and therefore needed to focus on a small number of broadly based instances rather than a large number of small units of analysis. For this reason case research seemed to be more appropriate than survey techniques.

Classical case research (as set out by Yin, 1989), is primarily oriented towards testing of hypotheses, which, in turn, are usually derived from previous theoretical propositions. Eisenhardt's seminal paper (1989) on building theory from cases extends this to cases where the researcher has no preconceived ideas and thus starts with a 'clean slate'. Alas, no satisfactory method is provided on how not to 'dirty' the slate with the inevitable bias any researcher will always bring with him. Given this researcher's 12 years of practical experience with international information systems, such a bias could be expected to be a serious factor.

Grounded Theory, developed by Glaser et al. (1967) for sociological research, on the other hand, provides a method for not only avoiding this bias, but indirectly turning it into an advantage. The dictate of developing any categories through coding straight from the elementary data forces the researcher to keep an open mind. It also rigorously grounds in fact any initial conceptualizations that are made. From then on, however, the researchers previous experience is called upon to first empower the ideation of relationships and linkages. Secondly, experience then expedites the practical reification of concepts and relationships into theories which 'work'.

Grounded Theory had been used in sociology since the 1970s and had found its way into business and information systems research by the late 1980s. Glaser et al. (1967) developed it originally to work with people, in individual interviews and micro-observations, which could be extended and added to freely. Strauss & Corbin (1990) heavily codified and procedurised it for precisely such studies. The method was thus not immediately useful for application to case stories, where organizational and political – i.e. 'people-centric – phenomena interact with technology issues.

However, the basic principles of grounding concepts in fact and refining theories with focused additional data (using theoretical sampling), seemed to be well capable of being actualized for research involving cases. The methodology set out by Glaser et al. (1967) looked flexible enough to lend itself to adaptation, whereas Strauss & Corbin's more structured prescriptions did not seem readily conducive for extension to cases – a fact at the centre of Glaser's (1992) criticism of their regimen. The method used in the research project was thus based on Glaser et al.'s (1967) approach to the discovery of Grounded Theory.

1.4 Structure of the Book

The book is structured as follows:

- Next, the literature on international information systems is reviewed; then the

- Research problem is set out and the research questions are spelt out; thereafter the
- Methodology for the research is set out in two sections: one to develop the methodology; and the second to then derive from this the practical method with which the research was conducted. In order to provide an 'anatomy'[8] of the research process, the two sections start from a deeper foundation and elaborate more fundamental considerations than may be usual in the average research project;
- In the main part, the three cases are described, followed by an analysis of their findings – again describing in greater detail than usual the conceptual abstraction process inherent in the Grounded Theory method. After the first case a First Theoretical Framework is defined. After each of the following cases, the framework is updated, theorems are added and modified. The 1st, 2nd and 3rd Theoretical Frameworks provide an illustration how the theory developed, how core categories were identified, extended or amalgamated with others and how relationships between them were discovered and refined with each step;
- The 3rd Theoretical Framework is then subjected to a process of delimitation to densify the – by then – considerable body of theorems, theses and postulates into its most parsimonious form. This was then shaped into an final Substantive Theory of International Information Systems;
- Discussion of the theory and its implications for practice and research closes the book.

To provide an even deeper level of detail, the original, extended case stories as well as the theoretical and conceptual workings for each case are set out in a series of web pages at a companion Website. Please contact[9] the author for access.

---

[8] Defined as the 'artificial separation of the parts of an organized body in order to discover their structure'.

[9] Best via email under Hans.Lehmann@vuw.ac.nz

Chapter 2
International Information Systems in the Literature

The following sections first put the research literature on international information systems in the wider context of information systems research in general. The second part will discuss the development of international information systems research literature and set out the 'state-of-the-art' at the end of 1994, when this research project was started. An overview of the literature since then concludes this review.

2.1 Scope and Depth of the Research into International Information Systems

International information systems are still a minority interest in the wider field of information systems research. The ABI/INFORM database lists 32,919 papers (with 'information systems' as a keyword) for the period from the beginning of 1985 to the end of 2005. For the same time period, keywords to do with international information systems occur in 234[1] papers, i.e. in less than 1%. By contrast, a traditional sub-area of information systems research such as Decision Support Systems has 3,607 listings in the last 15 years, or 11% of all IS papers. When the current research was started towards the end of 1994, there were a total of 69 papers listed for the 10-year period 1985–1994 – only 14 of them in '1st Tier' journals.[2] Interest then seems to have increased and over the next 5 years 165

[1] This compares well with Gallupe et al. (1999) who found 314 articles between 1990 and 1998, albeit in the much wider field of 'information management', i.e. in a wider spectrum of journals.

[2] These are defined as: *MIS Quarterly, Information Systems Research, Communications of the ACM* (research articles only), *Journal of Management Information Systems, Decision Sciences, IEEE Transactions on Communications* and *Software Engineering,* and *Management Science*.

H. Lehmann, *The Dynamics of International Information Systems*,
Integrated Series in Information Systems 23, DOI 10.1007/978-1-4419-5750-4_2,

papers were produced – 20 of them 1st Tier. The foundation of two journals for the field (in 1993 and 1998[3]) was indicative of this upturn in attraction.

However, on closer inspection, some of these papers do not qualify as global information technology research, which Palvia (1998, p. 4) defines as being concerned with information systems that are global in scope; operate in different cultures; and offer unique insights in comparison to a uni-cultural environment. About one in four of the 234 papers are studies about 'IS/T in another country…offering no unique insights…' and just because they are 'conducted in a country other than [the researcher's] own does not make it automatically global information technology research'(ibid.).[4]

On the other hand, one in ten papers covers aspects of the nature of international information systems, such as their structure and design, and one paper attempts to set out a framework for their research.

The remaining papers cover a considerable diversity of subjects. Information Technology in developing countries and cases of specific technology applications dominate the literature, as do cross-cultural studies and surveys (of, e.g. key issues in IS/T management) in more than one country. Nineteen further categories formed a large group of 'Other' research topics.

2.2 Research into International Information System Until 1994

A first attempt at identifying transnational IS issues was developed by Mandell et al. (1979) in a survey of European multinationals. They suggested that linkages between parent and subsidiaries could be divided into four types: organizational, data, technology, and communications. Each linkage presents a unique set of issues and problems. Early research into international information systems, however, seemed to focus mainly on issues of trans-border data flows, i.e. 'movements of machine readable data across national boundaries' (Sauvant, 1986). This area (summarized by Hamelink, 1984) was of increasing concern, firstly because of privacy mandates (Maisonrouge, 1981), but increasingly because regulation of trans-border data flows and international communication 'may make or break companies doing business multinationally during the next decade' (Moore, 1984, p. 30).

1982 saw two landmark publications: one was the first case history of an enterprise-wide[5] information system to be implemented in 40 banks globally. In it, Keen et al. (1982) first identified the common/local structure of a global system. The other paper, by Buss (1982), was the first to offer a comprehensive

[3] Journal of Global Information Management and Journal of Global Information Technology Management, respectively.

[4] Gallupe et al (1999) found an even higher percentage: 46.2%, of papers had 'Single Country' studies as their research theme.

[5] Kneitel's (1980) case about Du Pont's polymer sales system covers one application only.

discourse on the managerial and organizational aspects of international information systems. He underscored the need for IS planning and noted the lack of any planning frameworks. He observed that multinationals differ greatly from domestic firms in the arrangement of hardware and software and in the role of their corporate IS. Further, he argued that 'this diversity of approaches is confusing and there are few models to follow.' He recommended that multinationals should plan their IS by creating the right organizational framework and by defining the roles of key players.

Such a comprehensive planning framework was suggested by Selig (1982) who compared it with the actual planning practices of 25 US multinationals and found that there were significant differences in structure and detail. He concluded that the differences were attributable to contingency factors such as market and industry diversity and corporate roles.

It then took until 1989 before such 'contingency factors' were identified. Thompson et al. (1989), building on the work of Prahalad et al. (1987) and Bartlett et al. (1989) about business strategy of multinationals, suggested that two factors – degree of market integration and degree of home country rule – be used to categorize firms into one of four globalization stages, with salient IS management concerns for each stage. Reck (1989) took this a step further. Recognizing three fundamental operating strategies for multinational corporations – which he dubbed 'imperialistic, multidomestic, and global' – he posited that they also define IS issues such as technology architecture, data architecture, and communication architecture.

The notion that strategies could influence the information technology supporting them led a number of researchers to look more closely at those 'drivers' for global information systems. Applegate et al. (1996) and Ehrlich (1989) link the business reasons for global expansion to the nature of information technology employed. Ives et al. (1991) defined a set of ten 'business drivers for global information technology'. Whereas most of those are operations oriented, Butler Cox (1991) and Neo (1991) also found the marketing dimension as a significant factor in shaping global information technology. From a more technical angle, Hsu et al. (1991) identified the need to integrate data more stringently across 'heterogeneous, distributed environments' and Vinea (1992) developed an outline of the necessary software and architectures to achieve that.

Uniting most of this early research into global information technology was Palvia's seminal edition of *Global Issues of Information Technology Management* in 1992. In addition to topics on technology diffusion in developing countries and studies of specific industries and applications, for the first time a sizeable section was devoted to issues of managing global information technology and organizing for it. Keen (1992) set out strategic planning issues and Roche (1992b) summarized the lessons learned from seven cases about the development of international information systems. Furthermore, both Sethi et al. (1993) and King et al. (1992) attempted to establish a framework for international information systems, the former addressing the firm-internal environment and the latter also including the external influences on the international firm.

Two years later, Deans et al. (1994) edited *Global Information Systems and Technology: Focus on the Organization and its Functional Areas.* Concentrating on application systems issues, this germinal anthology brought together research from other disciplines, predominantly International Business.

Information systems research in the field, meanwhile, began to concentrate on the structure and architecture of IIS and how these fit with the overall organization of the multinational firm. Jarvenpaa et al. (1993) found distinct differences in the way firms organize their information technology – and that over half of the 109 firms investigated showed significant inconsistencies between the way information technology is structured and the organization of the firm itself. Cummings et al. (1994), in a survey of 67 subsidiaries of US firms in the oil and gas industry confirms a perceived complexity in the relationships between information systems, organizational structure and the environment.

Earl (1989) defined the architecture of an information system as 'the technology framework which guides the organization in satisfying business and management information systems needs'. To this, Keen (1991) and Weill (1992) and Weill et al. (1994) added the concepts of 'reach', i.e. the penetration of global sites, and 'range', i.e. how many of the operations are supported by an 'infrastructure', mostly of common technology.

A number of researchers have compared the architecture of international systems with the business strategy of the international firms that use them, using classifications developed by Prahalad et al. (1987) and Bartlett et al. (1989). Both classify the multinational's business strategy along two dimensions of global control versus local autonomy, as Figure 2.1 shows below.

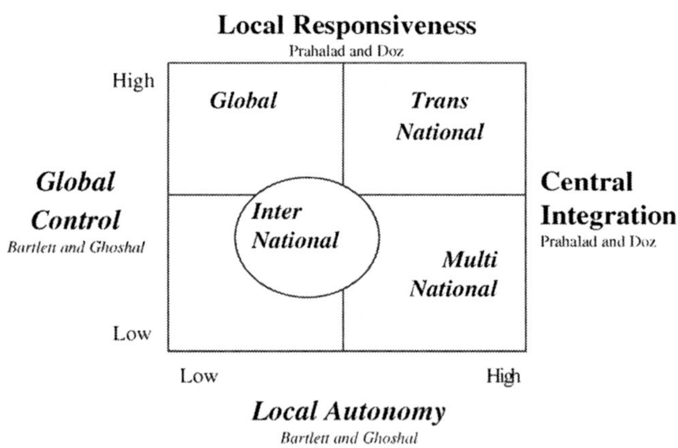

Figure 2.1 Global business strategies of multinational firms: the *Bartlett* and *Ghoshal* and Prahalad and Doz's integration-responsiveness models

Bartlett and Ghoshal's model, which integrates both global business strategy and organizational forces, has proved to be the most often selected framework by researchers into the linkage between international information systems' architectures and the strategic stance a multinational firm takes. Its four strategy archetypes are:

The '*global*' business strategy shows a high degree of global control at the expense of local autonomy;

Juxtaposed to this is the '*multinational*' strategy with little global guidance and high local control;

'*Transnational*' organizations balance tight global control in certain aspects with a policy of vigorously fostering local autonomy, particularly for the diffusion of innovation. These firms 'think global and act local' (Bartlett and Goshal, 1989). This strategy is considered optimal for many multinational corporations;

Defined as an interim, or transitory stage, the 'international' firm shows considerable variety between global and local control, often with neither control modus dominant.

Butler Cox (1991), furthermore, put a developmental perspective on the Bartlett–Ghoshal framework. While they use a different terminology, companies seem to become active internationally first as 'Exporter' of their goods or services – usually applying a '*Global*' [6] business strategy. Increased activity in any one location encourages autonomy for local operations, taking on the role of 'National Adapter', similar to the '*Multinational*' classification. In the next phase this degree of autonomy is counterbalanced by some global control as 'Central Co-ordinator', i.e. an '*International*' firm. Finally, as global operations mature, firms move towards a status of 'Global Co-ordinator' (equivalent to the '*Transnational*'). This migration does not necessarily follow a set pattern of clear stages, nor does it move synchronously in all locations, or with all products, at the same pace. Figure 2.2 below shows this migration.

Butler Cox (1991) also developed a model of IIS where there is a direct, one-to-one relationship between Bartlett and Ghoshal's global business strategies and these systems architectures. They distinguish between:

'Centralized' systems;
'Replicated', i.e. multiple copies of one central system;
'Autonomous', local systems;
'Integrated' systems, developed at local and central sites.

Other researchers propose similar relationships between information systems structure and global business strategy. Konsynski et al. (1993) describe (in the same sequence as above) 'centralized', 'inter-organizational', 'decentralized' and 'integrated' architectures. Sankar et al. (1993) define three global information architectures by the way their elements are linked, namely:

Integrated (separate elements, logically connected);
Centralized (together and connected);

---

[6] Italics denote the Bartlett & Goshal classification.

Decentralized (separate and disconnected).

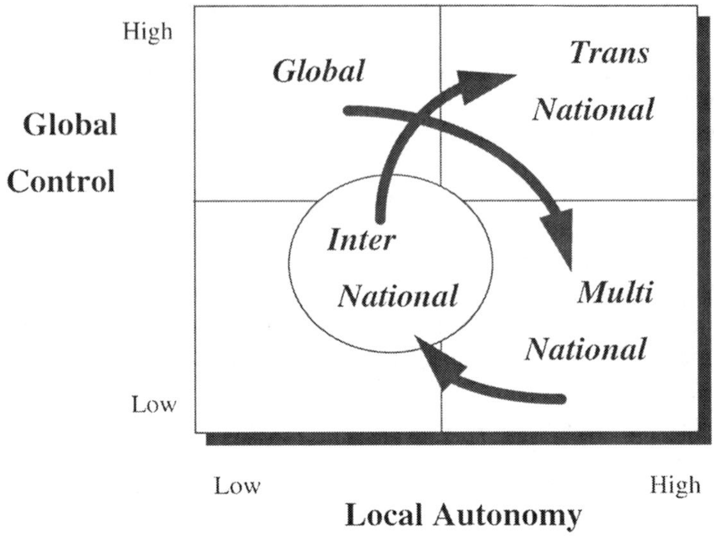

Figure 2.2. Migration through global business strategies

Jarvenpaa et al. (1994), in a study of organizational fit and flexibility in international information systems describe a framework of 'Global Information Technology Configuration' that also maps directly onto the Bartlett Ghoshal typology. That study is also supported by a series of previous case studies (Ives et al., 1991, 1992, 1994).

Gibson (1994) used statistical analysis (factor analysis, etc.) to arrive at seven-element definition of information technology architectures. Investigating them in the context of multinational companies, he found that they grouped into four distinct patterns as generic architectures, which, again, corresponded to Bartlett & Ghoshal's categories. Table 2.1 summarizes the results from the five studies:

Table 2.1. Comparison of architecture styles/configurations identified in the literature

Bartlett & Ghoshal	Butler Cox	Kosynski & Karimi	Sankar et al.	Ives & Jarvenpaa	Gibson
Global	Centralized	Centralization	Centralized	Headquarter driven	Centralized
Multi-national	Autonomous	De-centralization	De-centralized	Independent	De-centralized
Inter-national	Replicated	Inter-organizational	(Undefined)	Intellectual Synergy	Co-ordinated
Trans-national	Integrated	Integrated	Integrated	Integrated	Integrated

It seems that just as the 'international' business strategy is an intermediary stage, so are the corresponding global information technology configurations. If these replicated/inter-organizational/intellectually-synergized and co-ordinated structures are regarded as embryonic 'integrated' architectures, then just three generic architectures (*centralized, decentralized* and *integrated*) could suffice, as Figure 2.3 below shows.

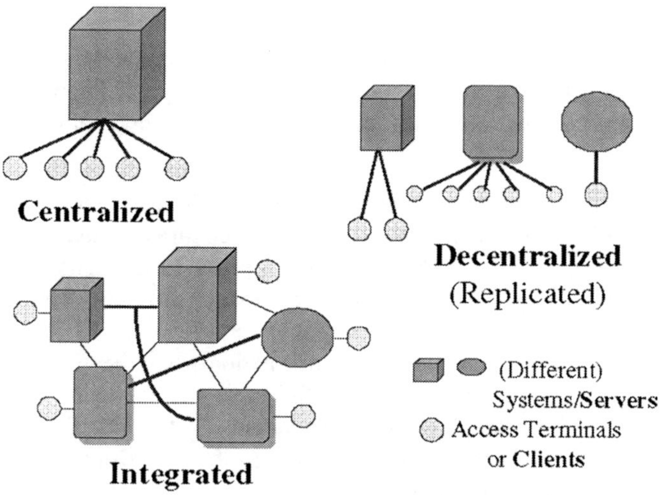

Figure 2.3. The three generic architectures of international information systems

Gordon (1994) analyzed the difficulties with centralized and globally standardized international information systems with a specific focus on telecommunications. The role of decentralized systems and the nature of the 'integrated' structure/architecture in an international context, however, had not yet been an object of rigorous empirical study.

By the end of 1994 international information systems research was well into what Palvia (1998) termed the 'first generation' of global information technology research. He characterizes the research in this phase as predominantly

- Descriptive studies, sharpening the understanding that international information systems are different from domestic systems, and perhaps significantly so;
- Exploratory studies, where first conjectural theses about the nature of these global/international information systems were formed, the major one being the connection between Global Business Strategy and the structure/architecture of the international information systems supporting them; research was, however, still mainly;
- Opportunistic, because of an absence of guiding frameworks that were specific enough to be useful: the first ones developed by then were – by necessity – either very broad [Deans et al.'s. (1994) embraced all of MIS research, just as

King et al.'s (1992) incorporated all of the multinational firm's global external environment] or too narrowly focused on just one aspect of global information technology, such as Ein-Dor et al. (1993) and Nelson et al. (1992) who concentrated solely on cross-cultural issues.

2.3 Relevant Research Since 1994

Following the establishment of a number of conjectures, a number of researchers set about trying to verify some of them. Significant examples concerning the nature, structure or architecture of international information systems are:

- Tractinsky et al. (1996), using Q-methodology (33 items on 18 project managers of multinational firms), confirmed empirically that a global context contributes significant variability and complexity to IS design and established that global systems need a design approach different from other large, distributed systems;
- Grover et al. (1996) found no such confirmation when they tried to validate the previously posited link between global business strategy and architecture of the global IS. Their data (from 344 respondents in the US, France and Korea) supported only minimal consistency between the organization of firms and the configuration of their information systems;
- Similarly, Burn et al. (1996) found that the concept of alignment or 'fit' between organizational and technology management structure does not work well in a global firm. Their results showed that problems with global information technology stem predominantly from 'social' issues – whereas information systems management is often aligned along technical lines.

1996 also saw Palvia et al. issue a follow-on collection of research papers, *Global Information Technology and Systems Management – Key issues and Trends*. Building on the previous anthology's foundations, this collection staked out specific concerns such as the technology environment, issues of national infrastructure, technology architectures and themes of systems planning, development and management. Of specific interest is Roche's (1996) analysis of the internet's likely impact on global information technology – one of the first acknowledgement of border-less electronic commerce. In the same spirit of more concrete, predictive, research, Targowski (1996) provided a detailed analysis of the technology infrastructure for global systems. Deans et al. (1996) put together the first textbook on international information systems for use by post-graduate students of International Business.

Detailed issues of international information systems design were taken up by Simon (1996) with the introduction of 'control' versus 'co-ordination' as determinants for the centre-subsidiary division in the configuration of information systems. His work builds on foundations already laid by Palvia's (1995) distinction of a global versus a domestic dimension. This topic had also been addressed by Apte et al. (1995), who re-affirmed that global systems have a local and a global component, corresponding to the dis-aggregation of the underlying information services of the multinational firm. Nelson (1996), further underscoring the distinction of global/international information systems, established a comprehensive set of quality dimensions for global information systems.

Christmann (1998) and van den Berg et al. (1999) carried on the emergent tradition of research into the development of international information systems. The former emphasizes the importance of developing a vision, specific for global information technology. Van den Berg et al., investigating four systems in operation across European borders, concluded that the key issues with such systems are with people, not with technology; the design and implementation, not the actual building, are the danger points in their development; and internal, political issues are of greater import in the life-cycle of their creation than external, cultural issues.

Three important frameworks were created:

- Gallupe et al. (1999) analyzed the research literature on information management over the last 10 years and distilled a comprehensive framework and taxonomy for research in this field. This now provides a detailed and practical guide for selecting and classifying areas of research;
- King et al. (1999) revisited their 1992 framework and in a large research project (150 multinational firms from 25 industries, represented in 20 countries) established an empirical base for an authoritative model of the organization of transnational systems. Their model confirms a link between the firm's organization and the configuration of its global technology – but they also found the relationship to be of considerably higher complexity than postulated in previous research;
- In a similar vein, Peppard (1999) extended the two domains (business organization and information systems architecture) to propose a higher level of sophistication for models of the interaction between business and information technology in the multinational firm.

In the last 10 years, research into international information systems has become a more accepted branch of IS research. This is visible in the quantity – and often the quality – of publications. There are also a larger number of discussion forums for researchers in this field: a number of first tier conferences now have tracks dealing with global information technology. 'Informatics in Multinational Enterprises' is the focus of the Working Group 8.7 within the International Federation of Information Processing (IFIP). The group holds regular working conferences in conjunction with the International Conference on Information Systems (ICIS). Last, but not least, popular undergraduate textbooks on information systems, such as Laudon et al. (1995) and O'Brien (editions since 1998), now contain chapters on international information systems.

Chapter 3
Research Problem and Research Questions

Whilst scholarly research has concentrated on the wider issues, within the practitioner community there was a widespread consensus emerging that international systems are a not only a major element of any global business strategy but also a major, and potentially disastrous, stumbling block for global operators. By 1994, a considerable body of – mostly anecdotal – evidence[1] for the difficulties with these systems had been assembled in the practitioners' literature. A selection of this is presented below.

As early as 1980, Kelley had observed that when firms install information systems overseas, they encounter problems such as lack of appropriately qualified systems and support engineers, difficulty in obtaining emergency service, poor quality communications equipment, and government bureaucracy. Keen et al. (1982) added that apart from globally common functionality, such international information systems also have a 'local' part that can be the key to the system's success. The fact that some 10 years later only 8% of a large sample of European multinational companies had managed to implement international systems satisfactorily (KPMG, 1993) indicates the seriousness of the difficulties encountered. The commonly acknowledged issues seemed to fall into two categories, namely technology problems and cultural diversity.

The technical problems with international information systems seemed to affect all functional areas of the traditional systems management and development framework, as the following examples show:

- Failure to link information technology and business strategy (Popper, 1990; LaPlante, 1991) in the multinational firm;
- Unsuitable development methods (Passino, 1990; Popper, 1990; LaPlante, 1991);

[1] Most of the 'evidence' is now contained as the (often historical) international cases in anthologies and monographs on large information systems failure, i.e. Glass (1992, 1998), Flowers (1996), Yourdon (1997), Collins et al. (1999).

H. Lehmann, *The Dynamics of International Information Systems*,
Integrated Series in Information Systems 23, DOI 10.1007/978-1-4419-5750-4_3,

- Technical complexities, often introduced by adverse legal aspects, e.g. with telecommunications (LaPlante, 1991; Kobielus, 1992);
- Hardware incompatibility and failure to establish interconnectivity (LaPlante, 1991);
- Lack of and/or incongruence of technology standards (Palframan, 1991);

However, the diversity bedeviling the technical aspects of IIS was matched by an array of differences in the way the international users carried out their business – often rendering large tracts of global systems useless. The assumption that international business is just a replication of domestic business, had been – formally – refuted for general business by Doz as early as 1980. Buss (1982) was the first to show that this assumption is also wrong for information systems. By 1994 a number of studies had identified the significance of such cultural issues. Robey et al. (1989), Goodman et al. (1992) and Heitzman (1990) found steep difficulties in implementing systems across[2] cultural divides. Saraswat et al. (1991), in a wide-ranging analysis of multinational's information technology deployment in developing countries confirmed that serious issues were equally caused by developmental divergence. Barsoux (1992) showed that an equally significant differential exists between styles and roles of information technology management across the nations of Western Europe.

At the start of the research project in 1994, recognition was taking hold among practitioners that, because of their diverse environments, international information systems were especially difficult. Invariably large, they were exceedingly expensive, complex to build, onerous to install and had a strong tendency to end up less than successful. Risk-reducing insights and suggested remedies were few, limited and based on anecdotal evidence from isolated experiences.

Academic research, on the other hand, was sparse and mostly focused on the analysis and taxonomy of the external conditions surrounding international information systems. By implication, academics still regarded them as no different from any domestic, large and distributed systems.

This dichotomy is the nucleus of the problem this research is setting out to address. On the one side are the practitioners' significant difficulties with international information systems, with only ad-hoc remedies to guide them. Academia, on the other hand, had carried out some research, but very little of an applied nature, and none of it expressly aimed at finding fundamental, systemic solutions to the problem.

As pointed out in Chapter 2, an underlying cause for this fragmentation is the lack of a theoretical framework into which research could be integrated. Such a framework would firstly need to contain a description and blueprint for the environment and structure specific to IIS – to distinguish them from other large-scale systems. Furthermore, a compendium of the factors that determine an IIS, and the relationships between them, would need to be established. This could then

[2] Latin America, South East Asia and the Middle East, respectively.

provide a foundation from which to develop the depth of understanding required to set out ways in which the difficulties with IIS could be overcome.

The research problem thus consists of two parts. Firstly, the generic nature of international information systems needs to be clarified:

1. What is specific about the nature, structure and characteristics of International Information Systems?

The second part is concerned with the implications for the way in which international information systems are designed, built and installed:

1. What is the nature and interaction of the specific factors that shape an international information system such that it is acceptable to its users?

Inability to cope with diversity is often caused by the rigidity of the structure and functionality of a proposed IIS. This rigidity is a main reason for failure – either political or technical, and often both. Finding a structure that can cope with a wide spectrum of environments, i.e. the answers to question 1, could significantly contribute to eliminating this failure factor. Answers to question 1 have a dual purpose: they firstly establish the causes and determinants for those structural/functional differences. This knowledge would enable the creation of designs that minimize conflict with the IIS's multifarious environments. Secondly, understanding the factors' interaction would permit the derivation of specific approaches and/or methods to build – and subsequently install – international information systems more effectively.

Chapter 4
Research Methodology

In this chapter, an appropriate approach and methodology for in the research project is developed. How the methodology is then translated into an operational investigation procedure is set out in the next chapter.

Because of the lack of a sufficient theoretical foundation for applied research in the IIS field, it seemed prudent to firstly derive an appropriate methodology by deduction from first principles, using the nature and characteristics of the research questions as a guide. Next, the nature of the theory to be built is examined and the origin of the theory building process is clarified. Finally, criteria for the goodness of such a theory are established.

4.1 Assembling the Research Approach

There are three fundamental characteristics of the research project:

1. The main object of the study is 'information systems'. A *hybrid* of human, social and technical research objects, they exist as co-operative conglomerations of hardware, software, data, processes and people (Kroenke et al., 1994);
2. The research objects, i.e. the 'nature', 'attributes', 'factors' and 'interactions' are likely to be abstract, broad and conceptual. They do not lend themselves easily to measurable definitions in quantitative terms. For this reason, the mode of enquiry will need to be a *qualitative* one.
3. Research is often based on knowledge gained from previous investigations and builds on the theoretical constructs distilled from it. In the case of international information systems, however, the body of research is narrow, mostly conjectural and often weak in terms of detailed predictive power. This limits its use for the formulation and subsequent verification of hypotheses. IIS research is therefore more likely to be concerned with *building new theory* rather than deductively extending old ones.

H. Lehmann, *The Dynamics of International Information Systems*,
Integrated Series in Information Systems 23, DOI 10.1007/978-1-4419-5750-4_4,

Compared with the quantitative research field, qualitative research methods are relatively new in information systems research and the discussion about their validity is still lively with respect to a number of issues. However, a wide area of qualitative research methodology has been in use in the social sciences now for some 60 years. Its validity has been firmly established and a reliable canon of good practice has been developed.

The 'hybrid' nature of the research object together with the dearth of theoretical guidance from the literature means that there are no ready-made, suitably tried-and-tested approaches and methods available. This makes it necessary that a new methodology for this study needs to be developed or – preferably – adapted from an existing one. Denzin et al. (1994) set out a five-step process of structuring qualitative research. This stepwise definition process has been selected for determining the most appropriate research method for this study because it begins to construct a methodology from its philosophy of science fundamentals and finishes with the details of data collection and findings interpretation. This comprehensive procedure is somewhat exhaustive, but it ensures that the resultant methodology is internally coherent and logically sound.

Denzin's five steps to define a methodology consist of the following building blocks:

1. The researcher's position within the Research Tradition;
2. Theoretical paradigms and perspectives;
3. Research strategies;
4. Methods of data collection and analysis;
5. Interpretation and presentation of findings.

In the following sections these points are discussed and the methodology position taken in this study is set out.

4.1.1 Position Within the Research Tradition

The internal characteristics of the research object and the nature of the research question determine the study's place in the information systems research tradition:

- In line with the qualitative nature of the research object, the research is *qualitative* in nature. This implies an emphasis on processes and meanings that are not rigorously examined, or measured (if measured at all) in terms of their quantity, amount, intensity or frequency (Denzin et al., 1994);
- Because its core research object is an information system, which is a social construct, the study follows the *social sciences* research tradition,. Although it has a technical component, the systems is more that just the sum of its technological components;

- The intellectual intent of the investigation straddles both *understanding* (*Verstehen*[1]) and *explaining* (*Erklären*). Exemplifying the nature of international information systems (and their attributes) requires the 'understanding of meaning, grasping the actor's definition of a situation', which is how Schwandt (1994) interprets the concept of *Verstehen*. However, the quest for 'factors' and 'interactions' introduces a causal element, which needs 'scientific explanation', which is how Schwandt (1994) defines *Erklären* with an underlying assumption of it to be quantitative. However, Schutz (1967), in an exposition of the different senses of the term *Verstehen* also defines it as a 'two-step process, peculiar to the human sciences'. A first-order sense of the term refers to how the researcher makes sense of the study objects and actors themselves. The second-order *Verstehen* then is the attempt to make sense of the processes, interactions, and relationships between the objects identified in the first instance (Schutz, 1967) – introducing, as it were, a qualitative 'version' of *Erklären*. This implies a response to the neo-positivist argument hat *Verstehen* is a 'pre-scientific, heuristic device useful in the context of discovery, but without value in the context of justification' (Schwandt, 1994).
- The research is fundamentally *nomothetic*[a, 2] in terms of its motivation. Ultimately, the 'nature' and the 'factors' should be forged into constructs that can be used to understand, explain and predict phenomena outside – and beyond – the immediate study situation and environment.
- The study, however, will initially focus strongly on *idiographic*[a] exploration – as there is no theory to posit a priori the scope, structure and content of the study. This precludes an etic[a] stance and thus means that the research
- is *emic*[a] in its commitment.

Positioning the research project in this way follows the notion described by Denzin et al. (1994) of the 'researcher–as-*bricoleur*'. An important aspect of this view is that the results of the research, the 'bricolage', is an 'emergent construction' (Weinstein & Weinstein, 1991), which 'changes and takes on new forms as different tools methods and techniques are added to the puzzle' (Denzin et al., 1994).

4.1.2 Theoretical Paradigms and Perspectives

'Paradigm' has many facets of meaning. A common definition is that it is 'a philosophical and theoretical framework of a scientific school or discipline within which theories, laws, and generalizations and the experiments performed in

---

[1] Schwandt (1994) uses the German terms in reference to Max Weber (1947), who first made this distinction with respect to the social sciences.

[2] a, b, c… refers to endnotes.

support of them are formulated.[b] Kuhn (1970) defines them similarly as 'accepted examples of actual scientific practice...from which spring particular coherent traditions of scientific research'. Denzin et al. (1994) provide a working definition of a paradigm as 'a basic set of beliefs that guide [the researcher's] actions...the *bricoleur's* [scientific] *Weltanschauung*'. For the purposes of the setting out the basic assumptions on which this study rests, a 'paradigm' is defined[c] as a set of *fundamental directives which governs the rules and standards for scientific practice in its realm.*

'Perspectives', on the other hand, are not 'as solidified, or as well unified, as paradigms, although they may share...a common set of methodologies' as Denzin et al. (1994) point out. They cite as examples for perspectives (with particular reference to qualitative research in the social sciences) such items as *feminism, ethnic models of inquiry* and *cultural studies*. Their logical independence from the paradigms makes them a separate dimension of research characteristic – possibly classified as the *bricoleur's* socio-political (as opposed to scientific) *Weltanschauung*, to paraphrase Denzin et al. (1994).

Whereas the position of the research project with respect to paradigms is an important issue, the first object of the study, the internal nature of information systems within multinational companies, seems neutral with respect to socio-political issues and *perspectives*. It may be possible that the shaping 'factors' and their interactions would contain such characteristics. Overall, however, the probability for such influences to be significant seemed low at the outset of the study. The selection of a specific, suitable 'perspective' seemed therefore not needed for this research.

There is a bewildering array of labels for research paradigms with often overlapping definitions. In order to obtain the clarity needed to make selection decisions, a brief excursion into the historical development of the major paradigms seems useful.

The traditional paradigm for scientific research, accepted for – at least – the last three centuries, rests on beliefs centered on the existence of reality, a way of furthering science by logically deriving hypothesis from overarching theories and verifying them in experiments of one sort or another. This view was considerably refined over time, not least by the positivist school of philosophy. In the early decades of this century, however, this 'positivism' paradigm [the 'received view' as Guba et al. (1994) refer to it] came under criticism from two sources:

Social science grew to rely more and more on research into areas where (numeric) measurement was difficult or impossible and thus the overly reliance on quantitative methods in conventional research was of little use. Furthermore, unlike most 'hard' science, social scientists do not deal with insensate research objects, but with 'units of analysis' who can – and do – interact with the researcher. For this reason, the very fundamental assumptions of traditional 'science' were questioned;

Philosophers of science themselves began to question the metaphysical undergirding of the 'received view'. Popper issued his first critique of the 'inductive method' in 1935, concluding that 'verification' of postulates is logically impossible. Kuhn (1970) introduced the concept of *normal science* (which 'follows the rules') and *scientific revolutions* (which don't), and maintains that the latter are the only means of significant progress in science. Feyerabend (1988) finally took this to its logical conclusion and maintained that any adherence to prescribed 'method' would only hinder the process of scientific discovery – thereby replacing *derivation* with *discovery* as the main characteristic of scientific pursuit.

Consequently, an adaptation of the conventional positivistic stance occurred. The resultant paradigm is referred to as Post-Positivism.[d] Guba et al. (1994) further recognize two additional research paradigms: Critical Theory and Constructivism. Table 4.1 below shows the position of each of the three 'new' paradigms with respect to traditional Positivism.

Table 4.1. Comparison of the 'new' paradigms against the 'received view', i.e. the research paradigm of traditional positivism (after Guba et al., 1994)

Positivism Critique	Post-Positivism	Critical Theory[e]	Constructivist[e]
Internal (intra-paradigm) critique			
Stripping of context and relevance	Accepting qualitative 'facts' increases relevance	'Facts' are embedded in context	'Facts' are any form of social/individual 'construction'
Exclusion of meaning and purpose	Qualitative 'facts' allow (some) expression of meaning/purpose	'Facts' are social and transactional, statements	'Facts' include experiential and social 'constructions'
Etic/emic dilemma	Accept 'emic nature' of social 'facts' and include emic settings	The (historical) reality is the emic situation	'Reality' is 'local' and 'specific' in nature
Nomothetic/ idiographic disjunction		Idiography of the research setting includes researcher	'Constructions' are refined from simple to complex
Exclusion of discovery	Discovery is a valid methodological objective	Product of the dialectic/dialogic research process	'Findings' are 'created' by the investigators and their subjects
External (extra-paradigm) critique			
Facts are theory-laden		Reality is 'virtual', shaped by exogenous values	Research is the refinement of 'constructions'
Facts are value-laden		Facts are 'value-mediated'	'Constructions' are experiential 'realities'
Under-determination of theory	Falsification and 'critical multiplism'[f] accepted	'Theory' is substituted by subjectivist view	'Constructions' are as rich as the investigations creating them
Neglecting the effects of the inquirer-inquired dyad[g]	Probabilistic view of 'reality' accepted	Investigator and subject transform views in dialectic dialogs	'Findings' are 'created' by investigator and subject

Orlikowski et al. (1991), in extending ideas first outlined by Chua (1986) to the information systems realm, had previously developed a similar taxonomy of research paradigms. Their taxonomy recognizes 'positivist' (the conventional, 'received view' variety) and 'critical theory' (as defined by Guba et al., 1994) which they also use as a representative of other research philosophies related to ideology. A third basic paradigm is named 'interpretive'.

This represents an amalgamation of terms, which Guba et al. (1994) later on split into two distinct categories: the enlightened elements of *post-positivist* (in Guba et al. (1994) terms) and the less radical notions of *constructivist* (i.e. a 'weak constructivism' in Orlikowski et al. (1991) terms). Myers (1997) also employs this tripartite taxonomy.

Judging from the literature it seems that the choice of these paradigms is sometimes a reflection of the researcher's own belief system, more often, perhaps, in the case of the Critical Theory paradigms. However, Morgan et al. (1980) assert that the 'appropriateness [of a qualitative research paradigm] derives from the nature of the social phenomena to be explored' (p. 491). In this sense, the specific nature of international information systems (and of their determining factors) was used for these decisions. Moreover, given the state of the paradigmatic debate, it seems prudent to also apply conservatism (*is it proven?*) and parsimony (*is it sufficient for the job?*) as guiding criteria in paradigm selection.

Guba et al. (1994) show that a research paradigm's 'profile' is determined by the position taken in its three constituent elements:

- *Epistemology*: the research object is of a (partially) technological nature and the investigation is a recording of historically ordered, but otherwise static, situations. This means that relatively little interaction of the kind that may taint or unduly bias the findings will be expected. This makes the traditional 'dualistic' principle of separateness of researcher and subject sufficiently rigorous;
- *Ontology*: the technology element in the study is embedded in the social structure of commercial enterprises, forming a union which is in constant flux. The 'picture' painted by the research is a conglomerate of 'snap-shots'. These are derived from people's memories, documentary evidence and a small element of direct observation. The results and findings of the study will thus be a diffuse reflection of an aspect of reality as selected by the subjects and retrieved by the researcher. In both cases this will have been filtered through what both thought 'relevant' at the time. The acknowledgement of these shortcomings of the 'picture' precludes the 'naïve realism' of the conventional positivist stance. The technology content of the research object, however, introduces a harder, quantitative, element, so that the post-positivist stance of 'critical realism' would be suitable. On the other hand, the social nature of the enterprises, the cultural and economic diversity of the locations to be researched and the emphasis on developmental issues in the research topic all suggest that a philosophy of 'historical' or 'virtual realism[h] may well be equally

feasible. There would also be a strong tendency toward a 'relativist' interpretation of the findings as an ordered *bricolage* of the sum of all 'facts' retrieved. The preferred ontology stance is thus one of critical realism, with a possible relativist interpretation of the historical reality of the 'facts' assembled in the study.

- *Methodology*: there is no overarching theory of the nature, structural and factorial determinants for international information systems that could enable the researcher to take an etic position. Subsequently, discovery is the main principle of the research. The two main groups of 'actors' in the study are multinational enterprises, i.e. social and cultural conglomerates on the one hand and clusters of technology and systems on the other. This suggests that descriptive, situational inquiry, searching out the actors' natural environment will be the main thrust of investigation – in the first instance. These emic viewpoints, descriptions and positions of 'all' research objects then build an understanding (*Verstehen*) of the 'nature' of international information systems and the 'factors' that shape it. This, in the second instance, then becomes the foundation for the construction of relationships and interactions between the 'factors'. A method for this development process cannot rely solely on 'dispassionate, independent observation', but needs to engage in some discussion between researcher and 'actors' with a view to refine an emerging 'reality', most likely in an iterative way. The methodology for this explanatory part of the study (*Erklären*) is thus essentially dialectical in nature.

The elements most suited for the study do not align themselves conveniently behind one dominant research paradigm. Guba et al. (1994) provide an analysis of the paradigm positions against its constituent elements with respect to practical research issues. Using this as a framework, Table 4.2 below shows the positions taken with respect to selected issues and paradigm elements with relevance for this study.

The summary shows that the paradigmatic make-up of the methodology most suited for this study is strongly oriented towards a post-positivist stance in Guba et al. (1994) terms. However, mainly because of the – initially – descriptive nature of the research goals, the paradigm is also somewhat 'constructivist' in its guiding principles.

In addition, the 'insight' character of the expected findings introduces an element of 'critical theory'. On the whole, in the nomenclature of Orlikowski et al. (1991), the research paradigm most appropriate for the study would be *interpretivist* in its ontological and methodological position, but with a strongly *positivist* epistemology.

There seems to be some disagreement whether these paradigms can be accommodated within one study, or if they are 'opposed by necessity' (Myers, 1997).

Table 4.2. Profile of paradigmatic positions (after Guba et al., 1994)[i]

Paradigm elements	Spectrum of Paradigm Positions			
	Traditional positivism	Post-positivism	Constructivism	Critical theory
'Voice'[3] *epistemology*	Dispassionate observer			
Inquiry aim *epistemology*	Explanation of the 'interaction' between the 'factors' that shape the 'nature'.		Understanding of 'nature', 'structure' and 'attributes'	
Nature of knowledge *Ontology*		Hypotheses from 'facts', which are…	… 'mimetic' constructions, that may include…	… structural and historical insights
Accumulation of knowledge *methodology*		Possible cause-effect postulations	Generalization by similarity of incidents	

Guba et al. (1994), support the dichotomy view and mention specifically that 'proponents of [critical theory and constructivism] join in affirming the basic incommensurability of [positivist and non-positivist] paradigms...[which] are believed to be essentially contradictory'.

On the other hand, there is material support in the literature for multi-paradigmatic approaches to qualitative research. First of all, there is a clear precedent in information systems research: Lee (1991) had shown that an integration of positivist and interpretivist paradigms in one study – such as suggested for this research – is a practical possibility. Denzin et al. (1994), too, maintain that qualitative research *eo ipso* is characterized by 'separate and multiple uses and meanings of [its] methods'. They assert that there is 'common acceptance of a multiplism of qualitative research methods', such as is proposed for this study. In a statement on qualitative methodology Nelson et al. (1992) observe that 'qualitative research is interdisciplinary, trans-disciplinary and sometimes counter-disciplinary…it is many things at the same time. It is multi-paradigmatic in focus. Its practitioners are sensitive to the value of the multi-method approach'. Finally, Guba et al. (1994) point to a possible avenue for reconciliation among conflicting paradigms by applying different research approaches to individual sets of research objects: '…one might wish to resolve the problem [of finding the right paradigm] differently in considering the physical versus the human realms'. Using epistemology as an example, they suggest it may be preferable to select one paradigm befitting the set of inanimate objects and another one for the study of conscious research. The dual nature of information systems as technology/human hybrids would then justify the use of two seemingly juxtaposed ontological paradigms in this study.

[3] This is the position of the inquirer *vis-à-vis* the research subjects, especially with respect to the impact any research findings may have on them.

4.1.3 Research Strategies

This is the step to 'put the paradigms of interpretation into motion' (Denzin et al., 1994). It first sets out 'what information most appropriately will answer [the] specific research questions', and, having decided that, goes on to establish 'which strategies are most effective for obtaining it' (LeCompte et al., 1993).

There are two epistemological parts to this study's research question. Firstly, it is 'fact finding' about information systems employed by international enterprises, their nature, structure and characteristics. The second part is concerned with 'inference building', i.e. uncovering what factors create the specific characteristics and establish how their elements depend upon, relate to, and are inter-linked with each other.

The research design, therefore, has to take into account both parts of the research question. The following sections discuss each part in turn.

4.1.3.1 'Fact' Finding

The selection of 'facts' to research is often predetermined by a theoretical proposition on which the research is based. In the absence of a pre-existing theory in the field of international information systems, 'fact' selection is therefore governed by the inherent qualities of the research object itself.

The hybrid nature of the research objects means that the 'facts' in the study have a number of dimensions:

- The information systems themselves can be viewed as purely a manifestation of technology, i.e. research objects of the inanimate kind. The technology is, however, inextricably related to its application in support of business operations, i.e. is more than just an inert inventory of hardware and software.
- The business operations, in turn, are an interplay of technology, procedures and people. Information systems, therefore, also need to be considered as – technology-enabled – social entities;
- The people, who make up the 'conscious' part of this socio-technical hybrid, are more than just users of an information system – they are also the actors in what makes up the 'business' as a social entity. Without them, the business would just be the real-estate shell holding the hardware inventory. This incarnation of the 'people' as business-cum-systems actors is of central interest to the investigation;
- Furthermore, qualities of the overall enterprise, i.e. the entity created by the accumulation of people and their systems, are in themselves information realms and research objects of significant relevance for the study;
- Lastly, the focus of all these individual activities, the 'business' or 'industry' the enterprise is in, is of interest for putting into context the 'facts' about the individual firms' information systems and their use. This ultimately puts into

place the framework of scope, extent and strength or size within which all the other elements interact.

The chosen research design needs to be capable of catering for this diversity of characteristics.

Galliers (1991) developed a taxonomy of information systems research approaches. Defining an 'approach' as 'a way of going about one's research', this term is sufficiently similar to the definition of research design by Denzin et al. (1994) to make his results and conclusions applicable to this discussion. He categorizes designs into two groups, namely 'interpretivist' and 'scientific', in which he includes Denzin et al.'s (1994) 'received view' of traditional positivism.

Galliers's (1991) 'interpretivist' designs include 'Futures Research', 'Subjective/Argumentative' designs, 'Historical Reviews' 'Action Research' and 'Games/Role Playing', none of which is suitable for this study. 'Descriptive /Interpretive' designs, in the more narrow sense, 'immerse [the researcher] in the life of the people he studies' (Lewis, 1985), 'seek to place the phenomena studied into their social and cultural context' (Myers, 1997) and are a 'general approach to the wide range of possible studies relating to the investigation of information systems' (Pettigrew, 1985). Their intended use for the social aspects of information systems makes this approach useful for the descriptive part of 'fact' finding within this study.

Galliers (1991) then separates the traditional 'scientific' approaches into those where the environment and the variables under investigation can be controlled, as in experiments or surveys. Case studies are considered suitable when there is a higher degree of complexity, a larger number of variables and limited capacity to control them. The case study design is thus the most suitable 'scientific' (in the strict positivist sense) approach for this study. Adding the descriptive/interpretive requirement established above, case study with a descriptive disposition is therefore the most desirable approach.

Stake (1994) distinguishes between different types of case study approaches. His *instrumental* mode,[j] where cases are used to 'provide insight into an issue' and 'facilitate our understanding of something else' (ibid., p. 237) is useful for this study. Given the likelihood that one case will not supply sufficient information, *collective* cases will be needed to provide 'a zone of combined purpose' (ibid., p. 238). Yin (1994) furthermore classifies case study approaches by the type of research questions they are designed to answer. Of his three types, the 'Exploratory' and 'Descriptive' designs are of most use[k] for this investigation.

In conclusion, the research design most suitable for the 'fact finding' part of this investigation would thus be a combination of *exploratory* and *descriptive case study* strategy. Given the inherent diversity of multinational enterprises, this should be applied to *instrumental* cases, in a *collective* mode.

4.1.3.2 Relationship Development

To satisfy the second part of the research question, the 'facts' established in the cases need to be brought into context with each other in the 'inference' part of the study.

The traditional way to do this would involve the verification of hypotheses, derived from a higher order theory. The absence of a theory of sufficient density for this field renders this method inappropriate. The main object of the 'inference' part of the study is thus to build new theory, not to test or extend an existing one.

There are two components to the 'theory' this study sets out to build:

1. Firstly, the 'factors' that shape an IIS; they need to be distilled from the descriptive material assembled during the fact finding;
2. Secondly, the 'interactions' between them need to be examined to establish how the factors 'shape' the IIS.

This sequence of investigative progression means that the variables elicited in the first instance will be strongly emic and idiographic in make-up, and their meaning will be limited to the immediate, local, substantive environment of the case their descriptions came from. The same goes for the relationships educed between these variables. This, however, is in contradiction with the requirement above (under Section 4.1.1 on p. 24) that the study be essentially 'nomothetic', i.e. any theoretical constructs it yields should be relevant outside the immediate case environments they were derived from. A research strategy is therefore required that will widen the scope of the variables and thereby also extend the applicability of any correlations and causalities established between them beyond emic confines.

Denzin et al. (1994) offer a list of qualitative research strategies[l] which they have separated from the concept of research design – a useful distinction for the two-phased research objective in this study. They begin with Case Study strategies, which both Galliers (1991) and Eisenhardt (1989) confirm as appropriate for building theory. Then follows a number of descriptive-interpretivist approaches,[m] which are not appropriate for this part of the study. The list concludes with the Grounded Theory approach. This is a general research strategy, specifically oriented towards developing theory that is derived from – i.e. 'grounded in' – data that has been systematically gathered and analyzed. This is in contrast to the theory generating research that begins with a theoretical construct and, through study, changes, enhances or negates it. Remarking that it may well be 'the most widely employed interpretive strategy in the social sciences today', Denzin et al. (1994) characterize it as a 'specific set of steps to follow, which are closely aligned with the 'canons of good science' and [are] an explicit commitment to theory development'. Similarly, Martin et al. (1986), define Grounded Theory as an 'inductive,[4] theory discovery methodology that allows the

[4] Josephson et al. (1994) would classify it as an 'abductive' method.

researcher to develop a theoretical account of the general features of a topic while simultaneously grounding the account in empirical observations or data'. This gives 'primacy to realism of context and theoretical and conceptual development as research goals' (Pettigrew, 1990, p. 283) and develops context-based, process-oriented descriptions and explanations of the phenomena under study (Orlikowski, 1993; Myers, 1997). A key characteristic of Grounded Theory is thus a duality of an interpretivist base in the descriptive nature of the data on the one hand, whilst at the same time evolving structure and theory from this data through a 'continuous interplay between analysis and data collection' (Strauss et al., 1994). The theory generated is developed from a strictly localized concept to a 'substantive' level first, before any further developments (or 'elaborations', in Vaughan's, 1992 terms) allow further generalizations to extend the scope of the theory. This bestows the method with the capacity of moving seamlessly from the emic surrounds of the first, idiographic case data to a level of nomotheticicity entirely commensurate with the predictive qualities of the data. This inherent progression of theoretical constructs from emic concepts to etic theorems makes the Grounded Theory strategy a suitable choice for the 'inference' part of this study. Moreover, its explicit linkage to the 'canons of good science' makes this strategy 'firmly entrenched within the modernist, post-positivist tradition' (Denzin et al., 1994). This makes the Grounded Theory research strategy compatible with the paradigmatic stance selected for the overall approach.

Although Grounded Theory approaches are becoming accepted as 'scientific' methods (Haig, 1996) and are appearing with increasing frequency in the IS research literature (Myers, 1997), they are primarily concerned with the human, social and organizational aspects of computing. The research object under study is not entirely homocentric, but a hybrid of technology and human elements. As Strauss et al. (1994) point out, however, Grounded Theory is 'a general methodology'. Glaser (1996) confirms that the principle of the theory is applicable to any subject where the data is capable of being coded and analyzed by comparison.

As a 'general method' in the post-positivist tradition, Grounded Theory was thus selected as suitable for the 'inference' part of this study.

In summary, the most suitable research design and strategy for this study is a combination of two research modes:

The case study research design of the 'exploratory' and 'descriptive' kind, applied to *instrumental* cases in a *collective case* arrangement, seems well suited for optimizing the results from the first, 'fact' finding, aspect of the study;

In order to investigate 'why' those 'facts' are shaped in a particular way, a strategy of inquiry based on the *Grounded Theory* mode of research was chosen as the most appropriate. It provides a means for categorizing the descriptive facts from the case study phase(s) and allows their amalgamation in such a way that correlative and/or causal linkages between facts can be conceptualized. *Grounded Theory* methods furthermore generate theory that can be generalized beyond the immediate case environs.

The use of Grounded Theory methodology with cases as the cardinal unit of investigation is a new concept and no precedents for such a constellation of research designs and strategies could be found in the literature.

4.1.4 Collecting and Analyzing Empirical Materials

This fourth step of research process has to do with the collection of the empirical data and other materials to be used in the qualitative research undertaking. Whilst there seems to be a great multitude of possible sources of empirical materials for the researcher, Schwandt (1994) puts this into perspective when he observes that: 'at base all interpretive inquirers watch, listen, ask, record, and examine. How these activities may best be defined and employed depends on the inquirer's purpose for doing the inquiry. Purpose, in turn, is shaped by epistemological and methodological commitments'. (p. 119). In addition to the paradigmatic commitments, however, the nature and reality of the research objects is a second decision factor for the selection of data collection and analysis strategies. In the following sections the methods suitable for use in the study are discussed in more detail.

4.1.4.1 Data Collection

There seems to be consensus among researchers with an interest theory building that it is imperative to use as wide a network of inter-dependent information sources as possible (Glaser et al., 1967; Eisenhardt, 1989; Orlikowski, 1993, 1995; Pettigrew, 1990). Denzin et al. (1994) present a comprehensive list of representative methods of collecting data, information and materials in qualitative research studies to achieve this goal. In Table 4.3 below they are evaluated as to their utility and suitability for this study.

Denzin et al. (1994) maintain that the interview is the favorite tool of the qualitative researcher as well as a 'paramount part of sociology, because interviewing is interaction and sociology is the study of interaction' (Benney et al., 1956). Defined as an 'individual, face-to-face verbal interchange' the interview has a wide variety of forms and a multiplicity of uses.

Table 4.3. Data collection and analysis methods (after Denzin et al., 1994) and their appropriateness for the research objects of the study

Methods of collection and analysis of research data	Suitability for the study
Interviewing	Main source of interpretive information
Observing	To augment the interviews
Artifacts, documents, and records	Main source of facts about the technology and main source of historical corroboration of the verbal data gathered in interviews; a list of the documentation is set out in Table 4.5 (on p. 42)
Textual analysis	Specific implementation of a Narrative Analysis method: coding of interview transcripts and other primary materials in the Grounded Theory tradition
Data management methods	Basic filing techniques are adequate for textual data
Computer-assisted analysis	Used for auxiliary assistance in two ways: as a repository and text management tool for coded interview transcripts (using the NUDIST software for part of the materials); In a limited way, spreadsheet technology was used to produce comparative and supplementary analysis of some quantitative support data and information (such as provided in annual reports and internal statistical documentation and records)
Visual methods	Not applicable
Personal experience methods	Not applicable

The interviewing in the study is characterized by the following:

- The absence of detailed, theoretical propositions in this research limits the use of structured interviews significantly. The suitable interviewing technique is therefore the unstructured interview in the tradition of the open-ended, in-depth 'ethnographic' interviewing (Fontana et al., 1994).
- Interviews should be intensive and take place in an uninterrupted setting. They should also be carried out in the 'field' to provide an opportunity for participant observation.[5] This confirms with Lofland et al. (1995, p. 19) requirement of 'mutuality of intensive interviewing and participant observation as the central techniques of naturalistic investigation';
- The interviewees should be a mixture of active users of the IIS on the one hand and of the information systems people involved in the development and maintenance of the IIS on the other hand. In this way, the interviews serve a dual purpose: they provide a personal[6] and experiential[6] account of the research object; and also serve as an oral history[6] of the relevant organizational context.[7]

[5] Mostly in the form of a demonstration of information systems or business operations features.

[6] Denzin et al. (1994) canons for good interpretive/descriptive research.

[7] The historical accounts were then corroborated by as much documentary evidence as possible.

Further important data were the field-, interview- and observation notes, coding comments and theoretical memos. Notes provide reminders of points of particular importance from individual interviews, observations on systems or the general environment, which can then be related to similar experiences in different environs or contexts. Coding comments are taken to provide a record of thoughts and ideas behind the conceptual classification, grading and comparisons carried out. They are 'designed to tap into the initial freshness of the analyst's theoretical notions and to relieve the conflict in his thoughts" (Glaser et al., 1967, p. 107). Complementing these comments are the theoretical memos. Defined as "the theorizing write-up of ideas about codes and their relationships as they strike the analyst while coding' (Glaser, 1978, p. 83), they often 'provide an immediate illustration for an idea' (Glaser et al., 1967, p. 108). Memos are also a forum for 'taking apart the story within [the] data' as the analyst 'sufficiently fractures' the idiographic constraints of individual incidents. They make possible the 'breaking down and out of the story [which] is necessary for clear integration of the theory' (ibid., pp. 108–109). Together, interview transcripts, observation notes, coding comments and theoretical memos 'provide the content behind the categories, which become the major themes of the theory later presented' (ibid., p. 113).

'Internal' material about the enterprise in question, such as company memoranda, and correspondence relevant to the case story, minutes of meetings, company-internal reports and similar material should further complement the interview and observation related documentation. 'External' material can include publicity documents, annual reports, special brochures, news reports, investment analyses and other public sources. Together they can be used to provide the essential widening of the contextual background to complement the narrower, more focused and 'emic' realities in the cases.

These 'texts'[n] formed the primary source of data analysis.

4.1.4.2 Data Analysis

The choice of Grounded Theory as the preferred research strategy pre-determines the principles of data analysis to a large extent. The following sets out a comparison of Grounded Theory procedures with other methods in qualitative research. Secondly, a choice is made between the two main schools of thought in the Grounded Theory field.

Grounded Theory, with its close relationship between data coding and analyzing, was new and revolutionary in 1967. However, by the mid-1990s a number of its principles had been assimilated into mainstream qualitative research methodology, such as in the data analysis steps suggested by Lofland et al. (1995), Miles et al. (1994) and Carney (1990). Grounded Theory, in the meantime, had developed into two main variants, namely

- the original process and sequence of phases as exemplified by Glaser et al. (1967) and further augmented by Glaser (1978); this is labeled 'Glaser' in the following discussion;
- the methodology as outlined by Strauss (1987) and then prescribed in procedural detail by Strauss & Corbin (1990); this is labeled 'Strauss'.

In Table 4.4 below, the two mainstream methodologies are set out in comparison with the steps in both schools of Grounded Theory methodology.

Table 4.4. Comparison of data analysis steps and phases. *Italics* denote a method's proprietary nomenclature

Lofland & Lofland	Miles & Huberman	Glaser after Glaser & Strauss (1967)	Strauss after Strauss & Corbin (1990)
'Framing' (in social science frameworks)			Formulation of the research question
Coding: initial coding	Creating a text to work on	Open coding	Open coding
Coding: focused coding	Trying out coding categories to find what fits	Theoretical coding	Axial coding
	Identifying themes and trends in the data overall	Memo writing (ongoing throughout all phases)	Axial coding and applying the 'paradigm'
Memo writing; and diagramming	Testing hypotheses and reducing the bulk of data for analysis of trends in it		Selective coding
		Theoretical sampling (iterating back to open or theoretical coding)	Theoretical sampling
			Identifying the process & contingencies
			Setting out the conditional matrix
Thinking flexibly: the final analysis	Delineating the deep structure	Theory formulation: substantive or formal	Theory writing

Lofland & Lofland's is the least prescriptive method outline. It follows a traditional, positivist paradigm by starting with a pre-defined hypothetical position, anchored in a social science framework germane to the research area and object.

Miles & Huberman's 'ladder of analytical abstraction' is somewhat similar in structure to the logic of the Glaser version of Grounded Theory. The significant difference is, however, that there is no element of theoretical sampling continually to steer the investigation along a route of increasing conceptual and theoretical density. Although some leeway for adapting categories to the data is provided for, theirs is fundamentally a non-iterative research design, more suitable for well-defined studies in the incremental tradition of Kuhn's *normal science.*

Strauss's procedural method compendium is the most elaborate and also the most prescriptive process of the designs under comparison. It seems to have developed into a set of 'exceedingly complex processes' (Lofland et al., 1995, p. 192), trying to do two things at once:

1. preserving the richness of application and elegant simplicity of procedure inherent in the 'Glaser' version of Grounded Theory methodology; while at the same time
2. attempting to avoid its reliance on the researcher's conceptualizing skills and theoretical sensitivity – by replacing it with a deeply structured process, trying to have a clear rule for every eventuality.

The original 'Glaser' framework was chosen as the methodology for this study because it does not require a preceding theory (as Lofland & Lofland's), it is extensible (which is difficult in Miles & Huberman's methodology) and because it provides more freedom of interpretation than Strauss's multi-step analysis procedure.

The shortcomings of the 'Strauss' process for the study at hand are manifold:

- It has been specifically designed for predominantly 'homocentric' research settings, i.e. with specific emphasis on human-to-human interaction.[o] This is, however, only one of the research objects in this study, which also spans technology, social, and organizational objects.
- Strauss' strict rules for open, axial and selective coding were designed for research where the individual is the main unit of analysis and the individual interview or observation the predominant 'slice-of-data'. It is questionable whether they could be adapted for an investigation where the unit of analysis are cases about information systems in multinational firms, i.e. multi-person, multi-layered (and eventually multi-organizational) settings with a strong content of inanimate technology;
- Strauss et al.'s (1990, p. 99) 'paradigm' for constructing and linking categories is too restrictive for the open-ended research question in this study. It forces the categories and their properties into a uniform, pre-defined causal structure. The relationship between facts is, however, a central element of the research question and its nature needs to be left to emerge from the investigation. The

narrowness of the 'paradigm' could thus preclude the correlative, 'covariant' relationships between facts expected in multiple cases;

- Moreover, Strauss's 'paradigm' is fully contained in the first of 18 'coding families' set out by Glaser (1978, p. 74–82) to illustrate some possible frameworks[8] for 'theoretical' coding (which furthermore encompasses the 'axial' coding in the Strauss terminology);
- Similarly, Strauss a priori forces a 'process' nature onto the underlying concepts (Strauss & Corbin, 1990, p. 143ff). This may or may not be justified, but in any case should be left to emerge from the data.[p]

A further deciding factor against the 'Strauss' procedure was the blanket refutation it received from Glaser (1992). His main argument is that it is 'an over-codification of the basic Grounded Theory method', resulting in 'conceptual fracturing… forcing preconceived notions on data', which, in the end merely produce 'full conceptual descriptions', but not theories which are grounded in data.

In the Grounded Theory tradition the first unit of analysis is a singular 'slice of data' (Glaser, 1996) pertaining to 'actors' in the study. In the sociology setting of traditional Grounded Theory, the 'actors' are usually individual people, and the theories tend to focus on their relationships to each other and/or their sharing of a common circumstance. In the first instance, *open coding* is applied to that raw data to develop categories and their properties and to crystallize them into concepts. *Theoretical coding* is then used to 'firm' the categories around a set of 'core categories' and to bring them to 'saturation'. A family of such saturated categories eventually forms a 'grounded theory' about what makes the 'actors' behave in the way they do.

In the case research approach in this study the 'slice-of-data' relates to a convoluted artifact made up of both technology and human elements, i.e. the nature and workings of an international information system. The sum of all the singular instances of 'nature' and 'workings' conveyed by interviews, observation and document analysis firstly needs to be amalgamated into a case story about the international enterprise whose information systems are under study. This larger 'text' is, however, just as much 'raw' data in terms of the comparative analysis, as are the interviews, observations and the other documentation.

Although the unit of analysis is significantly different from the traditional subject of Grounded Theory, the implications for the application of the method are few. Coding, open as well as theoretical, applies to the individual 'components' of the larger text in the same way as it does to the individual data elements of the traditional method. In addition, the larger text – the case story itself – becomes subject to another round of coding, mostly theoretical. There are some practical differences in the timing of the coding activity and in the use of memos (as set out

---

[8] Another set of frameworks are the relationships between 'basic social processes' and 'social structural units', Glaser (1978, p. 109–113)

in detail below). They do not, however, deviate at all from the purpose of coding and memo-writing as set out in the Grounded Theory method by Glaser et al. (1967) and Glaser (1978).

In the same way as there is no material difference in the substance of the data, there is also no difference in the logic of acquiring it. The traditional Grounded Theory method assumes a sequential process of data acquisition, in order to add relevant 'properties' to 'categories' until their 'saturation' makes any further data redundant. This process is in principle equally valid in the case environment. However, because the unit is an information system in an enterprise, considerably more data will have to be gathered about it all to first form an initial picture, before enough material on categories is assembled to begin steering the future data acquisition by theoretical coding and sampling *within* and *without* the case. For international information systems contained in an enterprise, there is, moreover, a limit to the amount of data that may be gleaned from one case. This means that additional cases may need to be brought into the investigation because it has not been possible to reach 'saturation' of specific categories in the single case in hand. Nevertheless, this is in effect[q] the same as when, in the traditional Grounded Theory method, a change to another group of 'actors' is undertaken for reasons of theoretical sampling: the motivation of the change is still to achieve 'saturation'. The additional case would be selected following the traditional theoretical sampling principles.

These considerations showed that an amalgam of cases and Grounded Theory is viable in principle and could be made to work in practice. The details of the adaptation of the Grounded Theory method for the specific requirements of this study are set out in the next chapter, which describes the actual research design.

4.1.5 Interpretation and Presentation of Findings

Denzin (1994) sets out a series of steps for the 'complex, reflexive process' of bringing the results of research 'from the field to the text to the reader' (p. 501).

The Grounded Theory method, as applied to cases, complies adequately with Denzin's generic steps for the interpretation of qualitative research. Coding notes and memos form the base documents for the write-up of the theory. The process of building the process will be continuous (as required by the Grounded Theory method), albeit with milestones when the theory-in-progress will be stated in the form of successive theoretical frameworks.

Table 4.5 below sets out

- Denzin's steps; together with the
- Comments of what steps are appropriate for this study and how they have been implemented.

4.2 Theory Building Issues

As set out before, this study is about building theory. The literature on this topic is 'sparse and uneven' (Weick, 1989) and often represents an 'incredible anarchy of language, concepts, proposals, interpretations and results of formal theorizing' (Freese, 1980, p. 189).

On the other hand there seems to be broad understanding of the processes researchers use for interpreting and delivering qualitative research findings and analyses. Denzin (1994) outlines the steps and stages of this generic process. In Table 4.5 below this process is presented in the form most useful for the research project at hand.

Table 4.5. The interpretation and presentation process for qualitative research findings (after Denzin, 1994)

Interpretation steps	Interpretation documentation appropriate for this study
Field text: accumulated field notes and documents	This constitutes the original 'chain of evidence' and contains: interview recordings (tapes); interview transcripts; observation notes, descriptions and illustrative materials; internal documentation from the case enterprises: minutes, memoranda, internal reports and other communications; external (public) material from the case enterprises: such as annual reports, brochures, product advertising and publicity material; external material: news reports, etc.
Research text: notes	This will comprise: coding annotations; the case stories, sufficiently interspersed with illustrative excerpts from interviews and other documentation and containing graphical and diagrammatic summations and explanations
Research text: interpretation aids	This will comprise: theoretical memos (setting out, developing and commenting on elements of the theory under construction); interim summations and other conceptualizing background materials
Interpretive working document	This, in Denzin's terms, is a 'recreation of the research 'text' to make sense out of what has been learned'. In this study, the emerging elements of the theory will be summarized and related in a set of 'theorems', which will eventually make up the proposed theory. This follows the continuous write-up tradition [9] in the Grounded Theory method. Although continuous, there will be a milestone after the completion of each case. After the first case, the theory will be written up in the form of a 1st theoretical framework. Constant comparison with successive

[9] Glaser & Strauss (1967, pp. 113ff) and Glaser (1978, pp. 128ff). There are some modifications to this in order to adapt it to the case-based study. They are detailed in the next chapter.

Interpretation steps	Interpretation documentation appropriate for this study
	cases adds to the framework, which will be re-stated after each case. The 'final' substantive theory will be written up after the core categories have reached a satisfactory level of saturation
Quasi-public text: for peer review	The 'first draft' efforts of the final work (e.g. for editorial discussion/evaluation with a publisher) would fall into this category
Public document: final text	Containing the case stories; the theory constructed from them; and how it relates to the literature on the topic There is also supplementary information such as a review of the literature on the wider topic and a description of the derivation of the methodology used

It seems thus appropriate to firstly define what a 'theory' is in the context of the study, then establish how to assess its quality and, lastly, where to begin with the building process.

4.2.1 Theory Definition

Theory as a philosophical construct consists of its objects on one hand, and of relationships – between these objects – on the other. In this sense Merton (1968, p. 39) defines a sociological theory as 'logically interconnected sets of propositions…from [which] empirical uniformities can be derived'. Bacharach (1989, p. 498) refines this definition to include concrete as well as abstract objects in these propositions. Sutherland (1975), supported by Sutton et al. (1995), provided a more precise definition of Merton's 'uniformities' as 'generic behaviors or structures assumed to hold throughout a significantly broad range of specific instances'. His definition, however, by only including *generic* behaviors occurring in a *significantly broad* range of instances, implicitly excludes the concept of theories as idiographic behavioral constructs, applicable in emic settings.

Glaser et al.'s (1967) distinction of 'substantive' and 'formal' theories, however, closes this gap by introducing a distinct specification of a theory's scope. The predictive power of a *substantive* theory is limited to the circumstances in the specific area from where it was developed (e.g. information systems in international enterprises). A *formal* theory transcends this limit and extends its applicability to as far as the conceptual entity it is based on has relevance in the wider research area (e.g. distributed information systems in diverse business environments). Figure 4.1 illustrates the Glaser et al. (1967) framework of theory evolution from ideas through to 'Grand Theories' (i.e. Merton's 'general theories').

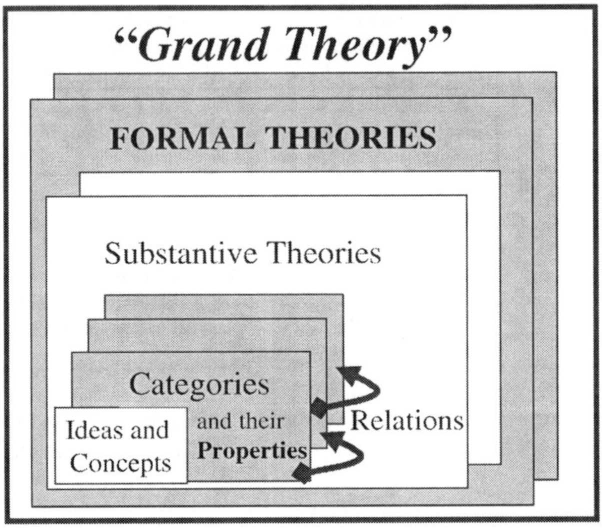

Figure 4.1. The progression of theory development in the grounded theory methodology

Merton (1968) introduced the umbrella concept of middle-range theories which are 'intermediate to general theories of social systems which are too remote from particular classes of social behavior…to account for what is observed; and to those detailed orderly descriptions of particulars that are not generalized at all….[they] involve abstractions, of course, but they are close enough to observed data to be incorporated in propositions that permit empirical testing'. Merton's examples, such as 'theory of reference groups, of social mobility, or role-conflict…' seems to suggest that they fall within the definition of Glaser et al.'s (1967) 'substantive' theories. Yin's (1989, p. 37) illustrative theory types are also in this class.

Whetten (1989) has brought all the above elements of a theory together in his four component framework. A theory must address each of the following:

1. *What* factors, variables, constructs, concepts, etc. should be included in the theory? They are judged by their comprehensiveness and parsimony;
2. *How* are the factors related? This introduces the relationships between the *what* objects and both (objects and relationships), form the 'domain' or 'subject' of the theory; typically these relationships embrace causality[r];
3. *Why* are the factors behaving like they do? This aspect of a theory supplies the plausible, cogent explanation for 'why we should expect certain relationships in the *what* and *how* data' (ibid., p. 491). Weick (1989) refers to this as *relevance* and Glaser (1978, p. 93) adds an element of urgency when he points out that theory should 'account for…which is relevant *and problematic* for those involved'.
4. *Who, where, when* are the temporal and contextual factors that set the limit on the theory's range, i.e. determine how generalizable it is. Bacharach (1989)

adds 'values' (which he defines as the theorist's *assumptions*, especially those of a paradigmatic nature) as another set of *who*-variables that bound a theory.

Because it incorporates all salient aspects, Whetten's comprehensive definition will be used as a guiding framework for the development and description of the theory to be built in this research.

4.2.2 Quality and Goodness of a Theory

To ascertain the quality of the model or theory[s] that will be developed in this study, it is important to set out the criteria that should be applied to assess its 'goodness' for explaining and predicting the nature and structure of information systems in multi-national enterprises.

Mayhew (1981) and Pfeffer (1982) confirm the three traditional criteria for a good theory as its clarity, parsimony and logical coherence. Whetten (1989) adds 'integration', i.e. how well it fits into a larger set of theories. Glaser et al. (1967) add to this a number of criteria specific for Grounded Theory:

- *Density*, refining the *parsimony* requirement;
- *Scope*, delimiting the environment the theory applies to, i.e. how *substantive* it is;
- *Fit*, with 'the situations being researched…i.e., categories must be readily, and not forcibly applicable to and indicated by the data under study' (ibid., p. 3);
- *Ability to work*; i.e. the theory 'should be able to *explain* what happened, *predict* what will happen and *interpret* what is happening in an area of substantive or formal inquiry' (ibid., p. 4);
- *Have relevance*; i.e. be 'meaningfully relevant to….the Behavior under study' (ibid., p. 3);

The 'comprehensiveness' requirement that both Whetten (1989) and Weick (1989) stipulate is implied in Glaser et al.'s definition of *scope* – which also embraces Osigweh Yg's (1989) notion of 'concept stretching'. Missing, however, is the element of surprise and the touch of elegance Weick (1989) asks for when he says that good theory should 'delight'.

In addition to, and sometimes in modification of, these general criteria for assessing a theory, specific benchmarks, such as *reproducibility* and *generalizability* have been set out for Grounded Theory by Strauss et al. (1990) in line with their enhancements and extended 'procedurization' of Grounded Theory methods. These have been hotly contested as 'wrestling with the canons for judging quantitative method research which are inappropriately applied to Grounded Theory' in Glaser's (1992) refutation of Strauss & Corbin's methodology.

Strauss et al. (1990) also set out two sets of seven criteria, which base the goodness of the Grounded Theory to a large extent on adherence – or not – to their own methodology. Glaser (1992) considers them irrelevant and maintains that the value of a theory should be in the theory itself, not in the adherence to any specific procedure. This, together with the fact that this study follows the 'Glaser' methodology school, makes the 'Strauss' criteria less applicable as quality benchmarks.

In conclusion, seven criteria for judging the quality of the theory developed in this study were defined. They are:

- Clarity;
- *Parsimony*; includes Glaser et al.'s (1967) 'density';
- Logical coherence;
- *Scope* of the theory; includes Osigweh, Yg's (1989) 'concept stretching' and Whetten's (1989) 'comprehensiveness';
- *Integration* of the theory into other theories in the same and related fields;
- *Falsifiability*; including Glaser et al.'s (1967) 'fit' of the theory to the data in which it is grounded, this is also closely related to Bacharach's (1989) notion of 'construct validity' and to Weick's (1989) requirement that a good theory must be 'real';
- *Utility*; in the terms of Glaser et al. (1967) a theory 'works' and is 'relevant' when it can explain and predict its constituent phenomena. This mirrors Bacharach's (1989) 'explanatory and predictive potential' and is extended in Weick's (1989) stipulation that a theory be 'interesting' and should 'delight'.

These criteria will be applied to the substantive theory at the conclusion of this study.

4.2.3 Origin of the Theory Building Process

Whilst there is ample guidance on the process of theory building research, discourse on what the 'starting point' in a theory building exercise should be is remarkably slim in information system research. Eisenhardt's (1989) seminal paper puts a strong emphasis on '[beginning the research] as close as possible to the ideal of no theory under consideration and no hypotheses to test'. At the same time she underscores the importance of a 'well focused research question' without, however, giving any indication where, in the absence of preconceived thought, the research question should come from.

Galliers et al. (1987) elegantly bypass this subject altogether by beginning their theory development progression straight off with 'case study/action research' as the sources from which a research question is to be developed. They, too avoid indicating how the case was chosen for study or why the action research was undertaken. Jarvenpaa (1988) juxtaposed their sequence with one that starts with a research question and then proceeds to build 'theories' from survey research – seemingly making 'hypothesis' and 'theory' interchangeable concepts. Figure 4.2 below illustrates these two theory development sequences.

The implausibility of the 'clean slate' that Eisenhardt posits, is a well known fact for philosophers of science such as Husserl (1970, 1982), who coined the specific phrase of *'ausklammern'*[10] for the necessity to remove the layers of prejudice that condition our powers of cognition.

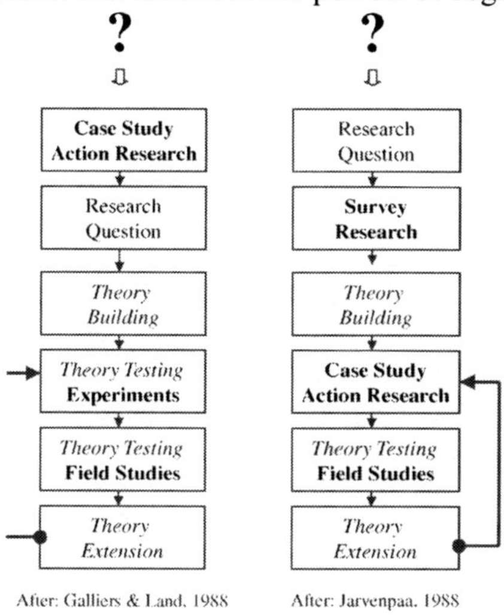

Figure 4.2. Theory development sequences proposed by Galliers et al. & Jarvenpaa

Weber (1947) pointed out that the 'value-laden nature of assumptions can never be eliminated'. Bacharach (1989) explicitly includes, as the natural boundaries of any theory, the 'theorist's creative imagination, ideological orientation or life experience'. Gadamer's (1976) altogether negates, by implication, the existence of a 'clean' starting point in his notion of a hermeneutic circle, which achieves understanding of a complex 'whole' from 'preconceptions' of the meanings of its parts and their interrelationships. Klein & Myers (1999) principle of 'contextualization' defines each study object as an integral part of its context, again implying the impossibility of isolated research settings, free of preconditions.

Acknowledging this difficulty, Glaser et al. (1967, p. 67) encourage the use of 'anecdotal comparisons' as starting point for setting out the focus of a research study: 'Through his own experiences, general knowledge, or reading, and the stories of others, the sociologist can gain data…that offer useful comparisons. This kind of data can be trusted if it has been 'lived'. Anecdotal comparisons are especially useful in starting research and developing core categories…the researcher can…sensitize himself to their relevancies.'

Glaser and Strauss's notion that ideas, resulting from anecdotal comparison, start the theory building process seems to tie in well with the prevailing thoughts on knowledge acquisition within the philosophy of science. In a classic work, Wolf (1922) sees 'working ideas' formulated as 'principles' or 'postulates' turning into hypotheses by the application of a method. Kuhn (1970) defines a (new) 'paradigm' as the igniting force for the forming of new theory. This is a set of propositions 'sufficiently unprecedented …[and] simultaneously, sufficiently open-ended to leave all sorts of problems...to resolve'. Merton (1968) refers to 'seminal ideas', often developed with the aid of a 'serendipity factor', as the starting point of a process to formulate 'theories of the middle range'.

---

[10] Literally translated 'bracketing out', it refers to putting part of a mathematical expression in brackets to prepare for its elimination from an equation.

Figure 4.3 below contrasts the Grounded Theory method – as applied to cases – with the two traditional theory development and enhancement paths.

While all these researchers take ideational constructs as beginnings, Wartofsky (1968) sees as them as the end product of a process of stepwise abstraction, beginning with abstractions of sensory perception and ending with 'conceptual abstraction…as the beginnings of theoretical scientific inquiry.' Ziman (1984) sees such seminiferous thought processes as 'patterns of fact in need of simplifying generalization and definite association'. Donovan et al. (1988) refer to the need for 'guiding assumptions' as the prerequisite for any research undertaking. Selye (1964) recognizes the 'intuitive flash or hunch…the inductive element, without which no new ground can be explored'.

For this study, the author's 'lived experience' with building and implementing information systems for multinational enterprises provided the ideational concept with which to delimit the research area in the first instance. The notion of a common architecture as a possible central engine of a specific development paradigm for international information systems was formed from 'anecdotal comparison' of specific incidents within the 'lived experience' (see Lehmann, 1996b). This initiated the focus on the 'interaction' of factors' that shape the 'structure' of international information systems.

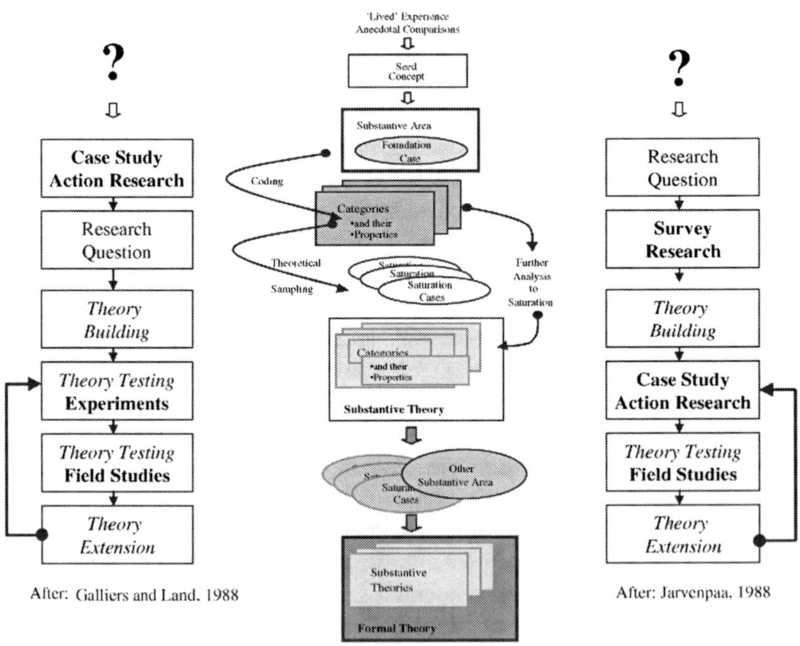

Figure 4.3. The grounded theory method, applied to cases, compared to the use of case study research methods in the – traditional – theory development paths suggested by Galliers and Land and Jarvenpaa

4.3 Conclusion

Following Denzin et al.'s (1994) five-step process of structuring qualitative research, a position within the research tradition was established, which then lead to definitions of theoretical research paradigms and strategy. From them, the most appropriate data selection and analysis techniques were selected.

The structure of the research methodology is characterized by the following:

1. Within the research tradition, the position taken was one of qualitative research in the social sciences tradition, straddling both *Verstehen* and *Erklären*, which is nomothetic in intent, but – at least initially – idiographic and emic in its stance;
2. An interpretivist paradigm with strong post-positivist leanings, reflected in a dualist/objectivist epistemological position;
3. The case study research design of the 'exploratory' and 'descriptive' kind, applied to *instrumental* cases in a *collective case* arrangement, was selected for the 'fact' finding part of the study;
4. Grounded Theory – following Glaser et al. (1967) and Glaser (1978) – was chosen for the 'inference' aspect of the research. It provides a means for categorizing facts from the cases and for conceptualizing correlative and/or causal linkages between the facts;
5. The Grounded Theory method (adapted for cases) has the interview as the main data collection instrument, strongly supported by observation and the enterprises' internal and external documentation. Coding – open and theoretical – is applied to the case story as the larger 'text' as well as to the individual 'slices-of-data' from which it is fabricated. Theoretical sampling applies *intra*-case as well as *inter*-case. Interpretation steps – coding, memo writing and theorizing – are carried out jointly with the data collection and write-up of the theory is continuous – albeit with milestones after each case when the theory-in-progress will be stated in the form of a theoretical framework.

The theory definition adapted for use in this study is Whetten's (1989) four component framework, i.e. a theory consists of

1. *factors*, which are linked in
2. *relationships* for which the theory provides
3. *explanations*, albeit within its
4. boundaries.

Seven criteria for assessing the quality of the theory were distilled from the literature, namely *clarity, parsimony, logical coherence, scope, integration, falsifiability* and *utility*.

The 'ideational construct' of a common/local structure specific for IIS, grounded in the 'lived' experience of the researcher, has been adopted as the starting point for the development of the Grounded Theory in this study.

Endnotes

a The terms nomothetic/idiographic and emic/etic are used following the context of Guba & Lincoln (1994). However, as Myers (1997) points out, considerable confusion and controversy continues to surrounds the use of these terms. For clarification, therefore, here are the definitions of how the terms are used here:

- *nomothetic*: relating to, involving, or dealing with abstract, general, or universal statements or laws
- *idiographic*: relating to or dealing with something concrete, individual, or unique
- *emic*: of, relating to, or involving analysis of linguistic or behavioral phenomena in terms of the internal structural or functional elements of a particular system
- *etic*: of, relating to, or having linguistic or behavioral characteristics considered without regard to their structural significance

(All citations: WWWebster Dictionary, 1996. Merriam-Webster, Springfield, MA [Online] at http://www.m-w.com/cgi-bin/mweb).

b WWWebster Dictionary (1996). {ibid.}.

c After Kuhn (1970), p. 11.

d For the purposes of this discourse, post-positivism shall include neo-positivism.

e A number of other alternative paradigms are included in the categories shown in the table. For example, Guba & Lincoln (1994) include in the Critical Theory category other ' related Ideological Positions', thus characterizing it as a summary category for generally 'ideologically engaged' paradigms. Similarly, such paradigms as Symbolic Interactionism, Structuration theory, Structuralism (including Post-Structuralist positions), Institutionalism are deemed to be in wider family which here is called Constructivist. It serves as a collection vessel for all paradigms that differ along the epistemology/ontology dimension. Although some of these 'excluded' alternative paradigms have been in sporadic use in recent information systems research, they bear little relevance to the research objective and have therefore not treated in any depth in the paradigm selection phase of this study.

f Selected validity of different, often mutually enhancing, methods of enquiry; Guba et al. (1994).

g 'Two individuals...maintaining a sociologically significant relationship'; WWWebster Dictionary, 1996. Merriam-Webster, Springfield, MA.

h Described by Guba & Lincoln (1994) as a 'congeries of social, political, cultural, economic, ethnic and gender factors, ...crystallized (reified) into a series of structures that are now (inappropriately) taken as 'real', that is, natural and immutable. For all practical purposes the structures *are* real, a *virtual* or *historical* reality'.

i Guba & Lincoln (1994) also compare the paradigm position with respect to *Goodness criteria, Values, Ethics Training, Accommodation* and *Hegemony* (of one paradigm over the others). These have been left out in the table because they are not relevant to its purpose, i.e. to select the research approach to be taken for this study.

j As opposed to (mostly single) *intrinsic* cases, where, 'in all its particularity and ordinariness, the case itself is of interest' (Stake, 1994, p. 236).

k 'Explanatory' case research explains a specific theory or proposition, stated a priori; this makes it similar to an experiment in the conventional, verificational, scientific tradition.

l As they contain a strong methodological element, Galliers (1991) would probably classify them midway between an *approach* ('ways of going about one's research') and a *method*, which he defines (after Weick) as 'simple ways to systematize observations'.

m These are: Ethnography and Participant Observation, Phenomenology, Ethnomethodology and Interpretive Practice, Historical method, Applied and Action Research and Clinical Models.

n There are many definitions of *text* in the literature, often conflicting and sometimes ideologically biased. For this reason, it is defined here in a neutral way as: 'something written or spoken considered as an object to be examined, explicated, or deconstructed'. (WWWebster Dictionary, 1996. Merriam-Webster, Springfield, MA).

o Strauss & Corbin's (1990) delineate the objects of the qualitative research they apply their version of Grounded Theory to as 'persons' lives, stories, Behavior, organizational functioning, social movements, or interactional relationships' (p. 17).

p This restriction would fatally limit the Strauss method's use for the 'fact' finding part of the study. In contrast, the Glaser method explicitly covers both 'variance' and 'process' constructs: '[it] can…be used to generate static theories [and also]…facilitates the generation of theories of process, sequence and change' (Glaser & Strauss, 1967, p. 114).

q But perhaps not in intention: the traditional data acquisition model seems to work under the assumption of an infinite pool of 'actors'; running out of data is not mentioned anywhere as a reason for changing groups.

r Whetten elegantly bypasses the (positivist) argument that causality may not be testable by commenting that 'restrictions in methods do not invalidate the inherent causal nature of theory' (p. 491).

s Following Dubin (1969, pp. 8–9) no distinction is made between the use of the terms *theory* and *model*. Dubin, however, also uses *system* as a synonym for theory – for obvious reasons this will not be the case in this study, wherein *system* will always only be a synonym for *information system*.

Chapter 5
Research Method: Grounded Theory for Descriptive and Exploratory Case Studies

Both Case Study and Grounded Theory methods are still minority research methodologies in information systems. A search of research papers published in higher tier information systems journals[a] between 1985 and 2005 showed that only 120 out of 7,372 articles were concerned with case study research. Case methods are, however, well established in organizational research and have become increasingly more accepted in information systems research too (for examples see Benbasat et al., 1987; Galliers et al., 1987; Yin, 1989; Lee, 1989a, b; Orlikowski et al., 1991; Zinatelli et al., 1994). In particular, Eisenhardt (1989) describes a process of building theory from cases, focusing especially on its inductive nature.

Grounded Theory research, on the other hand, is still a distinct minority method for information systems research: only 3 out of the 7,372 papers in 1st tier journals contain 'Grounded Theory' as a keyword. It, too, started in general business research first. Turner (1983) was the first to apply the approach to management studies. Since 1984, it had been used in a number of business studies (see Glaser's anthology, 1995). Orlikowski (1993, 1995) has pioneered Grounded Theory in Information Systems Research. Yoong (1996) and Atkinson (1997) are recent monographs based on Grounded Theory studies. Although Glaser et al. (1970) have also set out a research note on the role of cases in Grounded Theory, so far there have been no publications to show that this was attempted in practice.

In this chapter the adaptation of the traditional grounded theory method to case studies is set out. First the main principles of grounded theory will be exemplified and then compared with the traditional case study method. From this, the application of Grounded Theory in the context of cases is set out and the method to be followed in this study is described. Finally, a summary of the actual research activities is provided.

H. Lehmann, *The Dynamics of International Information Systems*,
Integrated Series in Information Systems 23, DOI 10.1007/978-1-4419-5750-4_5,

5.1 Principles of Grounded Theory Procedure

The constant comparative method of joint coding and analysis was first described by Glaser et al. (1967) and subsequently elaborated by Glaser (1978). The method, however, was not described in the sequence of events the researcher undertakes. In Table 5.1 below, therefore, the sequence of operations is set out and referenced back to Glaser et al. (1967).

Table 5.1. The constant comparative method of joint coding and analysis (after Glaser et al., 1967)

Steps	Detail of activity (Glaser et al., 1967)	Pages
1. Comparing incidents* applicable to each category	'Start by coding each incident in the data into as many categories of analysis as possible, as categories emerge or as data emerge that fits an existing category'	105
	[First] rule for the constant comparative method: While coding an incident for a category, compare it with the previous incidents in the same and different groups coded in the same category	106
	Second rule of the constant comparative method: Stop coding and record a memo on your ideas	107
2. Integrating categories and their properties	'The constant comparative unit changes from comparing incident with incident to comparison of incident with properties; in this way, incidents are compared only with the accumulated knowledge on a category...thus incidents integrate into properties; subsequently, properties become integrated. As they do, constant comparisons...force the analyst to make some related theoretical sense of each comparison'	108
3. Developing Concepts	'One generates conceptual categories or their properties from evidence; then the evidence is used to illustrate the concept. The evidence my not necessarily be accurate beyond a doubt...but [that] one fact then becomes merely one of a universe of many possible indicators for, and data on, the concept. Furthermore, the concept itself will not change, while even the most accurate facts change'	23
4. Theoretical sampling	'Theoretical sampling answers the questions: What groups next and for what theoretical purpose?'	47
	'The main criteria for choosing groups is their theoretical relevance for furthering the development of the emerging categories'	49
	'The [grounded theory researcher] 'is an active sampler of theoretically relevant data' not an ethnographer trying to get the fullest data on a group'	59

* *Incidents* are defined as 'text units', comprising the individual, self-contained topics or subjects in interviews, documents, etc., as well as elements of the case stories themselves – i.e. the 'larger text'

The four steps in Table 5.1 are iterated until the theory emerging from the data is of sufficient scope to 'work' for the substantive area chosen. Guidelines for when to stop the process of joint coding and comparative analysis, how then to achieve a satisfactory level of parsimony in the theory without sacrificing its scope and finally choosing the style of expressing the theory are summarized (and cross-referenced) in Table 5.2 below.

Table 5.2. Guidelines to scoping and formulating the emerging theory (after Glaser et al., 1967)

Steps	Detail of activity (Glaser et al., 1967)	Pages
1. Theoretical saturation	'Categories ...become theoretically saturated. Saturation means that no additional data are being found ...[to further] develop properties of the category [The analyst] learns to see whether or not the next applicable incident points to a new aspect. If yes, the incident is coded and compared. If no, the incident is not coded, since it only adds bulk to the coded data and nothing to the theory'	111 61 112
2. Delimiting the theory	'Delimiting occurs...at two levels: the theory and the categories: Solidification of the theory;... major modifications become fewer and fewer...they mainly clarify the logic and take out non-relevant properties; Reduction of categories means that the analyst may discover underlying uniformities ...and can now formulate the theory with fewer high level concepts; [This] achieves two major requirements of theory: parsimony of variables and formulation, and scope in the applicability of the theory to a wider range of situations while keeping close [to the] data'	110
3. Writing the theory	'The constant comparative method can yield either discussional or propositional theory. The former type of presentation is often sufficiently useful at the exploratory stage of theory development and can easily be translated into propositions...if a formal hypothesis [is required]'	115

Figure 5.1 depicts the Grounded Theory method from its inception through to the transition from substantive to formal theories.

The quintessential procedural *fiat* within the grounded theory tradition is the principle of theoretical sampling. While coding and comparative analysis are used by several methods, the continuous selection of the next 'slice of data' for its potential theoretical contribution is specific to the Grounded Theory method. It demonstrates a change in the logic of the method, as Glaser (1978, pp. 37–38) points out: 'Grounded theory research involves alternating between inductive and deductive logic as the research proceeds ... theory [development] is inductive: a theory emerges after data collection starts. *Deductive work* is used to derive from induced codes conceptual guides as to where to go next for which comparative group or subgroup, in order to sample for more data to generate the theory'. The sampling activity uses '*Conceptual elaboration*…[that] guides the researcher back to locations and comparative groups in the field to discover more ideas and connections from the data…groups [are chosen] on their *ideational properties'* (ibid., pp. 40–42).

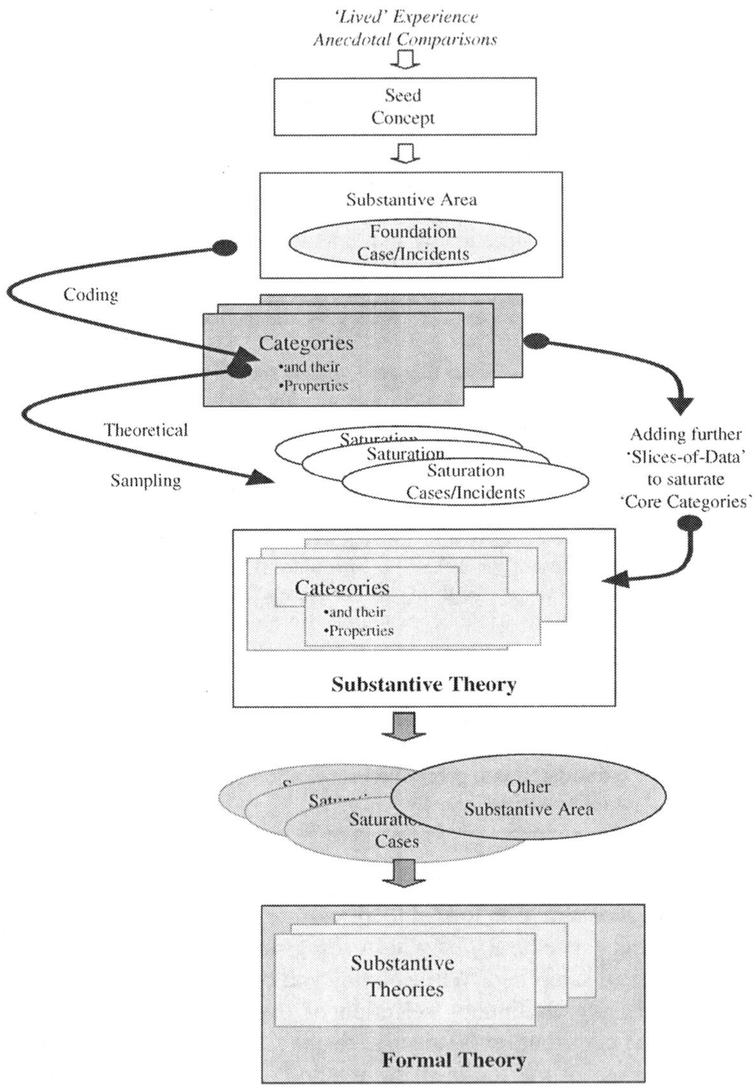

Figure 5.1. Theory development path in the grounded theory method

There are four major strategies for theoretical sampling: maximizing or minimizing the differences either between groups or between the data. Each strategy has a different objective, as Table 5.3 shows.

Table 5.3. Consequences of minimizing or maximizing differences in comparison groups for generating theory (after Glaser et al., 1967, p. 58)

Group Differences	**Data on category**	
	Similar	Diverse
Minimized	Maximum similarity in data leads to: Verifying usefulness of category; Generating basic properties; Establishing a set of conditions for a degree of category. These can be used for prediction	Identifying/developing fundamental differences under which category and hypotheses vary
Maximized	Identifying/developing fundamental uniformities of greatest scope	Maximum diversity in data quickly forces Dense developing of property of categories; Integrating of categories and properties; Delimiting scope of theory

This procedural definition of the Grounded Theory methodology can now be contrasted to the canons of traditional case study research.

5.2 Case Studies and Grounded Theory

Case study research, sometimes interpreted as a controlled, field experiment (Lee, 1989b), has traditionally followed the positivist, natural science model of hypotheses formulation from overarching theory and their subsequent verification or falsification in controlled studies (Yin, 1989). The grounded theory perspective, on the other hand, is not so clearly classified. Positivist in origin, it also 'reflects a naturalistic approach to ethnography and interpretation, stressing…observations, open-ended interviewing, the sensitizing use of concepts and a grounded (i.e. inductive) approach to theorizing which can be both substantive and formal'. (Denzin, 1994)

Despite those differences in *Weltanschauung*, case study research, using the Grounded Theory method as described in the previous section, can be designed to match closely the requirements of 'good [case study] practice', as set out by Yin (1989). Table 5.4 below compares Yin's case study approach with one based on grounded theory (Glaser et al., 1967).

Table 5.4. Comparison of case study approaches: Yin's traditional case study method and one based on Glaser et al.'s (1967) guidelines for grounded theory research

Yin's (1989) criteria for case studies and tactics (to improve each criterion)	Grounded Theory – corresponding process elements (where applicable)
Construct validity: Multiple sources of evidence Chain of evidence Informants review draft report	Joint coding and analyzing: Add data until theoretical saturation Transcripts, theoretical memos Add more data (if clarification is needed)
Internal validity; N.B.: not a criteria for exploratory and/or descriptive studies – they are not about causal relationships[b] Pattern matching Explanation building Time-series analysis	Constant comparative method: Coding/comparing of Categories/Properties Establishing relationships between Categories/Properties 'Time' could be a category itself
External Validity – definition of the 'substantive' area and generalizability of results: Replication logic in multiple cases: literal (same results expected) or theoretical (opposite results expected) replication	Boundaries of the 'substantive area' emerge from the data; Theoretical sampling determines multiple cases, which could aim at the same or contrasting categories. New data may add-to/change or confirm the theory
Reliability – the operations of the study can be repeated and achieve the same results[c]; Case study protocol Case study data base	Each unit of data gathering is documented in the form of (descriptive) transcripts, notes of their coding and a summary of observed relationships in theoretical memos; the totality of this documentation is equivalent to protocol and data base

The comparison shows different perspectives with regard to the traditional positivist requirements of generalizability, reliability and reproducibility. On closer inspection, however, they are mostly differences in terminology: Grounded Theory does not deny, but merely qualifies generalizability by defining the specific area of scope that the case study's theory will cover. Similarly, it substitutes reliability for the concept of 'saturation', i.e. when new data repeats (i.e. reproduces) the same categories without adding new properties.

In essence, therefore, an amalgam of Grounded Theory and Case Research should be as capable of producing good theory as its traditional counterparts on their own.

5.3 The Application of Grounded Theory to Case Research

As in the traditional Grounded Theory method, the unit of first analysis is an incident in individual texts. In contrast to individual, homocentric studies, cases represent a networked collection of primary texts, forming a larger text in itself. To simplify nomenclature, the incidents in individual interviews, observations, etc. are summarily referred to as 'texts' and the case-wide network of incidents is referred to as the 'story'.

As more cases are added, their texts go alongside each other for comparison and analysis purposes. In order to decide when cases are needed and what their nature and attributes should be, a two-layered cycle of theoretical sampling is necessary:

In intra-case sampling the theoretical focus is on selecting more 'slices-of-data' from within each case so that their incidents can saturate categories and maximize their conceptual yield. Once such new data does not add more properties and/or begins to repeat existing ones, then no more useful data can come out of the current case. A second round of sampling needs to occur;

In inter-case sampling the status of the theoretical framework, which is the result of all the previous cases' categories and constructs is assessed for 'saturation' of theorems and propositions. Theoretical sampling then selects the next case such that unsaturated theorems and propositions can be enhanced and strengthened in their explanatory and predictive qualities.

This process of adding cases on the basis of inter-case theoretical sampling is then repeated until the relevant 'core' categories and relationships are saturated and the scope of the resultant, theory is at the required level of nomotheticity. The theory is still provisional at this stage. It now needs to undergo a final stage of delimitation so that it can be restated in its final form as a substantive theory. Table 5.5 below sets out the detailed steps in the method together with the deliverables from each of them.

Table 5.5. Grounded theory method for case studies: detailed steps

	Analysis steps	Results and deliverables
1.	'Open' coding of 'incidents' in the interview transcripts and supporting documents, the 'texts'	Basic, 'raw' categories and properties
2.	Assembling the network of individual texts, i.e. writing the 'story' of the case	Case history/story
3.	Using the 'story' for reviewing, refining and collapsing the basic categories, based on uniform and/or overlapping properties; merging raw categories into families of 'substantive' categories and further reducing these to 'core' categories.	Hierarchy of 'core' categories embracing 'substantive' categories, formed from 'raw' categories
4.	'Theoretical' coding of the case 'story' for 'relations' between core categories; this is for the case in hand, although the categories and relations from previous cases are used in constant comparison	Identifying main interactive categories; distinction between primary and secondary interaction; identifying direction of linkages; defining the specific nature of each interaction;

	Analysis steps	Results and deliverables
5.	Establishing and refining categories and their linkages	Models of the interaction of all categories, in groups and in toto; preliminary theory write-up of descriptions and propositions
6.	Comparing between cases, 'stories' as well as individual 'texts'	Establishing the differences between the cases, by contrasting the case in hand with each of the previous cases in turn.
7.	Establishing and refining the theoretically relevant differences between the cases	Distilling any new, 'derived' categories and relationship 'constructs' from the comparative analysis
8.	Distilling theory elements from both the case in hand and from the comparative analysis	Theorems and propositions, forming the 'nth-generation' of the (provisional) Theoretical Framework
9.	'Densifying' the (provisional) Theoretical Framework by comparison with its previous 'generation'	'Revised 'nth-generation' (provisional) Theoretical Framework;
10.	Delimiting and 'axiomatizing' the last generation' (provisional) Theoretical Framework	Final substantive theory

The analysis steps fall into four categories, each of which, in turn, relates to a specific class of output in the form of a theoretical element. Figure 5.2 below depicts these analysis stages and the way in which they take the elements of the nascent theory to successively higher layers of abstraction.

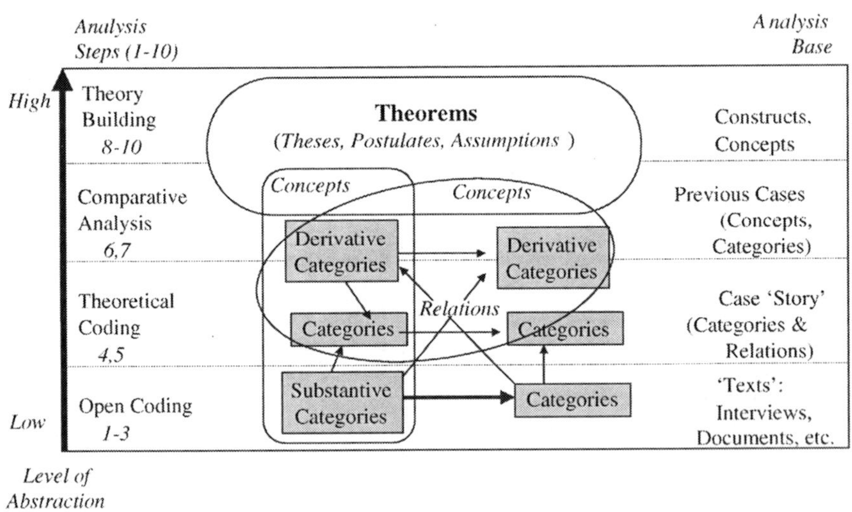

Figure 5.2. Theory building: analysis stages and levels of abstraction

The conceptualization process employed in the theoretical coding stage used a number of analytical schemes to elevate the explanation of the data from a descriptive level to a more theoretical way of thinking. This follows suggestions from Stern (1994), Lofland et al. (1995) and Miles et al. (1994). It is also consistent with Glaser (1978), who offers a number of schemata, diagrams and codes to use in the attempt to increase the 'theoretical sensitivity' of the theory building process. Weick's (1979) cause-and-effect diagrams proved very useful in the construction of inter-category relationships and other dynamic propositions, as did a number of other graphical analysis tools such as case dynamics network graphics as suggested by Miles et al. (1994). Much use was therefore made of graphic and diagrammatic illustrations in the analytical write-up of categories, relations and theorems.

5.4 Research Activities Summary

The research methodology developed and set out in the previous sections was applied closely in the methods used in carrying out the research study. In the following paragraphs a synopsis of the actual research activities will be set out.

The 'texts', the first accumulation of incidents, were prepared from in-depth interviews that were following theoretical guidance, but were otherwise unstructured, open-ended and wide-ranging. Their information content was supplemented by an extensive array of secondary material, internal and external. Maximizing the spectrum of information sources worked very well – corroborating Orlikowski's (1993) observation that 'triangulation across various techniques of data collection is particularly beneficial in theory generation because it provides multiple perspectives on an issue, supplies more information on emerging concepts, allows for cross-checking and yields stronger substantiation of constructs'.

Table 5.6. Summary of interview hours by type of interviewee and the extent of secondary materials used

Cases*	Business (hours and %)	IT people (hours and %)	Total hours	Documentation (approximate pages)	Documentation (number vol's)
Co-op	40.0	18.5	58.5	2,500	93
	68%	32%			
J Lauritzen	13.5	15.0	28.5	300	28
	47%	53%			
Panalpina	14.5	17.0	31.5	800	36
	46%	54%			
Total	68.0	50.5	118.5	3,600	157
	57%	43%			

* in the order of their participation

Table 5.6 above gives an overview of the hours expended in interviews and the extent of the secondary materials used.

The interviews were transcribed onto some 1,400 pages of notes. Together with about 3,600 pages worth of other internal and external materials (from 157 documents) they filled a small filing cabinet.

Held in closeted, uninterrupted settings, the interviews lasted usually for between 1:40 and 2:10 h. They are, overall, evenly spread between business people and IT management and staff, although the ratio shifted as the study went on. Most interviewees were interviewed twice: overall, 55 interviews were held with 30 case people in 11 locations worldwide. The interviews were recorded on audiotape and transformed into verbatim transcripts to accompany the interview notes for further analysis.

'Intra-case' theoretical sampling: guided the content of the interviews as well as the selection of the interviewees. In the first case more than two thirds of the information were gathered in interviews and from other sources in the firms Head Office. This reflects the emphasis on understanding the nature of the firm's business and its global strategies as well as the business role of information technology.

As the study progressed more information was needed to saturate the categories dealing with the actual use of any information systems by the firm's international users. Accordingly, the number of interviews with regional management and staff increased steeply, decreasing the share of the centre in the later cases.

Table 5.7 below summarizes the distribution of interview time between the centre and local users in the study.

Table 5.7. Distribution of interview contribution (hours) between head-office and regional offices

Case	Head office	Regions	Totals	
Co-op	44.5	14	58.5	49%
J Lauritzen	12.5	16	28.5	24%
Panalpina	3	28.5	31.5	27%
Totals	60	58.5	118.5	
	51%	49%		

Table 5.8 below shows the geographical distribution of interviews over the three cases.

For each case the 'stories' were written and, together with the results from the coding of the 'texts', formed the basis for the conceptualization of categories and their relations.

Table 5.8. Interviews (number) by case and global location

Interview location	Co-op	J. Lauritzen	Panalpina	Total
New Zealand-Auckland		4	3	7
'Australasia'	23 *,**			23
USA-San Francisco	1			1
USA-Los Angeles		3	2	5
UK-Surrey	3			3
UK-Kent			5	5
Denmark-Copenhagen		6*		6
Austria-Vienna			4	4
Switzerland-Basle			1*	1
Totals	27	13	15	55

* Head office location
** Includes regional management visiting at HQ

The first case, selected for its size and dynamics, was the 'Co-op'.[1] It yielded a very large number (133) of raw categories, which theoretical coding reduced to 27 families of substantive categories and finally to 13 core categories. Saturation was, however, lacking in all categories to do with the operational use of an IIS. Following extensive theoretical sampling, which employed a difference-maximization strategy, J Lauritzen was identified as the second case.

J Lauritzen contributed a wealth of information, especially in the area of operational use of an IIS and its acceptance by local users. Further inter-case theoretical sampling, this time applying a mixed strategy of minimizing 'group' but maximizing 'data' differences, pointed to the need for a larger, more mature operator of international information systems. PANALPINA was chosen as the result of this selection round. They are a mature, long-term user of global information technology, which plays a strategic part in their business. This third case contributed significantly to the saturation of new core categories added. Their conceptualization and embedding brought the temporary theoretical framework to a stage where its transition to a 'substantive' theory became feasible. Table 5.9 below summarizes the discovery of categories and the rate of their reduction to substantive and core categories.

Table 5.9. Growth in the number of categories across the three cases

	Co-op	J. Lauritzen	Panalpina	
		New categories added		Total categories
Raw categories	133	33	27	193
Substantive categories	27	8	8	43
Core categories	13	4	1	18

[1] The enterprise in question requested to be disguised.

Coding in the Co-op case was done manually, using a word processor to record and reference the categories. However, for both the following cases qualitative data analysis software was used to simplify and streamline the administration of the coding, as well as all the coding notes and theoretical memos produced during the coding processes.

Most of the data collection work was begun during the last months of 1996 and continued on to the end of 1998. Analysis (including a fair amount of validation, clarification as well as verification) took most of 1999. The process of theory development, although started in parallel with the data collection, was eventually finalized in 2001. Theory writing – and setting out the first formal report and summary on the research – went on until the second half of 2002.

The first case took nearly twice as much elapsed time as the others. The reason for it was that painting the first, initial 'text' requires disproportionately more data then the following, 'saturation' cases. In addition, the Co-op, as the 'foundation' case, provided an extraordinarily rich story, yielding a flow of – initially – some 130 categories of data. This allowed sharply focused theoretical sampling, leading to more 'efficient' data gathering in the next two cases. Developing the initial theory elements took the best part of the following year. Writing up the theory meant finding a way to cope with the richness of the stories and the enormous amount of detail uncovered in the study. Because of that – and because it was done part-time – 2½ years elapsed before the fist version of the research monograph was completed as a work-in-progress. By then it had been 6 years since the first data gathering and interviews had started. For this reason a round of update visits (with more data gathering) was undertaken during 2003 and 2004. The theoretical frameworks were updated and an extended version of the theory was published[d] in abridged form (Lehmann & Gallupe, 2005).

The case stories and their analysis are described in abridged format in this volume. Both are, however, supported by more detailed descriptions and analysis in the working paper chapters contained on the author's companion web-site.[2]

5.5 Conclusion

Applying Grounded Theory to Case Study was very successful. It produced a prolific amount of data and yielded a great richness of information. The reason for this was partly that all three cases were large firms, and two of the cases were from enterprises with a wide and dense global presence. Illustrating and absorbing their diversity necessitated the generation and collection of copious amounts of material. For a major part, however, the deluge of information was due to the efficiency with which the constant coding and comparison distils relevant categories and properties from the data. The case settings, furthermore, contained more varied data than could be expected from individual, purely

[2] Please contact Hans.Lehmann@vuw.ac.nz for access.

homocentric studies. Efficiency and abundance combined to make this method an exceedingly fruitful one. Whilst this is highly positive for the quality of resulting theoretical propositions, it presents a challenge for presenting the findings in a concise, readable format.

Endnotes

a The search filters included: *MIS Quarterly, Information Systems Research, Communications of the ACM (research articles only), Journal of Management Information Systems, Decision Sciences, IEEE Transactions on Communications and Software Engineering and Management Science.*

b Traditionally, both *exploratory* and *descriptive* studies were used as mere pilots for larger, explanatory studies in the second instance; it was the larger studies, following the pilot, which looked for relationships such as causality.

c If '*same results*' means that the contents of the data and observations will be the same, then this is not realistic for social, organizational and business research. It overlooks the fact that with time the observed entities, subjects, topics will have changed substantially – as Heraklith remarked: 'You cannot swim the same river twice'. A better method for checking 'reliability of the data' is the examination of the quality of the data gathering procedures and the quality of data recording. If 'same results' means that the findings and conclusions will be the same then the interpretative power of the individual researcher must be a very strong interference in any repetition of a case study. However, it seems that this criterion, seemingly taken straight from the quantitative method arsenal for the study of inanimate nature, is not in this form applicable to qualitative research in a social context. Reliability here needs to rely on the internal quality of the data collection and recording process and could be enhanced by quality audits (Yin alludes to this being an 'auditing' activity). Repetition would still have a place, but as a vehicle for secondary analyses of any case study data – a possibility Glaser et al. (1967) mention as a valuable source of additional data for grounded theory studies.

d Aspects of the cases, the theory and the method had, however, been published throughout the research, see Lehmann (1996a, b, 2000, 2001, 2003, 2004, 2006) and Fernandez & Lehmann (2005).

Chapter 6
Foundation Case: The Australasian Food Co-op

This chapter describes the first case study, the 'foundation' for the rest of the research project. The case itself is disguised, according to the wishes of the enterprise concerned. As mentioned above, the case is an extraordinarily rich one. This, in conjunction with the generative power of the Grounded Theory method, has meant that for reasons of readability an abridged version of the case and findings is contained in this chapter. A detailed version can be obtained from the author's companion website on demand.[1] The chapter is structured as follows:

- First, the case story is presented;
- Interpretation of the case is next;
- Third, the interpretation is expressed in theory terms as the 1st Theoretical Framework;
- Lastly, the rationale for the theoretical sampling to select the next case is set out.

6.1 Case History: Australasian Food Producers' Co-op

Marketing authorities for land-based industries (such as fruit growers, meat producers, dairy farmers, forestry, etc.) are often large companies with strong international presence. The Australasian Food Producers' Co-op[2] (the 'Co-op') with some $5bn revenue is one of the largest of those. Like the others, the Co-op is a 'statutory monopoly', as there is legislation which prohibits any other organization from trading their produce in international markets. With about a quarter of its revenue from raw materials and manufacturing outside Australasia, the Co-op is a mature transnational operator. Structured into nine regional holding companies, in 1997 it has a presence in 135 offices in 40 countries. The 15,000

[1] Please email Hans.Lehmann@vuw.ac.nz for access.

[2] All names and places have been changed; all money figures are in US Dollars.

H. Lehmann, *The Dynamics of International Information Systems*,
Integrated Series in Information Systems 23, DOI 10.1007/978-1-4419-5750-4_6,

primary producers are organized into 18 co-operative 'Production Companies' (ProdCos), where they hold shares in proportion to their production. The ProdCos, in turn, own the Co-op.

This tight vertical integration is seen as a big advantage. It allows the Co-op to act as one cohesive enterprise and to develop a critical mass needed in most of its major markets. Figure 6.1 shows this structure and the product flow.

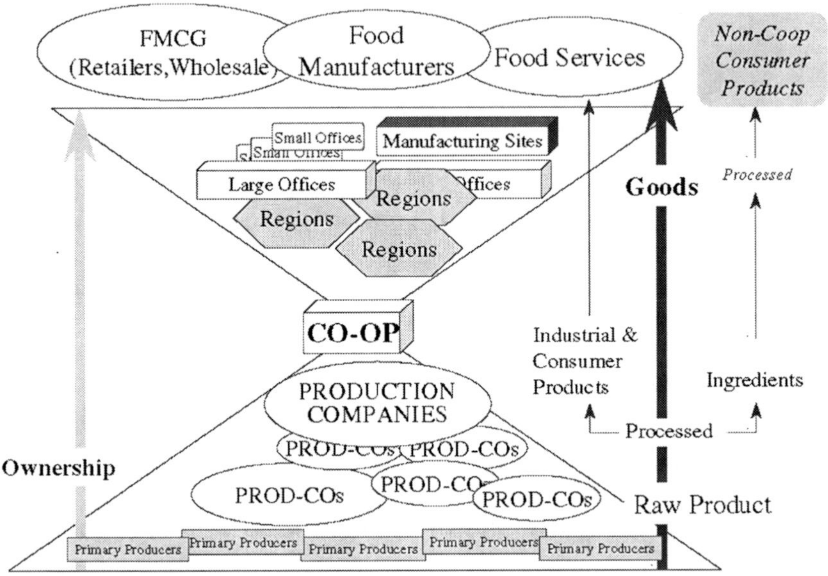

Figure 6.1. Business structure of the Co-op

6.1.1 Business Background

Prior to the mid 1970s Australasia exported some 85% of its produce to the United Kingdom, who, under Commonwealth rules, used to accept it all. Once the UK had joined the European Union (EU), however, the Co-op had to share access with all other EU members. This cut their market share immediately and severely. New markets were needed as a matter of survival. Subsidiary offices were rapidly set up all around the world and given free hand to sell as much as they could – by whichever means necessary. This policy of far-reaching local autonomy was very successful. Within less than a decade the Co-op had built a substantial presence in more than 30 countries and had managed, throughout, to secure a more than satisfactory return for all their primary producers. Overall, the expansion had made them a stronger and more profitable business.

By the early 1990s, the resulting enterprise was now a sophisticated, world-class operation of global reach and of often complex diversity. A comparison (shown in Figure 6.2) of value per tonne of product (as an indicator of product type), revenue per staff (commodity trading *versus* branded product marketing) and number of personal computers per staff (information technology literacy) shows an exceedingly wide range of diversity of business in the Co-op's regions.

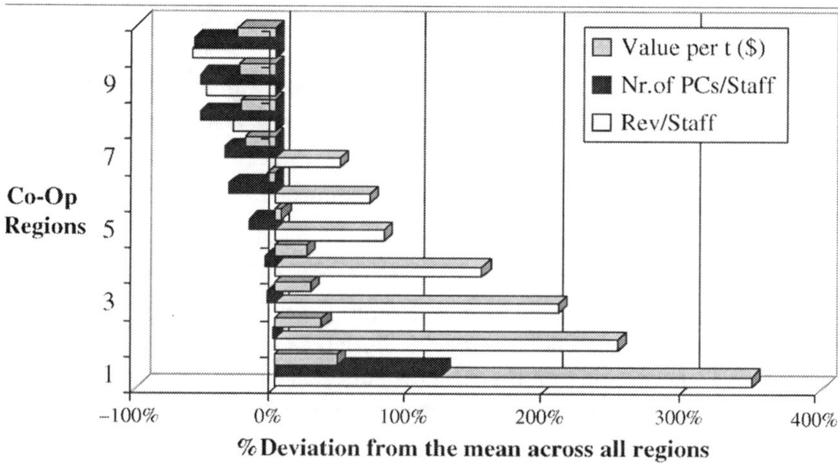

Figure 6.2. Business diversity across the Co-op's regions (deviation from the mean in % of the mean)

At the onset of the 1990s, however, competition in the Cop-op's main markets had become strong and increasingly global. With the emergence of global brands (such as Nestlé, Coca Cola, McDonalds) the Co-op needed to develop global brands themselves. For this, they had to have sufficient command and control to mount synchronized international marketing and logistics operations. With the arrival of a new Chief Executive Officer in 1992, the Co-op began a concerted campaign to shift authority and control over branding and global marketing policy back to head-office.

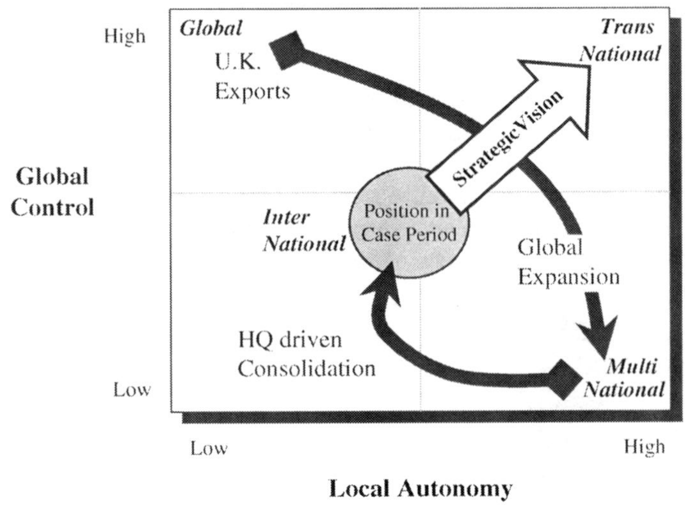

Figure 6.3. The Co-op's strategic migration

The CEO's vision was one of balanced central control and local flexibility. Figure 6.3 shows this development, using the Bartlett and Ghoshal framework.

The Co-op's IT people interpreted this new policy as an encouragement to have a critical look at the role of information systems throughout the Co-op's world-wide operations.

6.1.2 The IS Landscape in the 1990s

During the 'global' phase, the Co-op had built up a sizeable IS department with a mainframe operation at the head-office, linking up with all main subsidiary offices and ProdCos. Information systems concentrated on the needs of producers and local production – co-operatives and were traditional transaction processing systems, housed on a large central mainframe. Foreign activities were few and hardly needed computer support. The forced expansion drive in the 1980s, however, lead to an increased need by foreign operations to be supported with information systems. By 1992, most regional offices had bought computers and software. Some had built sizeable systems to suit their own, individual requirements. There were altogether seven different makes of information technology platforms, running diverse applications software, mostly locally supported.

6.1.3 The Global Information Systems Project

Against this background of a proliferation of uncoordinated local systems the Co-op's IS Department in April 1992 took the – unilateral – initiative to establish a 'Framework for Information Systems'. They interpreted the Co-op's policy of taking more charge of over global marketing as a return to a 'global' mode of central governance. Subsequently, they argued that such central standardization was necessary if a higher level of control was to be established. The Co-op's executive, who at that stage were not all too comfortable with information technology and described themselves often as 'benign illiterates when it comes to computers', sanctioned the initiative.

The 'Framework' was going to be the basis for a global standard for all information technology, including data, information and application software. The policy's objective was to have one common standard in force throughout all of the Co-op's 135 offices in 9 regions, across 35 countries. Subsequently, in late 1992, the 'Food Information Systems Technology' (FIST) project was initiated by the IS Department to implement the 'Framework'. The plan was to have three stages:

1. Development of a 'prototype' system; this was to be ready by early-1994;
2. Implementation of the prototype in a small number of 'pilot' sites by mid 1994; and a
3. 'Roll-out' of the 'global system' into all the 9 regions and 135 offices by late 1995.

In 1992 the North America region (NAR) had started to embark on a project to replace of its obsolescent IBM S/34. At the same time, the South East Asia region (SEAR) was looking to upgrade and consolidate their information systems configuration of numerous fragmented PC-based installations to cope with managing the rapid growth in the region. Both sites thus became candidates for the development of the prototype and also as pilot sites for further implementation.

6.1.4 Technology Selection and Pilot Projects

The FIST team was a small core-group of experienced data processing professionals, most of whom had been with the Co-op for a long time. Some were technical specialists, hired specifically for the project. They set themselves a first project milestone of June 1994 – 9 months hence. They were reasonably confident that by then they would have selected the global technology; developed the prototype, tested it for use as a pilot and gone live with the first global standard systems in North America and South East Asia.

To minimize language difficulties and other cultural barriers, the requirements for NAR were selected for use as a 'benchmark'. Requirements for all other sites could then be defined only in terms of their divergence from the benchmark. Traditional data modeling and business process modeling was used to specify a 'prototype' at the Co-op's head quarters. Despite criticism by NAR management as 'too high-level' to be useful for prescribing the functionality required, the 'prototype' was used as the base for a Request for Proposal (RFP). Asking for firm quotes for software, hardware, communications technology and support to be used globally, the RFP was issued to ORACLE, IBM, HP, EDS and UNISYS. After a rapid evaluation, HW[3] hardware and DBM[3] database software was selected. No decision was made about communications technology or world-wide user support. Although they had not been part of the tender, SOFT's[3] applications software was chosen on DBM's recommendation.

SEAR had been quite concerned when the FIST team restricted itself to developing a 'prototype' for North America as a global 'benchmark model' – and comparing it with the South East Asia region, instead of investigating their requirements *in loco*. Their concern grew after the selection of HW, DBM and SOFT as to whether they were reliably represented throughout South East Asia. When the FIST team subsequently found a '90–95% match' between the two regions, the head of SEAR office opted out of the Pilot. He felt strongly that, as North America's predominant business is in the industrial produce market, any model based on their requirements would not at all fit South East Asia ('nor Europe, for that matter'), as their business was mainly in the consumer and food manufacturing markets.

He was also very critical of what he called the 'top-down-approach' taken by FIST. With very little participation by the regions, he feared the systems, 'just like other past failures of the Computer Centre', would be missing most of the significant local requirements. By mid 1994, North America was therefore the only pilot site.

6.1.5 The North American Pilot

The FIST team then began with the implementation and modifications of the software in North America. For their own internal reasons DBM insisted on supporting the NAR project from their Australasian office, despite the fact that their global support centre was very close to NAR's head office. After these negotiations, actual work began in September 1994. Nearly immediately serious problems were encountered. The SOFT manufacturing and distribution modules – selected from the 'prototype' specifications – did not conform to the current business processes in NAR. Changes to make SOFT conform were estimated to

---

[3] To preserve the case's anonymity, the technology products are also disguised.

cost $1.8m. Moreover, at this time, DBM were starting negotiations with SOFT about acquiring them as their own applications software division. For the duration of these negotiations all work on the software was suspended. The deadline for the NAR pilot implementation was extended to mid 1995. The head of NAR refused to pay for the changes, saying, 'I told you so' and balking at having to survive with obsolescent technology for another year.

To overcome this strengthening resistance, the FIST team enlisted the help of the CEO, who issues a sharply worded edict to the NAR management team, ordering them to give FIST all the necessary support and co-operation. This silenced the North America executive. DBM had finished negotiations with SOFT. Both developments helped to bring the project back into life.

6.1.6 Europe and Business Process Reengineering

With NAR now underway, FIST began to look at the Europe Region (ER). The 'benchmark model' (i.e. the NAR prototype) was compared with Europe and a '90–95%' match was declared by the FIST team. However, the regional manager for Europe echoed the sentiments of his North American and SEAR counterparts when he remarked that 'These models are so general, they'd make Disney look like us.' Wary of the CEO support the FIST team could enlist he used this 'generality' of the models to distance ER from the project. He pointed out that ER's business is firstly fundamentally different from NAR: they are in different industries and different products. Secondly, as his region also incorporates Western North Africa, there is also a very wide spectrum in terms of size and sophistication throughout his operations. ER asked for – and was granted – suspension from FIST until after the NAR pilot implementation.

To counter this renewed, and strongly mounting, resistance to their vision of the same global system for every Co-op office, the FIST team, with the CEO's blessing, embarked on a business-process-reengineering exercise, again at the head-office. As a result the global standard design would be modified so that regional and local business management could accept it. They began to look at what 'Core' of application systems should be the same throughout the Group and which application areas could be different for each local subsidiary.

The main result of this study was a re-definition of all the main business operations as a streamlined 'Enquiry-To-Cash' process (ETC). This now became the global standard for the 'Core' information system. The 'Local' applications, to be selected by each office individually, were a residue of loosely defined 'manufacturing and marketing operations' support systems. FIST published this as the new 'Framework for Information Systems', and announced ETC as the new 'global operations paradigm' for all regions and operating subsidiaries.

6.1.7 From North America to the Middle East

All this had taken resources away from the NAR project, parts of which were suspended until ETC was completed. As a consequence, the NAR deadline was shifted to mid 1996. The NAR executive responded that their ageing system would not survive another year's extension. Furthermore they did not accept ETC, arguing that it 'did not fit the way their business works'. In response, FIST decreed that the North America region must change its operating procedures and processes to conform to ETC, as this was the new global operations paradigm. In order to implement the changes needed, a business-process-reengineering sub-project was to be embarked on throughout NAR.

Regional management, however, maintained that there was very little to be gained from such a major upheaval. They vigorously resisted the implementation of the reengineering project and, by mid 1995, reached an agreement with the CEO to 'suspend' FIST until they had replaced their – by now obsolete – hardware and information systems with an 'interim solution'.

In early 1995, the Co-op had opened a new office in one of the Middle East countries (MEO). By the end of 1995, there were 22 people working in the office. At the beginning of 1996, the FIST team selected MEO as the new pilot site for the global standard system for the Co-op, replacing NAR. The first 'global prototype' was going to be the 'Core' SOFT applications, implementing the ETC operational and business procedures. The first target date for completion was June 1996. However, for want of adequate local support, the systems could not be developed on site. It was therefore developed at the Co-op's Australasian head office. In November 1996 the deadline for full ETC implementation was extended to early 1997.

6.1.8 Final Resistance to FIST

In the run up to the conference of regional executives in mid 1996, the head of ER actively canvassed his fellow regional executives. With their support at the meeting, he raised serious concern over FIST, which by then had consumed some $9m in costs. He especially expressed doubts about the logic behind using MEO's information systems as a pilot and questioned how representative a tiny office in a fringe market could be as a model for a global system. After the meeting, he negotiated with the CEO to be 'temporarily excluded' from the FIST strategy in order to pursue urgent updates on their own, regional information technology and systems platform – work which had been postponed for 4 years, pending the imminent implementation of FIST.

FIST countered this by reducing the scope of the 'global prototype' to 'standard financials' and MEO went live with a set of basic accounting systems in time for the beginning of 1997. At the early 1997 regional executive meeting,

FIST now presented the MEO system as the first successful global pilot. They furthermore demonstrated a set of justifications for MEO which they extrapolated and forecast to show the global economics and benefits of FIST. Based on this, they announced a Global Roll-Out program, starting from mid 1997, to implement FIST throughout the world.

However, many of the regional executive members doubted the accuracy and relevance of the economic justification based on MEO. No agreement was reached as to how FIST would proceed.

The major, continuing difficulties with the FIST project, the missed deadlines, the significant costs without any noticeable results and the refusal by major regions to accept the FIST system had begun to raise doubts in the mind of the CEO. In mid 1996 he commissioned a major international consulting firm to audit and appraise the FIST project. Their report in early 1997 was critical of FIST, which they described as 'overly ambitious' and not 'achievable within the time frame or the existing project set-up'. This proved to be a turning point: The CEO re-aligned the IT portfolio – including FIST – into the Finance department. The General Manager Finance had been an open critic of FIST for a long time. In mid 1997 he terminated the project and called for a broadly based study of global versus local information technology strategy.

6.2 Findings and Interpretation of the Case

The case 'text' is based on some 60 hours of interviews and some 93 volumes/items of secondary documentation, totaling approximately 2,500 pages. 40 hours of interviews were held with the 'business' people and (candidate) users. With the exception of North America and the UK (head office of the European region), the majority interviews were held around Australasia, albeit not only with head office staff but also with a number of visiting regional executives.

In accordance with the research question – and also following Whetten's (1989) theory 'components' – the interpretation of the case is organized into three steps.

1. First, the 'factors', i.e. the categories and their properties at play in the case are identified.
2. They are then brought into relation to each other and, lastly,
3. The causes and reasons for the relationships are set out.

6.2.1 Categories and Properties

The 'text' was coded into 133 primary categories,[4] which fell into 27 sets of subject-related families. Theoretical coding reduced them to just 13 core categories.

The core categories found in the Co-op case fell into one of two domains, depending on whether they originated in the business or information technology arena. The core categories in both the business and information technology domains are made up of a number of sub-categories. In both domains the sub-categories were often the main point of interaction and contributed significantly to the dynamics between categories. The core categories in both the business and information technology domains are summarized in Table 6.1 below:

Table 6.1. Domains and core categories from the Co-op case

Business domains	IT domains
Nature of the business	Global standard IS design
Global business strategy	Analysis (methods and paradigms)
Lack of IT sophistication	Capacity
Migration of global strategy	IS professional skills
Tradition of local autonomy	Domestic mindset
Rejection of global IS	IS initiative
	IS by force

In the following sections the categories in both domains are described in more detail.

6.2.1.1 The Business Domain

The six core categories in the business dynamics domain, together with their most significant sub-categories are summarized as follows:

1. *Nature of the Business*,[5] i.e. the aspects of the Co-op's business specifically relevant for the global IS project; the political nature of the Co-op, their global diversity and the low information technology intensity of their basic business are influential properties of this category;
2. The Co-op's *Global Business Strategy*; the difficulties with balancing the dichotomy between local autonomy and central control, as well as the actual split of functions between head office and the regions are both significant, directing influences for the Co-op's information systems;

---

[4] To recapitulate: 'Categories, in Glaser & Strauss (1967) terminology, are the main influences that shape the 'text' – or parts thereof. They are the building block objects of the theory-to-be-discovered, and the 'factors' whose relationships form the explanatory and predictive statements of the theory.

[5] *Core Categories* and *Sub-Categories* are formatted as shown.

3. *Lack of IT Sophistication*: a partial consequence of the low information intensity, especially during its earlier global business strategy, this is the Co-op Executive's inexperience with information systems and subsequent lack of 'IT awareness' culture; it shaped the way in which the Co-op assessed the viability and progress of the global IS project;
4. The nature and history of the *Migration of Global Strategy* the Co-op underwent, where the current progression towards '*transnational*' [6] is of special significance: the IT people misinterpreted this as a return to the old '*global*' [7] strategy, which sowed the seeds for strong, politically motivated rejection by the business fiefs;
5. The *Tradition of Local Autonomy* reflects the *status quo* during the '*multinational'* phase of the strategic migration. This degree of freedom is vigorously defended by regional and local management against the global IS, which they see as an political instrument of subjugation;
6. *Rejection of Global IS* characterizes the actions and maneuvers by regional management to avoid the acceptance of a global standard system. Two sub-categories comprise most of the reasons for rejection: *Control/Politics* is the aversion and defense against any increase in central control, especially by political means. The concern that the proposed system does not do what the business needs is named *Misalignment*.

All these categories are deep-seated. They are well anchored in the way in which the business carries out its mission. The global IS runs against the very fundamental conflicts between the centre and the local parts of the Co-op's organization – which are at the very heart of its ultimate rejection.

6.2.1.2 The Information Technology Domain

There are seven core category families in the information technology field. They are set out below, together with a description of their most significant sub-categories.

The *Global Standard IS Design* is the largest core category in terms of attributable occurrences and the most influential factor for the *Rejection of the Global Information Systems*. The core is made up of three main sub-categories:

The *Global Nature* of the system is the collation of all the globally standardized, 'One-system-fits-all', elements of FIST's systems and technology architecture.

The *Common Core* category contains all the 'factual' (rational) arguments surrounding the scope of the common, globally compulsory part of the system.

[6] That is High central control over strategy as well as high local control over operations.

[7] That is Little autonomy as a result of strong central control over local operations.

Initially all systems were going to be standard; next, the streamlined, standardized ETC processes would form the global system; after all of the above had failed to materialize, a standard financial system was the last 'common core' proposed by FIST; complementing this,

The *Core/Local Split* is the distillation of the 'process' (political) difficulties – and ultimately the inability – of coming to an agreed definition of what should be the 'common core' and what should be the 'local' parts of the system.

The *Analysis* category sums up the main assumptions, methods and paradigms that govern the analysis of the business requirements for the global IS. It comprises of three sub-categories, namely

Equating Information with Application and Technology Infrastructure (further on this is referred to as '*I=A=T*' for short); this is the paradigmatic assumption that obtaining *equal* Information content requires *identical* Application systems, running on the *same* Technology Infrastructure. In design terms, it manifests itself as an uncritical belief that global, standard application system on standard hardware are the *only* solution to common information requirements;

Data/Business Modeling turned out to be an altogether insufficient tool for comparisons between the requirements of different local/regional offices. The modeling techniques were carried out at too high a level of abstraction, so *eo ipso* returned very similar models for significantly and substantially different businesses. In this way, they perpetually reinforced and deepened the fallacious

Business Sameness paradigm, i.e. the mistaken belief all the Co-op's businesses are essentially the same and can therefore be supported by the same information system, irrespective of location, size or nature of the business;

The fact that these assumptions, methods and paradigms are all either wrong, inappropriate or misguided means that the *Analysis* category represents an overall negative influence on the resulting global IS.

The category termed *Capacity* assimilates the qualities of being able to

understand, conceptualize and abstract the complex business process settings in the Co-op's regional operations; and to

develop from this base a set of solutions which are logically sound and practical, i.e. they can be implemented.

Similar to the *Analysis* category, *Capacity* manifested itself predominantly in its negative form, i.e. by a general inability to be successful in neither conceptualizing problems nor solving them acceptably.[a]

The quality of the *IS Professional Skills* brought to bear on the systems development process is an important category because it affects and shapes other core categories. Like its predecessors, this category, too, was apparent mostly at a low level. It has two sub-categories:

IS Professionalism, i.e. the adherence – or not – to what is considered good practice in information systems work;

Information Technology Conservatism, i.e. applying design and technology architecture concepts that are not at the 'state-of–the-art'.

The *Domestic Mindset* category describes the application of a set of predominantly domestic experiences, parameters and knowledge to the task of developing and implementing an international information system. Related to the *Analysis* and *Capacity* categories, this has two aspects:

Ignorance of the business conditions and cultural environments in the 35 countries where the Co-op's offices are situated; and

Underestimation of the time and effort required for analyzing and designing the systems as well as managing and progressing international projects,

The *IS Initiative* category embodies the fact – and its consequences – that the global IS project and had not originated from the business side, but had been initiated unilaterally by IS, with very little very little, insignificant user input.

Its main sub-category is the *IS Origin* of the project, as opposed to being business driven; Two further sub-categories are consequential to *IS Origin* and complement each other:

The business side always maintained that there was *No Economic Justification* for the global system, pointing to the efficacy of their – functioning – local systems. The cost justifications (in terms of people savings, etc) brought forward by the IS people – without the users' sanction – had little or no credibility with the business who regarded them as political window-dressing. This manifests itself as the

IS Control category, i.e. the interpretation of FIST as a political ruse to re-introduce higher levels of head-office control in the disguise of an information system;

The *IS by Force* category represents the use of politics and executive *fiat* to get the business to accept the global information system. Partly a consequence of *Capacity* and catalyzed by the political *Nature of the Business,* this category is characterized by four sub-categories:

Enlisting *CEO Support* in an effort to overcome rational arguments with political clout; this lead to the more general attitude of

HQ Rules, which means that the regions and local offices have to implement the global IS as, when and how they are told by head-office; it also means that

the *Business will Change*, not the system, in case of discrepancies between its functionality and the way the business operates; and, in general,

Political Arguments will be used to compensate for inabilities to resolve objections in a rational way.

The categories in both domains influence each other strongly, both within each domain and, more significantly, between the domains.

6.2.2 'Factor' Relationships: Dynamics Between the Business and IT Categories

In each domain, some categories interacted directly with the other domain. Other categories shape them and determine the nature of the interaction between the domains. In the following sections, the interrelationships between categories are described for each domain.

6.2.2.1 Category Interaction in the Business Domain

The business categories are the main originators of influence over the Co-op's position *vis-à-vis* FIST, the international information systems project. The *Nature of the Business* is the most fundamental influence. Its structural uniqueness determines the essential characteristics of the *Global Business Strategy*. Similarly, the particulars of its external – market and industry – evolution have caused this strategy to change in a distinct pathway, set out in the *Migration of Global Strategy*. All three of these factors combine to form a *Tradition of Local Autonomy* among the Co-op's local offices and regions. Although assisted by other influences, this well established culture of far-reaching independence for regional management is the main shaper of the *Rejection of Global IS* category, which in itself is then a major influence in the development of FIST, the global systems development project. The other information technology related category is a *Lack of IT Sophistication*, skills and experience with information technology matters at the Co-op's headquarters.[b] In turn, the Co-op's naivety in information technology at the centre reinforces the *Tradition of Local Autonomy*, this time with respect to managing the local information systems and technology installations. Five of the six categories, or 'factors', are akin to 'independent variables'. They condition and shape the character of *Rejection of Global IS*, the 'dependent' category, which is the one engaged in the major interaction between the IT and the Business domains.

Figure 6.4 below shows the interplay of the major business categories.

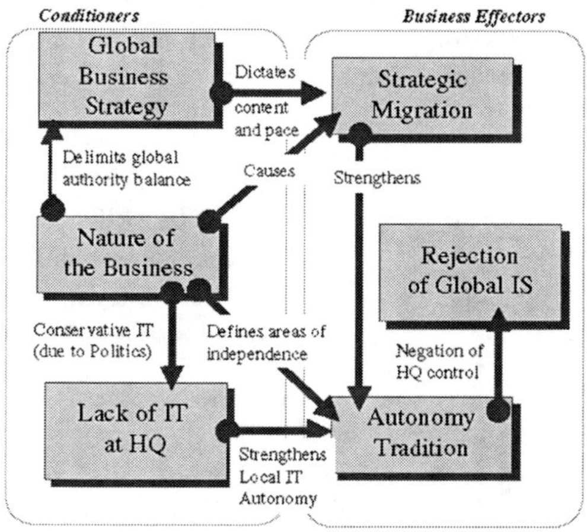

Figure 6.4. Business dynamics: major categories and relations

6.2.2.2 Category Interaction in the Information Technology Domain

Capacity, the most fundamental conditioning category, is the level and degree of conceptual capability brought to bear on the design of the system, i.e. the ability to conceptualize and think through thorny issues. It has the most detailed influences on the other categories – because of its nature as a fundamental and basic requirement for good information systems design and development. The greater complexity of an international information systems environment seems to place a commensurately greater significance on this factor. The lack (or low level) of *Capacity* is accompanied by the effects of *Analysis*, the application of mostly erroneous methods and assumptions used in the system building activity. The fallacy and inadequacy of these underlying paradigms acts as a direct influence on the character of the *Global Standard IS Design*:

the *Global Nature* of the application systems reflects the belief that they are all serving identical, merely geographically separate, businesses; this misconception is aggravated by the use of

Data/Business Modeling at too high a level; consequently, this leads to the stipulation of

Globally standardized technology in terms of the *I=A=T* sub-category, i.e. the erroneous assumption that identical information needs to come from identical applications, which, in turn, require identical hardware to run on.

Figure 6.5 below shows the interplay between the major categories within the Information Technology domain. These distorting influences on the design of the global IS were further complemented by the (often low) level of *Information Systems Professional Skills* the FIST team brought to bear on the one hand, and the evidence of an inadequacy to internalize international issues, summarized in the *Domestic Mindset* category. In concert, they are a major reason for the, the main interface with the business domain.

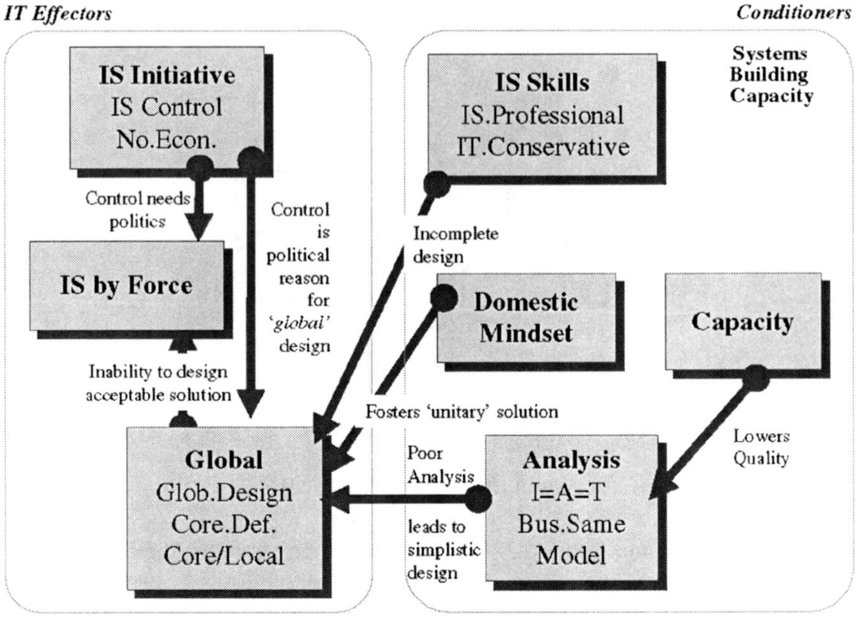

Figure 6.5. Categories and relations in the information technology domain

The two other 'dependent' categories are the fact that the whole project is an *IS Initiative*, created in response to perceived inefficiencies in the international operations of the Co-op. This category is a strong influence towards the standardized, centrist nature of the global IS, with the perceived intention of using the global IS as (covert) instruments of central control; *IS by Force* developed as a consequence of the inability to deal in a rational way with the business people's rejection of the global IS – and subsequently resorting to political power-play in an attempt to push acceptance of the system.

The summarization levels displayed in Figure 6.5 above mask the fact that the interaction between the information technology categories is multidimensional, often linked at the sub-category level and very richly interwoven.

6.2.3 The Nature of Factor Interactions: The Force Field

The Business and Information Technology Domains to set up an arena for the interactions between the business and information technology interests. In each domain, the individual category dynamics culminate in forming one category that is responsible for the primary interface between the business and information technology domains. In the IT domain, this is the *Global Standard IS Design*, acting as the first causal factor in the business domain's *Rejection of the Global System*. This then sets up a pattern of interplay between the domains, involving *IS Initiative* and *IS by Force* in a secondary interaction. A suitable model for describing such an interaction of socio-organizational forces is a 'Force Field', in the sense of Lewin (1952). Figure 6.6 illustrates this.

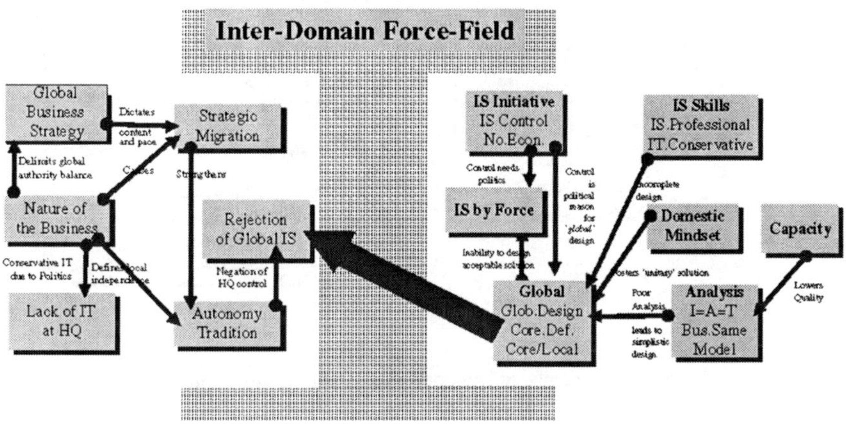

Figure 6.6. Force field of business and IT dynamics: interplay of the major categories

The forces acting in that field are of considerable magnitude. Initially, the conflict presented itself as a straightforward clash of divergent self-interests and goals. Regional management defended their 'fiefdoms' against the IT people's attempt to impose FIST as a means of stringent head-office control.

Furthermore, there is a deeper causal chain leading up to this confrontation, as Figure 6.7 shows. The numbers in the figure follow the sequence of the steps in the progression of cause-and-effect that finally resulted in the establishment of the Force Field.

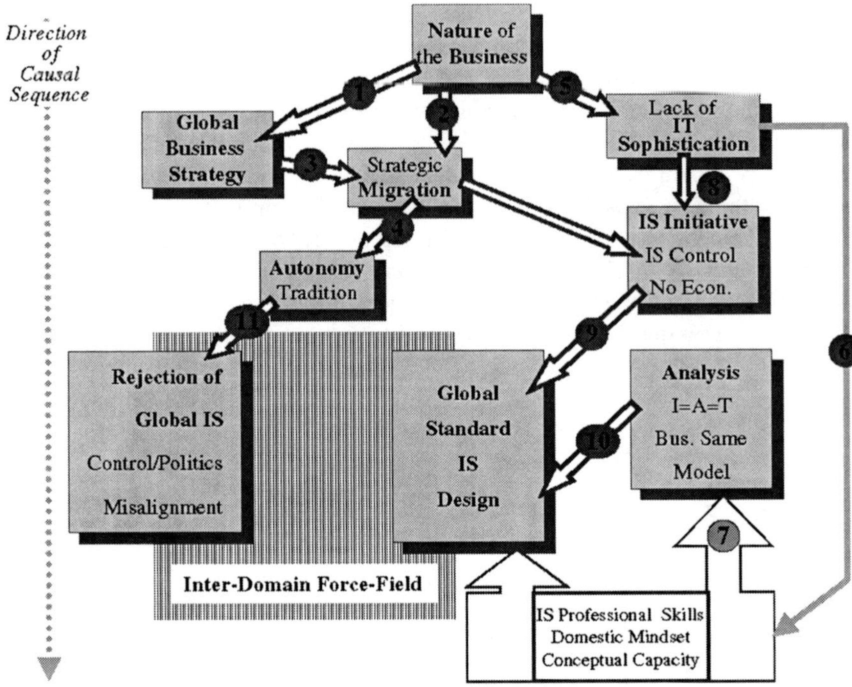

Figure 6.7. The causal sequence of category inter-relationships in the build-up of the inter-domain force field

Starting the sequence, the *Nature of the Business*

1. Dictated the content of the *Global Business Strategy*.

External changes (the UK's joining the EU) to the Nature of the Business then cause a

1. Migration of Global Business Strategy, as did, further on,
2. changes to the Global Business Strategy that were generated internally, i.e. by the CEO's vision;

The sound success of the first, traumatic migration to a *multinational* strategy (in Bartlett and Ghoshal terms) had created a number of 'local heroes' in the regions, who were the solid foundation for a

1. *Tradition of Local Autonomy* and independence from head office.

The Co-op's executive are mostly from a Primary Producer background, where information technology is not of importance. Furthermore, the political character of the Co-op breeds a culture of cautious conservatism towards issues with any level of failure probability. Both those traits explain the

1. Lack of *Information Technology Sophistication* at the executive level. In turn, this had a number of effects on the IT people in the Co-op:
2. The information technology culture followed the executive's conservative stance. This lead to a certain complacency with low *IS Professional Skills*, little conceptual *Capacity* and a pervasive *Domestic Mindset.* Lack of experience outside the Co-op's legacy mainframe technology, confined to the home country, compounded the situation. This syndrome also shapes the
3. *Analysis* as a collection of outdated assumptions (such as *I=A=T*[8]) and inappropriate methods (*Data/Business Modeling*) leading to influential fallacies *(Business Sameness).*

The second far-reaching consequence of the *Lack of IT Sophistication* and the parochial culture of the IT people at head office was the encouragement given to the

1. *IS Initiative*, a misinterpretation of the CEO's vision, was seen by the business people as an exercise in *IS Control.* Having *No Economic Justification*, the proposed
2. *Global Standard IS Design* was seen as naïve and unworkable, which reflected
3. the influence of the *Analysis* category.

The business, defending their *Tradition of Local Autonomy* against what they saw as a means of *Control/Politics*, united in a clear

1. *Rejection of Global IS,* ostensibly because of its *Misalignment* with business needs and strategy.

This first rejection by the business people was, however, only the beginning of a series of antagonistic exchanges, which eventually engaged the opposing sides in a cycle of rejection and reaction which in the end proved strong enough to stop the information systems project altogether. The scene for the conflict was set after a number of key developments in 1993 and early 1994 had set the scene:

- NAR and SEAR were co-opted to FIST as 'global pilot' sites;
- After some initial input from NAR a 'Benchmark Model' was developed by the FIST team at the Australasian HQ for use in a Request for Proposal (RFP) for the Co-op's global information technology and systems;
- Supplier's responses' were evaluated quickly and the global standard technology was selected by FIST: HW platform, DBM database and SOFT applications; no communications or support vendors were selected;

[8] The paradigmatic assumption that obtaining *equal* ***I***nformation content requires *identical* ***A***pplication systems, running on the *same* ***T***echnology Infrastructure.

Table 6.2 below re-casts the case story[c] to highlight the five dialectical interchanges of business rejection alternating with FIST's reaction observed in the Co-op case.

Table 6.2. Stages in the original cycle of rejection and reaction between business and FIST

Time	Cycle	Project activity
Mid-1994	Cycle 1: Rejection Reaction Cycle 2: Rejection	FIST 'benchmark' comparison between NAR and SEAR finds a '90–95%' match. SEAR points out it is in different markets with different products; refuses to accept 'Benchmark' and opts out of the pilot. FIST press ahead with NAR. SOFT has not enough functionality for NAR's actual requirements and needs extensive enhancements. However, NAR refuse to pay an estimated $1.8m for changes to obtain 'what we have now'.
Late-1994	Cycle 2: Reaction	FIST team enlist support of the Co-op's CEO, who issues a strong directive to NAR (and copies to all other regions) to accept FIST.
Early 1995	Cycle 3: Rejection	FIST 'Benchmark' comparison extended to European Region (ER) and finds another 90–95% match; ER rejects the finding, citing 'divergence in markets, intra-regional diversity'; obtain the CEO's agreement to hold off until FIST is implemented successfully in NAR.
Mid 1995	Cycle 3: Reaction	With the CEO's backing, FIST initiate the 'Enquiry-to-Cash' project (ETC), a business-process-reengineering initiative to align all Co-op operations globally with SOFT functionality (as modeled on and extended for NAR).
Late 1995	Cycle 4: Rejection	NAR opts out of the pilot project: after 3 years of delays, they now have to replace their obsolete technology and IS with an 'interim solution'; will thereafter decide whether and how to implement FIST.
Early 1996	Cycle 4: Reaction	Co -op opens new, small (16 person) office in the Middle East (MEO); FIST team select MEO as the new 'global prototype' and begin development to adapt SOFT at HQ in Australasia (as there are insufficient IS resources in MEO).
Mid 1996	Cycle 5: Rejection	Questioning MEO's suitability as a 'global prototype', ER opt out of FIST permanently. The CEO commissions an international consulting firm to carry out a performance audit of the FIST project.
Late 1996	Cycle 5: Reaction	MEO 'global prototype' is 'reduced in scope': General Ledger, Debtors & Creditors go live in time for 1997; FIST announce 'global roll-out' after this 'successful pilot' implementation.

Time	Cycle	Project activity
Early 1997	Termination	Consultants report to CEO: 'FIST is overly ambitious; probably unachievable within the set timeframe; realization of benefits is highly doubtful'. CEO re-assigns FIST Management; Scope of FIST changed to develop a global information systems plan.

Figure 6.8 below illustrates the principle of this cycle and the major categories involved in the dialectical interchange in the fashion of a cause-and-effect loop, after Miles et al. (1994) and Weick (1979). The cycle activities all take place in the force field between the main category domains in the case.

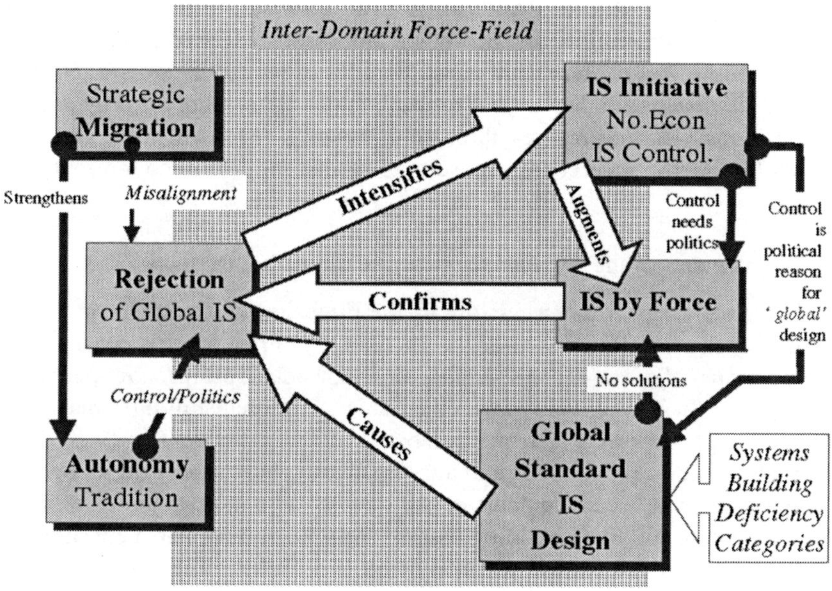

Figure 6.8. Interaction cycle: *rejection* of the international information system by the business people and *reaction* from the IT people

Repeated failure to arrive at an acceptable *Global Standard IS Design* lead to its rejection by the business people. Their refusal to co-operate further increased the isolation of the FIST team. This reinforced the *IS Initiative* category, which in turn strengthened the tendency to push the *IS by* (political) *Force*. Confirming their view that FIST was really a political power play, the business people responded in kind and with renewed *Rejection of* the *Global IS*. This isolated the IT people even further, leading to yet another round in the cycle.

6.3 The First Theoretical Framework

The following paragraphs set out the first formulation of a theory of the factors at work in an International Information System. Before that, however, it is necessary to clarify the rationale for the nomenclature used.

Whetten (1989) defines a theory as a set of linked elements: *factors* are interconnected by *relationships*, which the theory *explains* – in the first instance for the *range* of its substantive environment. The statements describing all this then form Merton's (1968) 'logically interconnected sets of propositions'. Ordering those is not difficult, when their number is small (Dubin, 1969). Zetterberg (1965, p. 86–94) suggests, however, that for more than three propositions simply listing them is not enough and a more structured mode of ordering them is advisable. He recommends 'inventories' of determinants and results, organized in chain patterns or even matrices, if their nature allows it. Following this suggestion, the theoretical propositions derived from the cases shall be ordered in 'theory areas' that group families of related *factors*. The patterns of their *relationships* are then set out for each major factor, supported by *explanatory* propositions. This discharges three of Whetten's requirements. The cases, in which the interim theoretical exposé is grounded in, determine the fourth, i.e. its *range*.

The elements of the nomenclature chosen for stating the theory are:

- The *Theoretical Framework*: this is the provisional, interim theory written up after each case. Referred to as the 1st (2nd, etc) Framework it consists of
- *Theorems*: these are propositions of factor relationships, grouped around a common theme, i.e. their 'theoretical area'. Theorems, in turn, may contain a number of supporting statements, labeled
- *Theses*: they are also theorematic in nature, but usually describe a single relationship between elements of the theory. The more complex relationships may require still more building blocks: these supporting statements are named
- *Postulates*: which explain and add detail to a Thesis. They can be premises or assumptions, either *paradigmatic*[9] or *axiomatic*[10] in nature.

In this section the first theoretical framework, based on the Co-op case, is set out.[11] It is first set out in the order in which it was developed. Secondly it will be grouped into theory areas of like factors.

---

[9] In this context, it means relating to a specific, substantive, *example*.

[10] i.e. relating to established principles, – such as canons of good practice in the field of Information Systems in general – which for the purpose of this discourse are accepted as *self-evident*.

[11] The theorems, theses and postulates are set out in summarized form in the following paragraphs. The detailed set of theoretical statements is contained in the working papers and in the detailed notes contained in the companion web site.

A fair proportion of the FIST team's difficulties arose from the structure of the IIS. At first this was to be a system, the same everywhere. Only later did FIST make concessions to local differences, but could not find a design that was acceptable to the regional users. Political arguments clouded this process further. The first three theorems aim to capture the underlying essence of these developments:

A. An IIS for a diverse international firm must have a *Core/Local Split*; i.e. a totally identical system for use everywhere is not the logical starting point.
B. Nature of the business and its autonomy structure determine the contents of the IIS core; the design of the IIS as a globally standard system reflects the *Misalignment* between the CEO's intention and the FIST interpretation.
C. The extent of the Local parts of the IIS is more determined by political factors than by rational/logical analysis. Because the potential of the *IS* as an instrument of central *Control*, the *Core/Local Split* involves more than just a rational allocation of functionality.

In a similar vein, the management structure and processes of any IIS project must align with the global firms governance, so that

D. the decision making authority for the creation and implementation of the IIS must reflect the business' authority structure, especially the boundaries of regional/local autonomy.

Theorem C., in particular, is the foundation for a more general observation, namely that

E. the implementation of an IIS that is perceived as an instrument of central control meets conflict from local management. This sets up a Force Field of antagonistic interaction between users and IT people.

The next group of theorems focuses on the conceptual, technical and professional difficulties that plagued the FIST team in their efforts to bring together a workable design. Albeit still expressed with a considerable degree of generality, they are beginning to outline the specific requirements for an IIS development methodology:

F. Creating and implementing an IIS requires international knowledge;
G. The analysis preceding IIS design requires an extraordinary high level of conceptual capability;
H. Backing by local business management (i.e., not just by the central executive) is required for design and implementation of the IIS;
I. State of the art skills and a high degree of professionalism are required prerequisites for the design and implementation of an IIS.

Acknowledging that the conflict between IT and the regional users is not limited to one interchange alone, the last theorem connects the users' and IT responses to the notion of the Force Field developed earlier in Theorem E.:

J. Response, i.e. Acceptance and Rejection are determined in Force Field interactions between Users and IT people

The theorems group into three areas of theoretical topics, focusing on

1. The architecture, i.e. shape, structure and elements of an international information system;
2. The interactions surrounding the nature of the users' response to the IIS and the shape and direction they take in the Force Field;
3. The requirements for structures, processes and skills in the management of the development of an IIS.

The grouping of theorems into the three topic areas is shown in Table 6.3 below.

Table 6.3. Theorems of the 1st theoretical framework ordered by theory areas

Theory area	The 1st theoretical framework – based on the Co-op case
Architecture of an IIS	Theorem A. An IIS for a diverse international firm must have a Core/local Split Theorem B. Nature of the business and its autonomy structure determine the contents of the IIS core Theorem C. The extent of the local parts of the IIS is more determined by political factors than by rational/logical analysis
Response and the force field	Theorem E. The implementation of an IIS that is perceived as an instrument of central control meets conflict from local management and sets up a force field Theorem H. Backing by local business management (not just by central executive) is required for design and implementation of the IIS Theorem J. Response, i.e. Acceptance and Rejection are determined in force field interactions between users and IT people
Development management skills for IIS	Theorem F. Creating and implementing an IIS requires international knowledge Theorem G. The analysis preceding IIS design requires an extraordinary high level of conceptual capability Theorem I. State of the art professionalism is required for the design and implementation of an IIS Theorem D. Decision making authority for the creation and implementation of the IIS must reflect the business authority structure

The first case yielded a large amount of data over a broad front. Each theorem is supported by several theses, covering a number of properties. The resulting theory is relatively unspecific, but of a wide reach and range.

More, and more focused, data is now needed to add depth to this first theory, to make it more expressive, to add clarity and to strengthen its explanatory power.

6.4 Theoretical Sampling for the Next Case

This method of selecting additional areas for further research addresses the 'basic question…[of] *what* groups or subgroups does one turn to *next* in the data collection?' (Glaser et al., 1967, p. 47). These groups are selected for their potential to add the 'slices of data'[d] needed to firm up on propositions or to provide new insights. Theoretical sampling concentrates therefore on the categories and areas that are not yet considered to be *theoretically saturated*.[e] The first step towards new data selection must therefore be the assessment of the saturation levels for the core categories identified so far. From this, a sampling strategy can be derived and the requirements for the next case can be established.

6.4.1 Assessment of 'Saturation' Levels

Table 6.4 below summarizes which areas, core categories and main sub-categories are considered to be in need of more clarifying detail.

Table 6.4. Assessment of the saturation level of major categories

Unsaturated categories	Saturated categories
Business	*Business*
Nature of the business	Lack of IT sophistication
Global business strategy	Migration of global strategy
Rejection of global IS	Tradition of local autonomy
Information technology	*Information technology*
Analysis (methods/paradigms)	
IS professional skills	IS professional skills
IS conservatism	IS professionalism
Capacity	
	Domestic mindset
IS initiative	IS initiative
IS as control	IS origin
	No economic justification
Global standard IS design	Global standard IS design
Common core	Global nature
Core local split	
IS by force	

They are then contrasted with those categories where current understanding and explanatory strength is considered to be adequate for the theory. These include categories that reflect items regarded as sufficiently common knowledge in the information systems' field so that they do not require further expansion or exemplification.

In the following paragraphs the saturation levels of the main categories are discussed, firstly for the categories – in both domains – that are considered saturated. Secondly, the discussion sets out where, and what, further investigation is needed to enhance the understanding of the 'unsaturated' categories.

6.4.1.1 'Saturated' Categories

Despite the fact that most core categories are broad rather than deep in their coverage, a number could nevertheless be considered 'saturated' after the Co-op case. In the *Business Domain* this comprises:

- *Lack of IT Sophistication*: this category has been established abundantly in interviews and other data; secondly, its detrimental effect on a complex project is plausible *eo ipso*[f];
- *Migration of Global Strategy*: a clear understanding of the direction of change in strategy is established in the history of the Board and a clear picture of how this affects other categories has been obtained. Furthermore, the significance of the Global Business Strategy for Information Systems policy is one of the few well documented findings in the field of international information systems research;
- *Tradition of Local Autonomy*: this is abundantly established through interviews, and well embedded in the case 'text' as a significant element of the Co-op's corporate history; as a consequence of the 'multinational' business strategy it is also well grounded in International Business research literature concerned with the status of subsidiaries of multinational enterprises.

Some of the categories in the *Information Technology Domain* discovered in the Co-op case are considered to be general knowledge in the wider field of information systems research. As such they apply to any information system, not just to global and/or international ones. Embellishing these categories any further will not contribute much to a specific theory in the substantive area of international information systems.

For this reason, a lack of *IS Professionalism* (from *IS Professional Skills*) will be detrimental to any information systems project, albeit even more so for a complex one such as FIST. Similarly, the lack of business backing inherent in *IS Origin* is well known as a contributor to IS failure, as is *No Economic Justification* (both from *IS Initiative*), i.e. asking for significant business changes without offering convincing business benefits.

Two categories more specific to international information systems are also considered 'saturated'. The negative influence of a *Domestic Mindset*, i.e. not knowing about international settings and environments not understanding how they are different has been well documented in the case history. The second (sub)category is the *Global Nature*, the only 'saturated' element of *Global Standard IS Design*. There is exhaustive confirmation in the case 'text' for the large probability that a globally identical system and technology platform will not work satisfactorily across businesses of varying sizes in different markets and environments. In addition to the case evidence, both categories are plausible within themselves.

6.4.1.2 'Unsaturated' Categories

Out of the 13 core categories, however, 9 are in need of further investigation. They are either new and need more data to enhance understanding, or they seem case-specific and their generalizability needs probing and confirming.

Three of the *Business Domain* categories require the latter. The effects of the Co-op's unique *Nature of the Business* on the character of its operations and the character of its IIS are amply manifest in the case. Whether these influences also exist in other circumstances, however, needs further exploration. The same goes for the *Global Business Strategy* category, where a possible connection between the 'core' of the IIS and the role of the centre and regions was indicated by the case story, but needs more investigation. The reasons for the *Rejection of* the *Global IS* are comprehensively contained in the case. However, the *inverse* category, i.e. business people's Acceptance of an IIS, only exists in the case history as conjectural speculation. This certainly warrants further grounding in empirical data: a 'Response' core category – of which Rejection could be but one incarnation – would be potentially very important.

In the *Information Technology Domain*, most of the categories in need of more data are new, or have a new application in the field of international information systems. The category describing the methods and paradigms of *Analysis* used in the design of an IIS covers three such new 'discoveries':

A. *I=A=T*[12]*;* although clear in its effect in the case, the concept is new and needs more understanding;
B. *Business Sameness;* the origins of this category, especially its possible correlation with the deficient conceptualization of international business operations will profit from more exemplification;
C. *Data/Business Modeling;* the lack of value of these techniques for the design of an international information system is surprising; their – possibly causal – link to *Business Sameness* needs deeper comprehension; another potentially critical linkage as a possible key influence to *Core/Local Split* also requires more empirical detail.

IS Conservatism (from the *IS Professional Skills* category) is all about being out of date about technology. This may not just (trivially) reflect ignorance, but could also be an expression of intentional caution, or even just stem from the long duration of global projects *vis á vis* the fast pace of information technology

[12] The paradigmatic assumption that obtaining *equal* ***I***nformation content requires *identical* ***A***pplication systems, running on the *same* ***T***echnology Infrastructure.

change. For this reason, further embedding in data is essential to add more, and more specific, utility to this category.

The importance of high conceptual ability (the *Capacity* category) in a general sense would be a truism, as important in the IS field as in any other, were it not for its link to – somewhat unexpected – difficulties with *Data/Business Modeling* or conceptual fallacies such as *I=A=T*. Their role and significance needs to better understood in the specific context of international information systems. A possible link to *Business Sameness*, i.e. using the wrong level of abstraction when conceptualizing international settings also requires further investigation.

IS as Control, a sub-category of *IS Initiative*, is about the use of information systems as a lever to impose a different level of control on international firms by means of forcing the necessary organizational and process changes. Both aspects are in need of more understanding, especially any linkage with 'Response', i.e. Rejection or Acceptance of the IIS.

The two sub-categories of *Global Standard IS Design* require more data. The existence of a *Common Core* in the architecture of an IIS is well established in the Co-op case, but not what determines its content. Also, the case points only to the difficulties of achieving an acceptable *Core Local Split,* i.e. the definition of what applications should be in the common core and in local variations. More data of what a 'working' definition would consist of and how it could be arrived at is required.

A number of issues pertaining to the political exchanges in the case contained in the *IS by Force* category require further investigation:

- That *CEO Support*, a stalwart, traditional success factor of IS projects, can function in a detrimental way is worthy of empirical substantiation beyond the current case;
- The role of *Political Arguments,* predominantly negative in the Co-op case, needs further investigation;
- *Business will Change* and *HQ Rules* dominated the interchange between regional/local offices and the centre in order to adapt an IIS's common core. These categories, obviously critical for successful systems implementation, needs further clarification.

After the identification of the areas of further investigation, a strategy for selecting the next case needs to be established. From this, the requirements of what qualities and attributes the next case enterprise should have can be derived.

6.4.2 Sampling Strategy and Requirements for the Next Case

After identifying the target categories for further saturation, the second decision about the theoretical sample is whether to aim for similar or different data and/or groups.

Glaser et al. (1967) recommend that the two strategies follow each other: 'When beginning his generation of a substantive theory, the [researcher] establishes the basic categories and their properties by *minimizing* differences in comparison groups. (*Note:* Good substantive theory can result from the study of *one group*, if the analyst carefully sorts data into comparative subgroups.) Once this basic work is accomplished, however, [the researcher] should turn to *maximizing* differences among comparison groups in accordance…with the requirements of his emergent theory'. (ibid., p. 56–57)

The first case had established a number of basic categories, their properties and linkages. Some of these are unsaturated because the case study has only been able to bring up one side, dimension or aspect of the category and a different setting is now needed to fill in the gaps. Others are new and more data is needed for confirmation, or otherwise, of whether they are uniquely specific to the Co-op's case or whether they have more general theoretical value. Maximizing differences was therefore selected as an appropriate strategy for the theoretical sampling for the next case.

In order to put the new case in juxtaposition to the Co-op, the new enterprise should have the following overall attributes:

- They need to have had implemented, or should operate currently, a successful international information system;
- Their business should be less diversified with respect to markets and operations,

In Table 6.5 below the desired characteristics of the next group, i.e. the next case for study, are set into the context of the saturation requirements for individual categories. One of the Co-op's main shipping partners was J Lauritzen, a Danish shipping company with a recently established international information system. J Lauritzen fits well within the sampling strategy of maximizing 'group' differences.

Contrary to the Co-op, however, J Lauritzen is in the business of selling a service, not a product. They are a much smaller firm than the Co-op and it is a closely held private firm, not a co-operative society under statutory rules.

Table 6.5. Theoretical sampling requirements of the next case study

Unsaturated categories	Requirements of the next case
Business Domain	
Nature of the business	The business should have a reasonably clear focus to allow an easy identification of any linkage between operations and the nature of the IIS
Global business strategy	There is no specific preference for any particular global strategy, as long as the case's strategy is a clear one and can be readily compared within the Bartlett & Ghoshal framework
Rejection of global IS	The case should be around an accepted IIS to allow ready investigation into what made the business accept it

Unsaturated categories	Requirements of the next case
Information Technology Domain	
Analysis I=A=T[13] Business sameness Data/business Modeling IS professional skills IS conservatism Conceptual capability	The case should provide examples of the methods/paradigms used, successfully, to develop and/or maintain the IIS
IS initiative IS as control	Business management should have been behind the IIS – to allow the original IS Initiative category to be extended by contrast
Global standard IS Design Common core Core local split	Study of these critical categories how the split between core/local was done; and what is defined as the common core should be easily possible
IS by force CEO support Political arguments Business will change HQ rules	The case should show how the system is distributed to the regional/local units; and how the local autonomy issues are addressed

J Lauritzen also fits well into the requirements of maximizing 'data' differences. The business is well defined, with a stable and definitive global strategy. According to the users of their system, J Lauritzen's IIS had adequate functionality and accepted utility. It had been implemented recently and should therefore clearly show the methods/paradigms used for its development and implementation. Furthermore, it should be possible to set the system's perceived utility into context with the way in which the *Core/Local Split* was carried out. Lastly, a clear concept of what the *Common Core* should be, would be derivable from this. In all of this, J Lauritzen seemed to fit the requirements for the next case rather well.

For this reason, the firm of J Lauritzen was chosen as the second case.

Endnotes

a Examples are:

- Confused and woolly ideas such as separate physical inventories for A and B Products (a marketing classification for the probability distribution between 'predictable' versus 'windfall' yields, necessary for forecasting production rates for natural products) could not be resolved into workable information systems concepts;
- A 60-digit, concatenated, 'standard product identifier' in response to the requirements of unified production planning and allocation is a demonstration of the inability to go beyond simplistic, trivial 'solutions' which are practically inoperable; and, similarly;

[13] The paradigmatic assumption that obtaining *equal* ***I***nformation content requires *identical* ***A***pplication systems, running on the *same* ***T***echnology Infrastructure.

- A 56-digit account code to implement a 'standard global account structure'. In addition to being impractical, such a standard would be illegal in most European countries, where firms' account structures are dictated by statute and tax law – reflecting the Domestic Mindset category at its most detrimental.

b The political nature of the Co-op's business structure and culture is a partial reason for this: self-preservation instincts dictate a policy of cautious conservatism in all things expensive that might go wrong.

c Glaser & Strauss (1967) recommend this as a good test to see whether the theory so far does 'work', i.e. can explain the 'text' by telling it in another way.

d This is what Glaser & Strauss (1967) refer to as a single 'datum' which provides a 'vantage point from which to understand a category and to develop its properties' (p. 65). There are 'no limits to the techniques of data collection,the way they are used, or the types of data acquired'(ibid.) for defining such new sets of data within the theoretical sample.

e *Saturation* is defined as the point in the investigation when 'new data does not add any more new properties or insights to a category and its properties' (Glaser & Strauss, 1967, p. 61).

f Glaser & Strauss (1967) specifically categorize this type of saturation criterion as '[the researcher's] own experiences, general knowledge and the stories of others' (p. 67).

Chapter 7
Case Two: J Lauritzen Ship Owners

This chapter contains the case story, its interpretation and the translation of the factor relationships, which is then expanded into the 2nd Theoretical Framework. Setting out the considerations for the theoretical sampling for the next case concludes this chapter. The details of the case and its analysis are, again, available from the author on demand.[1]

7.1 Case History: J Lauritzen Ship Owners

The J Lauritzen Shipping Company was founded by Ditlev Lauritzen in 1884. Since 1930s the Company has concentrated on specialized shipping which requires technically advanced vessels and a high degree of expertise and experience. Today, J Lauritzen is the second largest shipping group in Denmark – Maersk is number one.

This case study is about one division, namely Lauritzen Reefers . 'Reefers' are specialized ships for the transportation of perishable products with sophisticated temperature and environmental control capabilities. They cater for *unitized* cargo, i.e. pallets in the hold and/or (refrigerated) containers on deck.

Over the last two decades the shipping industry had been faced with considerable turbulence. Cyclical over-capacity combined with deregulation and removal of protection for national carriers in most OECD countries have led to predatory price cutting on certain key shipping routes. At the same time, *Danyard*, the J Lauritzen shipbuilding arm was making heavy losses and the drain on profits forced the group to divest 50% of *Sabroe Refrigeration A/S* to a Swedish-led investment consortium. To cope with all these developments, a major restructuring of the whole J Lauritzen group was carried out during 1997 and 1998.

---

[1] Best via email under Hans.Lehmann@vuw.ac.nz

H. Lehmann, *The Dynamics of International Information Systems*,
Integrated Series in Information Systems 23, DOI 10.1007/978-1-4419-5750-4_7,

7.1.1 J Lauritzen's Business

Lauritzen Reefers run a fleet of between 50 and 60 ships of between 2,500 t and 11,000 t capacity. They own about 40 of the ships and have the rest either under management or under contract. A small number of large customers account for 90% of their business. These are predominantly producers of fruit, vegetables, dairy produce or meat in the Southern Hemisphere, whose markets are the major economies in the North. For them the cost of transport has a major and direct effect on their bottom-line profits. For predictability, cargo contracts are auctioned annually, to the lowest bidder. J Lauritzen have usually about 60% of their available shipping capacity signed up under regular and firm contracts. These cover costs – profits come from the best use of spare capacity around the 'booked' business.

The local offices, i.e. the 'jobbers' in shipping parlance, are responsible for establishing the business with customers. This involves the preparation of quotes, the negotiations preceding the deal and, finally, the drawing up and closing of contracts for the business. In this, they enjoy a high degree of autonomy.

After a contract is agreed a 'voyage' (i.e. one element/segment of a *journey*) is established. The jobber then organizes with the customer to bring the goods to the pier. From this point on, the 'operator' in the operations department takes over. They keep records for each 'voyage', including position and travel details as well as actual costs against the estimates the original quote was based on.

A central schedule of the ships, the 'common resource' in this business, is kept at the J Lauritzen head office in Copenhagen. It relies on information about ships' movements that all the Operations Departments update into the system. In this way, it contains snapshot of positions, estimated arrival times, directions, ports, etc. of all 50–60 Lauritzen ships available. With the help of this schedule the local jobbers can find freight capacity from ships that maybe in the vicinity and are going 'on ballast' (i.e. are without lucrative cargo), or are heading towards a port from which they will then be going on ballast. The chartering department is the second central function, which controls all the 'supply' contracts (e.g. for provisions and fuel, the 'bunkering' in shipping parlance). They set the rates for each contract or consignment and thus control significantly the profitability of the firm.

This central *vs* local interaction: is illustrated in

Figure 7.1

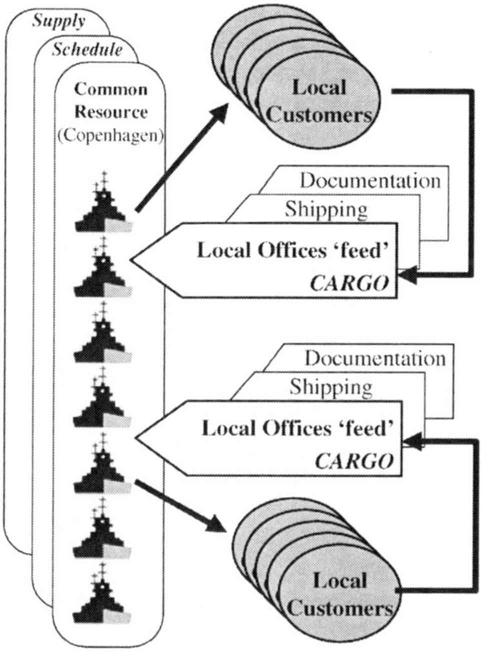

Figure 7.1. J Lauritzen's 'nature of the business'

There are two major areas within J Lauritzen's main business:

1. The main 'Reefers' business is 'tramping',[2] where the avoidance of 'going on ballast' is key. The firm relies on the local jobbers to fill the ships with cargo from one journey to the next. The jobbers rely heavily on central scheduling, which, in turn; relies on them (and the ships) for up-to-date, accurate and shared operations data. The 'season' for their typical cargo of perishable foodstuffs is from February to June, during the Southern Hemisphere's harvest season – with the exception of meat, which is traded all year round; there is also some
2. 'line' business, i.e. having schedules of journeys between a number of ports. The key success factor is, again, for the 'jobbers' to fill the space on each journey. Similar to the airline business, pricing flexibility is important, to optimize the contributions for each journey, as their cost structure is fixed. The jobbers rely, again, on central data for rates and to assess the flexibility of individual schedules.

---

[2] That is going to wherever freight is and taking it to where it needs to go.

7.1.2 J Lauritzen's Global Business Strategy

The interaction of the local offices with the central head office in J Lauritzen is quite straightforward: the local offices are responsible for acquiring trade, and in that they have a nearly entirely free hand. However, following the long traditions of European shipping, the centre keeps tight control of the ships (their common resource) and of all that affects them, from supply to maintenance and capital expenditure.

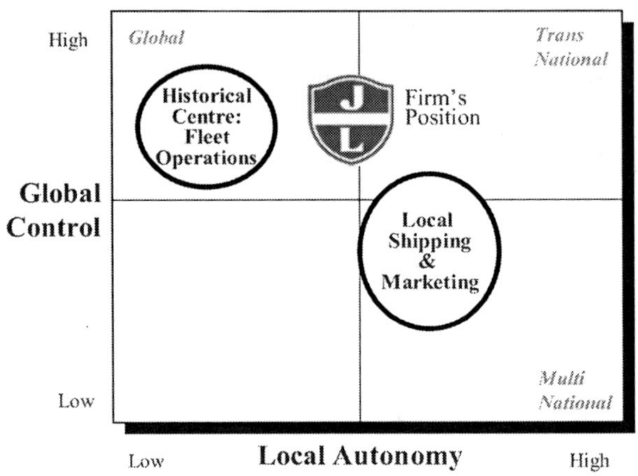

Figure 7.2. J Lauritzen global business strategy in the context of the respective strategic positions of head office and local subsidiaries

In this sense, J Lauritzen follow a *transnational*[3] strategy. The nature of the local office's 'independence', however, is somewhat less than the ideal of 'think global, act local' demands. Some of the local offices fulfill mainly contracts managed from somewhere else, while others represent only a sales function, with little or no operational responsibility. That moves the classification of J Lauritzen more towards the *global* business strategy stance.

Figure 7.2 above depicts the dichotomy between the centre and the local offices together with the resulting Global Business Strategy assessment of the firm overall.

Information systems have always played a role in J Lauritzen. In the following section their history is set out and the major information systems are introduced. Their role in the firm's operations are then analyzed and, lastly, management of information technology in J Lauritzen is described.

---

[3] In Bartlett & Ghoshal (1989) terms.

7.1.3 The History of Information Systems in JL

In 1981, Claus Ipsen, the J Lauritzen Group Information Technology Manager, introduced the first computer, an IBM/3090 mainframe into the firm. The first applications developed were the cost management of ships and the scheduling of the fleet of then 32 ships. These largely independent programs were consolidated into the first integrated information system in 1984 – the Shipping Information Processing, or SHIP system. The major geographical expansion during the second half of the 1980s posed the firm with the option to either introduce distributed computing or to stay with a central system. The decision was taken to maintain a central system on the mainframe in Copenhagen.

Over the last decade, three more central systems and one more central computer were added to the information technology portfolio. Local offices all over the world were connected – through a third party network – with terminals directly to the central systems. Computers and communications were also introduced to J Lauritzen ships during that period. In the last 5 years, most of the international offices were upgraded to using Personal Computers instead of mainframe terminals. In the larger offices, these are linked with Local Area Networks. The extent of the J Lauritzen's international network is shown in Figure 7.3 below.

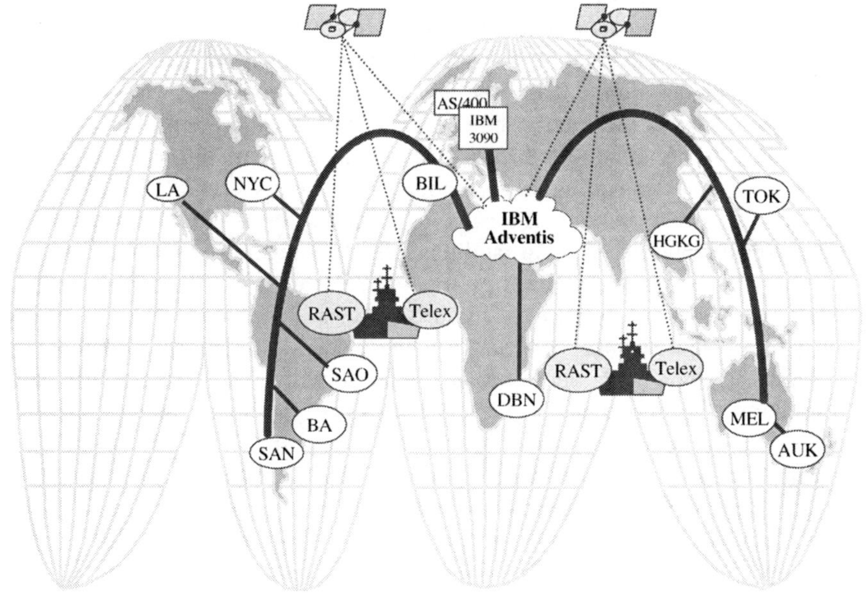

Figure 7.3. The extent of J Lauritzen's information and communications network in 1996

- By 1996 Lauritzen Reefers had information systems in six application areas,:
- *SHIP*, the operational control system is acknowledged by the users (jobbers, operators and accountants) as a robust and reliable working tool for the basic shipping requirements. It runs on the IBM/3090 in Copenhagen and its main functions are *Scheduling*, i.e. keeping track of movements of each of the ships under J Lauritzen's control and the *Simulation* system, used to prepare quotations and carry out 'what-if' investigations for customers during contract negotiations.
- The 'Economy and Accounting System', *ECAS* carries out the basic cost and management accounting function and also produces the group's statutory accounts and reports. It also runs on the IBM/3090 in Copenhagen;
- *TRADEWARE* produces the – prolific – documentation required for shipping. It was bought in 1993 from another J Lauritzen company, *Arctic Line*, who ran a shipping line between Denmark, Iceland and Greenland. A standalone system on an AS/400 in Copenhagen, it turned out not a particularly good match. The central system team have been modifying it ever since its inception, but by 1996 the jobbers in the local offices were still not satisfied with the system's functionality; for this reason, they had developed a number of
- *Local Systems* in subsidiary offices, which run on local PC networks and are in the main aimed at extending TRADEWARE's functionality; Statutory financial accounting for the subsidiary offices is also carried out locally; local systems are linked to the two IBM mainframes in Copenhagen by
- *LECS* (for Lauritzen Electronic Communications System), a messaging system based on mainframe data exchange technology. This was bought in 1990 from Maersk Data, the information technology arm of J Lauritzen's main competitor. A central database on the IBM/3090 in Copenhagen, to which every local office has access, allows the interchange of files and messages between all offices. However, by the mid-1990s LECS was already 15 years old and the facilities offered for communicating were adequate, but cumbersome. J Lauritzen uses the IBM network service *Adventis* to connect to its international offices. *Adventis* has satellite hook-up facilities, which now allowed on-line contact to the ships, either via the old telex protocol or using
- *RAST*, the on-board system on J Lauritzen-owned ships. In 1990 J Lauritzen went into a joint venture project with the Danish government to build high-technology ships with very low manning levels. This project was not a commercial success but its legacy RAST, an on-board maintenance and governance system on an OS/2 platform on – sometimes networked – PCs, now installed on all J Lauritzen owned vessels.[4] RAST manages on-board stores, communicates payroll information and sends operating reports back to head office.

---

[4] Chartered vessels, or those under J Lauritzen management, are usually only capable of communicating with telex – the reason why both SHIP and LECS still have to support telex protocols.

J Lauritzen's information systems are reliable, and support the operations where it counts. In line with the climate of austerity in the group, the do so in a rather minimalist fashion, with mostly second-hand software on mature technology.

7.1.4 Role of Information Systems in J Lauritzen's Operations

'In J Lauritzen A/S the information technology area is not defined as a critical success factor for the business areas, hence the information technology area is seen as a tool to improve efficiency on the tactical level of the organization.' So starts the 1996 strategic 5-year information technology plan for the J Lauritzen Group. This has two main consequences for information systems within Lauritzen Reefers: first of all, information systems themselves must be run cost-effectively; secondly, systems that support operations have first priority over others. Figure 7.4 below shows how business and information systems interact.

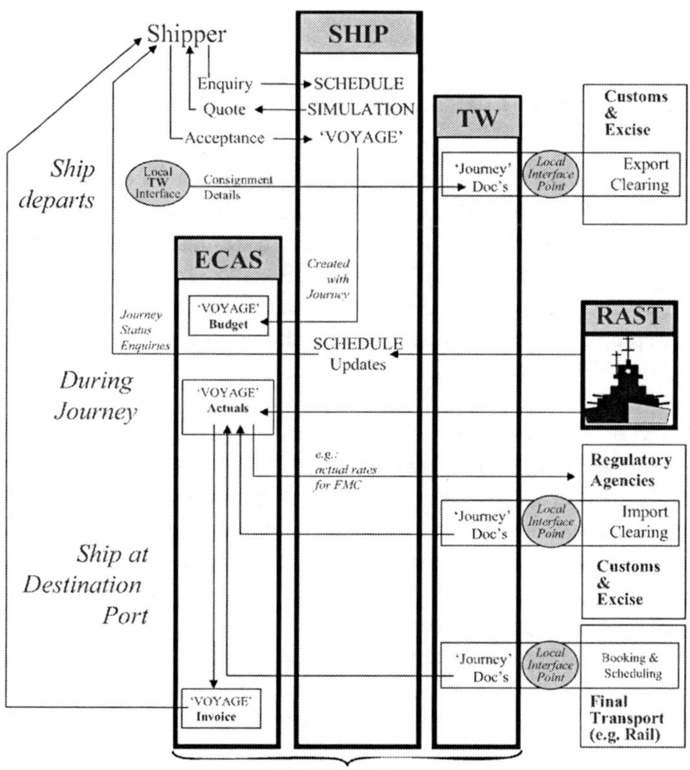

Figure 7.4. Interaction between information systems and the business cycle in J Lauritzen

Information technology has therefore been an integral part of J Lauritzen's business processes right from the outset – the very first systems[5] were operations support applications with strong decision support components. This tradition has continued until the present, with a major emphasis on 'wiring' the central control to ships and all the local offices in order to carry out the business in as much 'real-time' as possible.

A key characteristic of J Lauritzen's systems is that they are tightly interwoven into the business processes throughout the whole business cycle between J Lauritzen, its direct and indirect clients (i.e. the 'Shippers' and their customers) and local authorities in ports, such as maritime and customs agencies.

Enquiries are answered with reference to SHIP's *Schedule* and then *Simulation* is used to negotiate rates and put together a quotation. Once accepted, TRADEWARE and local systems interfaces are used to create the necessary documentation for the individual 'voyage' as well as for the overall 'journey'. Actual values of position, supply, etc. are updated from RAST and local systems into SHIP and ECAS during the journey. At its end, TRADEWARE produces all the necessary documentation for the 'consignees' as well as for the local authorities.

7.1.5 Central Versus Distributed Data and Applications

The central orientation of the information systems in J Lauritzen has been the result of long and ongoing discussions. The option to distribute some of the processing and/or data arose for the first time in the late 1980s when J Lauritzen had embarked on rapid geographical expansion. However, three convincing business arguments disfavored a distributed configuration:

1. In the shipping business data needs to be shared among many players, often at the same time. Therefore, *Data Integrity*, i.e. accuracy and being up-to-date, is very important;
2. *Confidentiality* reasons also contributed, as data can be kept secure easier in one central place than in distributed mode. This is important for two reasons:
2.(a) Protecting their *customers*; nearly all of them are in the commodity business, where information about shipping volumes and dates would allow competitive action. This could have a direct and adverse effect on market prices;
2.(b) Protecting *themselves*; particularly in bidding situations, competitive intelligence is very important and "confidentiality until the last minute and careful maneuvering with always an eye on the competition are essential ingredients to be successful in this business";
3. *Differences in local businesses and customs* were further deciding factors against adopting a distributed information systems architecture:

---

[5] That is the 'simulation' and 'scheduling' aspects of SHIP.

3.(a) *Mixed computer literacy* at J Lauritzen's various outposts, i.e. offices and agencies is a main issue. Mistakes and omissions, whether committed in negligence or ignorance, could compromise both data integrity and confidentiality far beyond the confines of the 'perpetrating' local office.

3.(b) *Cultural differences*, e.g. 'in South America even with IBM everything is *mañana*: the ship is leaving in 1 h, the system is down – but they always say they'll come tomorrow'.

As technology developed over the last decade, the data integrity and confidentiality issues are not as insoluble in distributed information systems platforms as they were in the late 1980s. Cultural differences and literacy problems, on the other hand, are changing at a much slower pace.

Furthermore, an equally important argument for a centralized information systems architecture is – in the words of their Operations Director – that 'for example, you can sit down, one in Japan, one in Chile, talking to somebody on the phone in Long Beach about a specific bill – and all three can see the same version of the bill; when they then need access to, say , the schedule, they just switch in Copenhagen at the same time, from the same system…'. There are a number of such 'real-time' requirements, involving several of J Lauritzen's systems, as Table 7.1 shows.

Table 7.1. 'Real-time' transactions in the J Lauritzen business cycle

Transactions	Systems/information	Interaction required between
Journey quotation	SHIP/schedule	Centre,[6] originator,[7] (receiver[8]) (ships)
Cargo enquiries	TRADEWARE/manifests; SHIP/schedule	Centre, originator, receiver, (ships),
Originating and terminating voyages	TRADEWARE/manifests, customs documentation	Originator, receiver, (customs), (regulators)
Supplying ('bunkering') ships	ECAS/cost accounts & budgets	Ships, centre

(optional actors)

7.1.6 Structure and Strategy of Information Systems Management

Support for Lauritzen Reefer's information systems comes through the main Information Systems support group, located within the J Lauritzen Group head-office. Reefer's, like the other group companies, have an Information Technology Manager who reports to the Group IT Manager in his functional role and to management within the subsidiary for day-to-day work. Within the group there

---

[6] The central operations department at J Lauritzen's head office in Copenhagen.

[7] J Lauritzen's representative at the *origin* of the proposed journey.

[8] J Lauritzen's representative at the *receiving/terminating* end of the proposed journey.

are user centers for each of the key application systems. This responsibility extends to the use of the system internationally. Each local subsidiary, on the other hand, is responsible for their own information technology configuration and platform. To illustrate: there is one full time support person in Long Beach and one full time person in Auckland. Both are, however, shared between Reefers and their local joint-venture partners and both have a 'functional' responsibility to Copenhagen.

The operation of the central mainframes is outsourced to IBM Services, as is the management of the network, which is handled by IBM's *Adventis* group. Some of the local offices, notably Tokyo and Melbourne, also have outsourcing agreements with IBM's local offices.

Cost effectiveness and cost reduction dictate information systems support throughout the firm as the following the key policies – from the 5-year strategic plan – show:

- The current mainframe applications will be modified only '*where this is of benefit to all users*'; furthermore, any local applications must fit in with existing central interfaces and 'the responsibility [for the interface] lies with the owner of the application *receiving* the data through the interface';
- Equally, 'different applications will not be used in order to cover needs that are basically identical';
- As a first principle, '*Technology* management and support will be outsourced wherever possible' and 'preference for local support is given to external support organizations';
- Management of information *systems* shall be 'stabilized and integrated into the business management of J Lauritzen';
- Standard software packages are the preferred choice for information systems acquisitions;
- In the local offices 'Homogeneous end-user applications (office automation applications) shall improve cost efficiency'.

The strategic 5-year plan then sets out in detail how to go about implementing this concentrated focus on a lean information systems portfolio with a declared objective to increase the efficiency of the business operations they are an integral part of.

7.2 Analysis of the J Lauritzen Case

To establish the J Lauritzen case 28.5 hours of interviews were held with 9 interviewees, 4 of which are business people and 5 are from the information technology side, representing the main stakeholders in the international information systems. Interviews and data gathering took place in Denmark (at J Lauritzen's head office in Copenhagen), California and New Zealand between February and April 1996. The face-to-face discussions and fact-finding talks resulted in some 380 pages of interview transcripts and coding notes and were augmented by some 300 pages of internal and public documents.

The steps in the analysis of the case and the results of each step are in principle the same as the ones carried out for the Co-op case. However, as this is the second case, an inter-case comparison was carried out after the initial coding. Similarly, the new theoretical framework based on the second case alone was then 'merged' with the first one, to produce the 2nd Theoretical Framework. This section is organized accordingly:

Section 7.2.1 provides a description of the salient characteristics of the new categories discovered in the second case and their interrelations;

Section 7.2.2 sets out the salient differences between the cases and investigates their theoretical relevance. This lead to the introduction of a number of 'second-order', *derivative categories.*

In Section 7.3, the 1st Theoretical Framework is amalgamated with the new theoretical insights gained from this case and the comparative analysis with the previous one.

The chapter concludes with a description of the theoretical sampling process that was applied to determine the third case.

7.2.1 Categories and Relations

The first 'open' coding of the material yielded some 70 categories. Of these, 37 confirmed or expanded categories defined in the previous case. 'Theoretical' coding reduced the 33 new categories to 4 new core categories.

Two of the new categories fall into the Business Domain and two are from the Information Technology arena. Including the four new ones, altogether 17 core categories have now been identified from both cases. Because of the differences in cases, however, two of them, *IS Migration*[9] and *Analysis*, were not active[10] in the J Lauritzen case and others, such as the *IS Skills* related categories, only acted indirectly.

Of the remaining ten 'active' categories six were responsible for the bulk of the important interactions in the case. Table 7.2 below gives a summary of the 'active' categories at work in the case.

[9] *Core categories* and *Sub-Categories* are formatted thus.

[10] Strategy is stable and no significant *new* development is undertaken

Table 7.2. Active categories in the J Lauritzen case

Active Categories	Status	Remarks
Strategic weight of IT	NEW	Clear, as opposed to unclear in Co-op
Historical factors IT history Business history	NEW	Reflects the influence of 'Tradition' in both business and information technology
IT management Style Architecture	NEW	Is related to IS by force, especially: business will Change and HQ Rules
IS mirrors business Operations (IS=Ops)	NEW	IS integrates 'naturally' into the business processes/cycle.
Acceptance of global IS New sub-category: Global IS/IT diffusion	NEW aspect: inverted from 'rejection'	Manifests the opposite end of a 'response' spectrum from the rejection of the global IS
Global IS design New sub-categories: Central and local Reasons	Significantly expanded	New explanatory power is added to the common core and core/local Split sub-categories
Nature of the business New sub-categories Common resource Economic constraints	Expanded contains inverted IS initiative	J Lauritzen's IS development policy focuses on business (not IS) initiative, with stringent economic justification (not none)
Global business strategy	Confirmed	Clear and stable global strategy
Tradition of autonomy New sub-category: Business politics	Confirmed, but weak in J Lauritzen	IS by force is used to a limited extent, in the form of political arguments
'IT professional factors' New sub-categories: Centrist skills Local IT literacy Multi-domestic mindset Cultural differences	NEW summary category: only indirectly active in J Lauritzen	Encompasses also elements of: IS professional skills, IS professionalism IS conservatism Lack of IT sophistication Conceptual capability Domestic mindset

[shaded box] Main interaction categories

The new categories in this case stem from the fact that the information system in question is an established business tool that has been around for nearly two decades. *IT Management* structure and processes are well understood. Furthermore, because shipping is steeped in long – and revered – tradition in Denmark, *Historical Factors* are a strong influence not only for the business, but also for the way in which information systems are developed so that *IS Mirrors* the *Business Operations (IS=Ops).* Shipping is international by nature and, given this level of integration into the business, 'internationalization' of the information systems was a factor in the their architecture from the outset.

Information systems are not given a high *Strategic Weight of IS* by the Group, but are regarded as an essential ingredient in the management and stewardship of ships and cargoes, the common resource of their business operations. This stance colors the organizational placement of the *IT Management* function, which is embedded in the – central – operations hierarchy rather than occupying a functional niche of its own.

Of the 'main' categories, *IS=Ops*[10] has the most profound impact on the way in which information systems work within J Lauritzen. Reflecting the fact that these systems are an integral part of the business operations of the firm, users don't regard them as special, they are just part of the normal work routine. This operational nature of J Lauritzen's information systems has two major corollaries. It is

A. the major factor responsible for shaping the *Design* of the global system; and
B. directly relates to the general *Acceptance* of the system by its users, the second important category in this case.

The *Acceptance of the Global Information System* manifests itself in the very fact that users regard it is as an ordinary part of their work procedures. As such, it is subject to the same satisfaction as well as scrutiny and criticism as any other part of the business processes they use. There is an understanding that the system is a 'living thing', that it has to change and that input to this change process is important.

The three categories are linked in a tight cause-and-effect cycle. At the centre of the interplay between categories is *IS=Ops*, which influences – and shapes – the *Global IS Design*. The information systems design determines how the technology is used to support the business operations. This, in turn, influences and shapes the way in which they are carried out. The resulting continuous and successful interaction between business and information technology people is the main reason for the *Acceptance of the Global Information System*. Acceptance, as a product of beneficial interchange between IS and operations then goes on to intensify *IS=Ops* by enhancing the readiness of the business people to integrate the international information system ever more fully into the business process. This further refines the Global IS Design, leading to another loop in the cause-and-effect cycle, as shown in Figure 7.5 below.

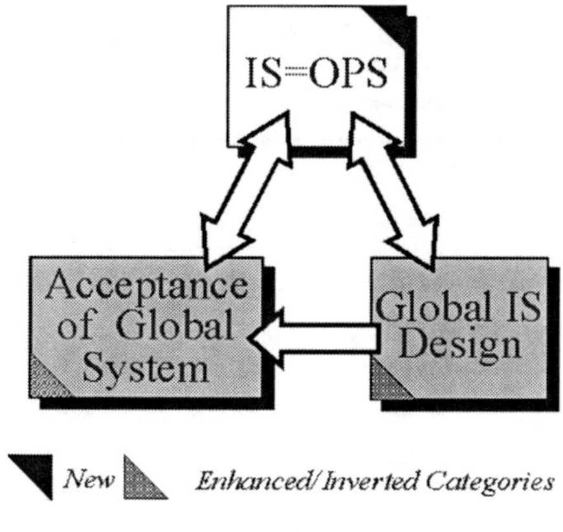

Figure 7.5. The cycle of integration and acceptance in the J Lauritzen case

This 'virtuous' cycle originates in the *Nature of the Business* of J Lauritzen. At the heart of their operations is the – central – management of the shipping fleet as a *Common Resource,* which is the main profit driver and with which everybody in the firm interacts continuously, contemporaneously and world-wide. The roots of the central nature of J Lauritzen's information systems are in this element of central control. They are further deepened because they reflect the firm's *Global Business Strategy.* Management of the fleet and its basic stewardship (of ownership structure and mix, supplies and maintenance) is best done by headquarters in Copenhagen. The job of the local offices is it to 'feed' the fleet, i.e. they are mainly responsible for marketing and customer relations.

This 'global' element of the firm's strategy is reflected in their *IT Management,* which accumulates most of the IT knowledge at the centre. This 'centrist'[11] frame of mind, in turn, has shaped the *Style* of IT support (for common systems only) and the basic *Architecture* of the international information system, which revolves around two central mainframe installations in Copenhagen. These mutually linked categories seem to be engaged in a self-fulfilling cycle, maintaining a structure of central control and systems architecture. They exert a significant influence on the *Global IS Design.* Figure 7.6 summarizes the interaction of the main categories.

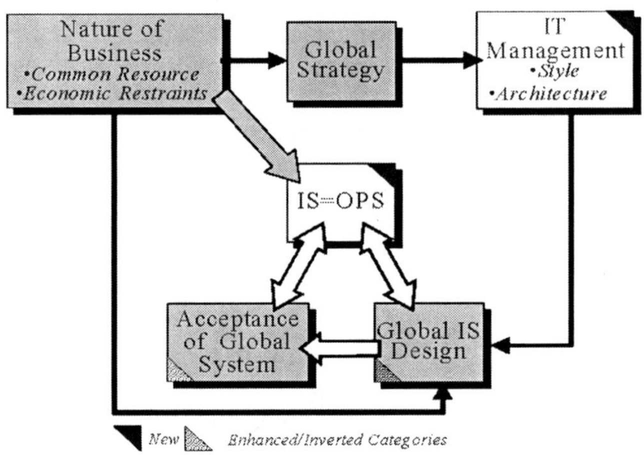

Figure 7.6. Interaction of all the main categories within the J Lauritzen case

The four other active categories play a minor role in the interaction of categories. *Tradition of Local Autonomy,* because of the firm's centrist

---

[11] This term, although usually found mostly in a political context, will further on be used to express the amalgamation of the four categories that deal, respectively, attitude (*HQ Rules*), paradigm (*IS=Ops*), policy (*Central Support for Local IT*) and strategy ('Global' *Business Strategy*), all of which have a central focus.

organization, it is not of great influence. '*IS Professional Skills*' are also of limited importance, as there are no large projects and technical functions have mostly been outsourced – reflecting the low *Strategic Weight of IS*. In turn, this weighting has its roots in *Historical Factors*.

7.2.2 Comparison of J Lauritzen and Co-op Cases

The J Lauritzen case is in a number of significant ways different from the Co-op case. Firstly, the international information system in place has been actively accepted by the business people who use it as part of their work – whereas the Co-op's story is one of accelerating rejection. The second difference is the stability of the global business strategy followed by J Lauritzen. Their stance of – predominantly – central control of the core business operations is well grounded in the history of the firm – whereas the migration through a number of global business strategies is an important characteristic of the Co-op case. Thirdly, there is no big, ongoing information systems project.

An assessment of these differences should sharpen the understanding of core categories and should lead to new insights.

7.2.2.1 Nature of the Business: Synchronicity

The businesses, operations and IT architectures of J Lauritzen and the Co-op are significantly different, with regard to their business mission, the way they operate and also with respect to their IT architecture.

Synchronicity of the business operations is the salient point of difference in this domain. It seems correlated to the degree of 'Centrism' of the IS Architecture – none for the asynchronous Co-op and highly 'centrist' for J Lauritzen. The Co-op's failure to implement a centrist, and globally standard, information system's regime could thus be explained by trying to adopt the 'wrong' type of system for their type of business operations. Furthermore, it could be conjectured that the *I=A=T*[12] fallacy discovered in the Co-op case could well be related to *Synchronicity:* if *I=A=T* is wrong for an asynchronous operations, it might well be right for a synchronous one.

[12] This is the belief that in order to obtain the same *I*nformation in a distributed system, all *A*pplications and *T*echnology had to be identical too.

Table 7.3 below illustrates this with a comparison of business mission, operations and information technology architecture.

Table 7.3. Business and IT differences between J Lauritzen and the Co-op

	J Lauritzen	Co-op
Business mission	Hiring-out of storage space in a fleet of ships. The fleet is a common resource for all business units and all operating activities are centered on it.	Distribution of produce in parallel to all subsidiaries; the operations do not have – or require – a common physical operational entity they focus on
Operations	Multiple operators make dispositions about the common resource in a synchronous and interactive manner*	Orders, information and physical movements are exchanged sequentially and asynchronously between HQ and local management
Information technology architecture	'Centrist' architecture	Distributed architecture (centrist architecture was rejected by business users)

* This defines Synchronicity

7.2.2.2 Architecture and Common Resource

J Lauritzen's information systems directly support management of the *Common Resource*. In contrast, there is no *Common Resource* in the Co-op's case. The *Common Resource* category had important, but opposite, implications for the IS *Architecture* and *Global IS Design* in both cases:

Common Resources determine J Lauritzen's information systems architecture, which is characterized by a common 'core' and 'local' variations. The nature of the commonality unambiguously defines the functionality of the 'core';

Absence of a *Common Resource* made it impossible for the Co-op to develop a common data/business model (except at a level of generalization that made them practically meaningless). Subsequently, they could not design a global information system that the users would accept – and the existing distributed information systems remained in force.

7.2.2.3 IS=Ops and the concepts of *Utility* Versus *Control*

The *Synchronicity* and the *Common Resource* categories in J Lauritzen both contribute to the emergence of *IS=Ops*, which gives the information systems a strong element of *Utility*. The business people respond to 'their' information systems in a positive manner, because they are useful, often essential, components of their work. This is an important catalyst for the *Acceptance of the Global Information System*.

Without a *Common Resource*, *Synchronicity* or *IS=Ops* in the Co-op case, the IIS had little useful functionality for the business people – as expressed in the *No Economic Justification* sub-category. Furthermore, the dearth of *Utility* in the system led them to conclude that the 'real' reason for the global system was the imposition of a higher level of central *Control*. The reaction to this was a *Rejection of the Global Information System*.

A comparison of the linkage between the relevant categories in the two cases is shown in Table 7.4 below.

Table 7.4. Relationships between *IS=Ops* related categories in the two cases

J Lauritzen	Co-op
Common Resource and Synchronicity	Common Product, but No Common Resource and Asynchronous business processes
lead to	lead to
IS=Ops	No IS=Ops and No Economic Justification
leads to	lead to
Clear Common Core and Core-Local Split in the Global IS Design	Vague and inoperable Global IS Design
lead to	leads to
Utility of the information systems	No Utility, but suspicion of central Control aspirations
leads to	lead to
Acceptance of the Global Information System	Rejection of the Global Information System

7.2.2.4 Strategic Directions: *Alignment*, Vectors and Response

J Lauritzen's strategy has only changed marginally over the last three decades. The Co-op, however, has been through a migration of extremes: from an initial 'Global' position to a 'Multi-National' strategy and now back, aiming for a – balanced – 'Transnational' policy.

In both cases, the direction of the business strategy diverges from the strategy followed by information technology management. In J Lauritzen's case, the difference in strategies is small: the information technology strategy gives more say (on IT matters) to local management. In the Co-op's case, however, the IT strategy aims at restoring more control to the centre, whilst the business strives to hand out more, but better balanced, control to regional/local management. The degree of concordance of IT and business strategies is usually labeled as their level of *Alignment*. In the case of J Lauritzen the level of *Alignment* is reasonably high, whereas there is *Mis-Alignment* between the Co-op's divergent business and information technology strategies.

Using 'vectors' to depict these strategies then the concordance or divergence of business and information technology strategy can be illustrated for both cases. Figure 7.7 shows this.

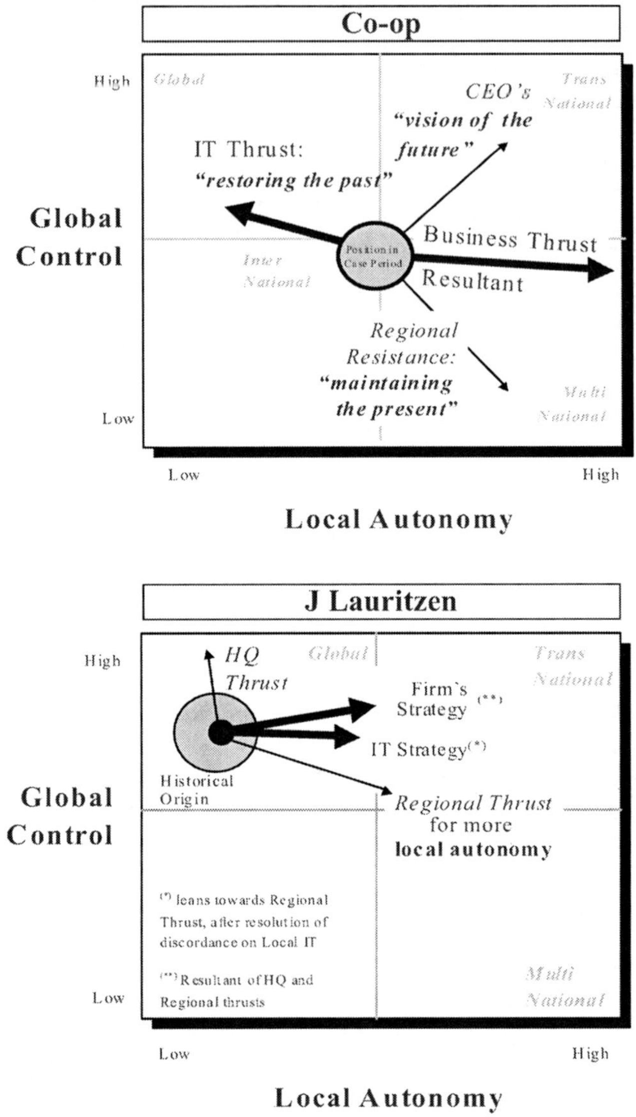

Figure 7.7. Conceptualized strategy vectors of J Lauritzen and the Co-op

Response [13] to the Global Information System was similarly different: Acceptance in J Lauritzen's case, Rejection from the Co-op's business people. Figure 7.8 below plots the respective *Response* and ***Alignment*** positions for both cases.

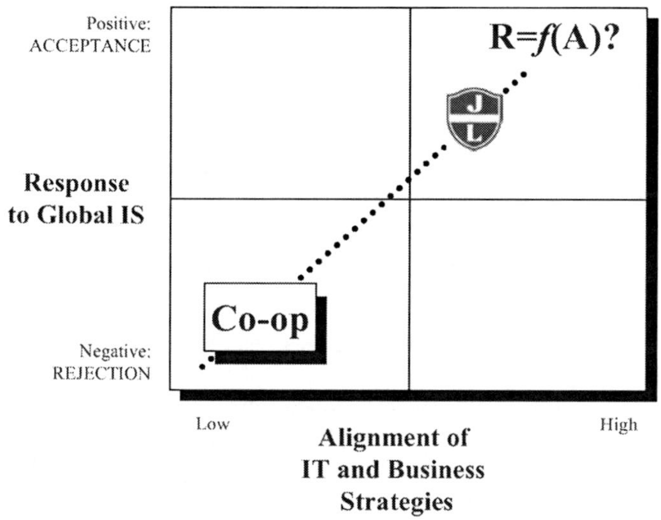

Figure 7.8. Correlation between alignment and response

The apparent connection between *Alignment* and *Response* could indicate the existence of a function such that the levels of one allow the prediction of the level of the other. The level of *Response* would be the obvious preferred dependent variable, i.e. the one to be predicted from the level of *Alignment*. Investigating the relationship between the respective strategy 'vectors' for IT and Business might clarify this notion.

In both cases, the vectors representing the business strategy are in fact 'resultants' formed by diverging strategic directions by central and local management:

J Lauritzen's IT strategy is formed by a compromise between the centrist IT management and their (few) local subsidiaries;

The Co-op's IT strategy towards 'Global' is a unified one but nearly diametrically opposed to where the business wants to go. The business vector is a resultant between the center's 'Transnational' vision, whereas the regions defend their 'Multi-National' stance.

The constellation of vectors *eo ipso* suggests a possible function linking *Response* to *Alignment*: The- size of the angle between the business and IT vectors could provide an indication of the degree of *Acceptance* or *Rejection*. Figure 7.9 below demonstrates this.

[13] As the collective label for both acceptance and rejection.

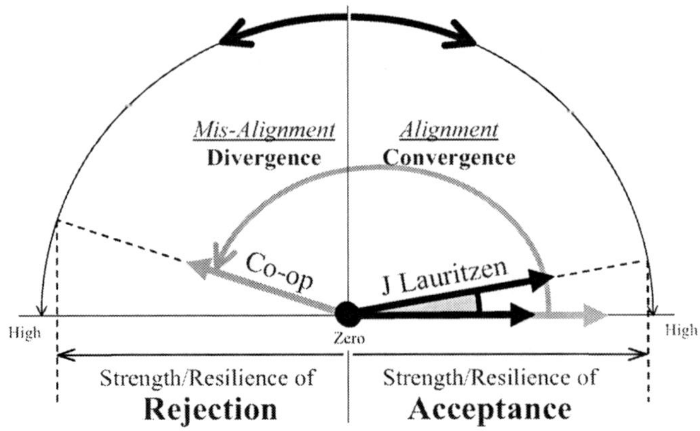

Figure 7.9. Relationship of response and alignment

The angle of strategy vectors seems to divide into two sectors: oblique angles, where the two strategic thrusts are converging, are related to *Acceptance* on the response spectrum. Obtuse angles between diverging vectors indicate that business and IT pulling away from each other, and relate to *Rejection*.

7.2.2.5 Force Fields and Politics

The force field of interactions between business and IT factions was strong and engulfed most 'of the 'dependent' categories in the Co-op case.

Table 7.5. Comparison of the force fields across the cases

	Co-op	J Lauritzen
Nature of the force field	Major activity, determines main interaction of categories	Minor activity, affects main categories only indirectly
Interaction	Antagonistic exchanges and adversarial politics	Rational exchange and limited politics over peripheral issues
Scope	All major effecter categories are participants in the force field constellation	Only the categories involved in the central/local debate are force field participants
Conflict resolution	Both parties are trying to 'win' and involve political means to achieve their ends	Consensus policy leads to rational discourse and an equilibrium solution

In J Lauritzen, the arena of interaction between business and IT was dubbed an 'Area of Discordance' because it is weaker and has a narrower scope. Table 7.5 above compares the two force fields.

There seems to be a correlation between the absence or presence of **Politics** and the notions of *Utility* and *Control*:

- in the Co-op case the information system's low Utility did not provide any incentive for the business people to accept it – hence the IT faction applied the politics of *IS by Force* to achieve its goal. The absence of Utility, moreover, aroused the user's suspicion of a hidden motive of Control – which seemed to add to the strength and acrimony of the antagonistic forces at play;
- High Utility and low Control in the J Lauritzen case, on the other hand, correlate to a low level of politics, weak antagonism and a prevalence of rational exchanges between business and IT factions.

7.2.2.6 Acceptance and Rejection: Response Cycles

In both cases the way in which the business faction reacts to the introduction of an information system by the IT people seems, to be governed by a stepwise, cyclical, and incremental interchange, as shown in Figure 7.10 below.

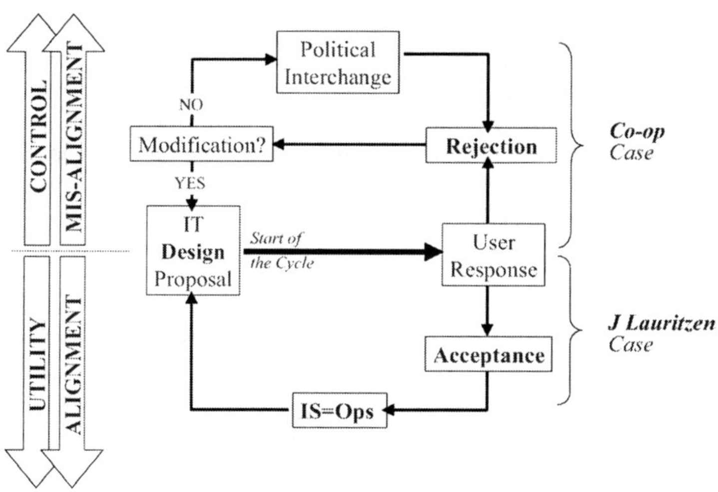

Figure 7.10. Anatomy of the response cycles

In the Co-op case – characterized by *Control* and *Mis-Alignment* – the interchange was predominantly negative, from the first rejection of an – seemingly inadequate – information systems proposed by the IT faction, to its ultimate defeat by business management after a number of rejection-reaction cycles. The cycle in the J Lauritzen case, on the other hand, is a benign one. *Alignment* reigns and information technology's existing integration in the business operations leads to an IIS design of high *Utility*. That, in turn, assures that business users and management accept the system – anchoring it further into the business processes – whence the cycle starts again.

7.2.2.7 Summary of the Derivative Categories

During the comparative analysis a number of new, 'derivative' categories emerged. They are grounded in a variety of other categories. For enhanced clarity, they are briefly summarized in the paragraphs below.

Alignment – and its opposite *Mis-Alignment* – stem originally from a sub category within the *Rejection of the Global Information System* core category in the Co-op case, which is now part of the *Acceptance/Rejection* dyad. It also has significant connections to Force Field strengths and the negative or positive character of the politics between business and IT.

The concept of *Synchronicity* –simultaneous, real-time international interaction – is dominant in J Lauritzen and stems from the *Common Resource* category their *Nature of the Business*. The Co-op, on the other hand, runs mainly asynchronous operations in its international dealings. The category explains J Lauritzen's 'centrist' IIS architecture – and why the Co-op failed to implement an *I=A=T*[14] system.

Utility, linked closely to *IS=Ops* and *Global IS Design*, encapsulates the international information system's usefulness for the business users. Seemingly juxtaposed to it is *Control*, the intent to use the system to impose central control. *Utility* and *Control* are correlated to contrasting and opposed strategies in the two cases, such as rational, constructive arguments *versus* political, destructive ones and Acceptance *versus* Rejection.

7.3 Enhancing the Theory: The 2nd Theoretical Framework

In the second case, the 13 core categories that formed the foundation of the 1st Theoretical Framework had now grown to altogether 20 conceptual constructs (including the 'derivatives').

The updated theory, too, had grown from 10 to 22 theorems, grouped into six (previously three) theory areas:

A. Architecture of International Information Systems;
B. Alignment, Response and Force Fields;

---

[14] The paradigmatic assumption that obtaining *equal* Information content requires *identical* Application systems, running on the *same* Technology Infrastructure.

C. The Response Cycle;
D. Utility and Control;
E. The Role of Design;
F. Development Skills for International Information Systems.

In the following paragraphs, the 2nd Theoretical Framework is set out.

7.3.1 Architecture of International Information Systems

The Co-op set out to implement a globally standard information system and failed. In the J Lauritzen case the functionality of the system's common parts was restricted to common business operations – a seemingly important criteria for its acceptance.

This leads to two deductions about the nature of international information systems, namely that

A. an IIS consists of a part common to all users – the 'core' – and other parts that are specific to users in various local sites – the 'local' functionality;
B. The core is defined by the *operational* needs of the business shared by all users; all other functionality is local – and at the discretion of local management.

A corollary of item B is contained in a normative deduction:

C. The structure and management of the IIS must tie in with the Global Business Strategy, especially with the level of autonomy of the local users.

This is borne out by the Co-op case where this was mismatched and became a prime cause for the systems rejection.

Synchronicity is also linked to architecture, mainly to the degree of its centricity. Using the *I=A=T* sub-category to describe the degree of standardization in an IIS, it can be posited that

D. Synchronicity determines how central and standardized the IIS needs to be. Minimum synchronicity requires only identical information, i.e. it would be I≠A≠T. High synchronicity, on the other hand, would require identity of not just information but also the application systems that produces it as well as the technology the systems run on, i.e. I=A=T. Interim levels of synchronicity would require correspondingly mixed degrees of identity between I, A and T; furthermore the case also seems to indicate that
E. Centrist architectures have a tendency to resist change – for historical as well as for economical reasons. This is especially so if Synchronicity is their main cause. The case further suggested the existence of a self-fulfilling cycle of centrist architecture and IT management, further adding to the resilience of central architectures.

The architecture[15] suggested by this part of the theory is depicted in Figure 7.11 below.

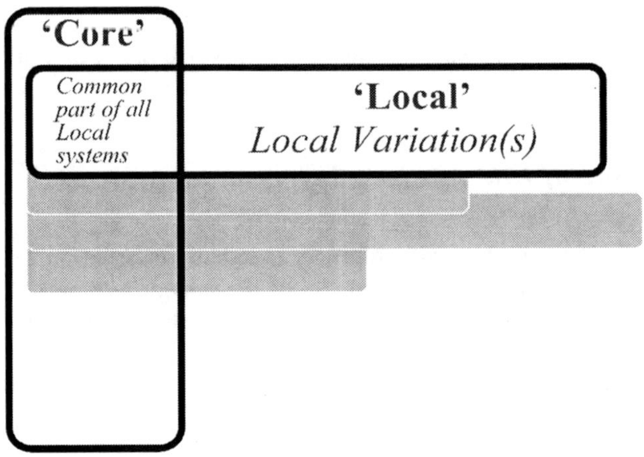

Figure 7.11. Generic architecture of an international information system

The horizontal box represents the totality of information systems and technology in any given local/regional subsidiary. The shaded horizontal boxes of different length indicate that individual local offices might have widely varying and different local systems and technology configurations. The vertical box, on the other axis, depicts the systems that are common/standard for *all* locations. The intersection of the boxes is the part all local systems have in common.

7.3.2 Alignment, Response and Force Fields

Both cases indicated the significance of differences between business and information technology strategies for response to the IIS. This lead to the following theorems:

F. Alignment (of IT and business strategies) is important for the design and implementation of an IIS.
G. Alignment determines Response: low alignment leads to rejection, high alignment fosters acceptance.
H. Alignment increases the business effectiveness of the IIS.

Alignment also correlates with force fields (shown in Figure 7.12 below):

[15] This builds on earlier studies (Lehmann, 1996a, b), which suggested a similar generic architecture.

I. Alignment creates weak force fields – which enhances Acceptance. Mis-Alignment creates strong force fields and fosters Rejection.
J. Alignment and weak force fields facilitate consensual conflict resolution, whereas Misalignment is connected to antagonistic stances in strong force fields.

Force field and conflict characteristics are also related to the nature of political interchange:

K. Alignment creates few and consensual politics, whereas Mis-Alignment is conducive to strong, antagonistic politics.

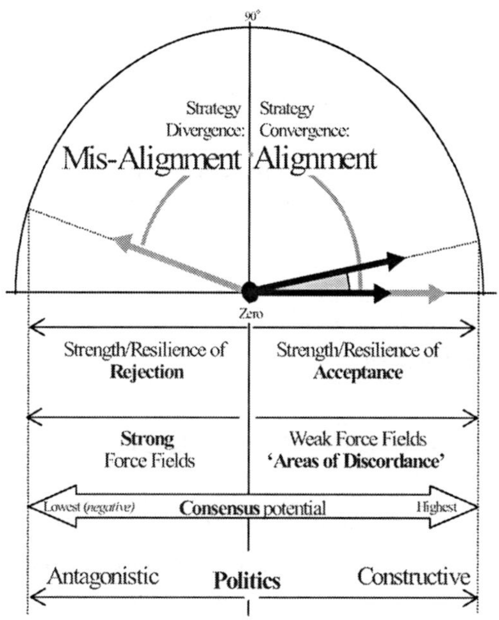

Figure 7.12. Summary of alignment dependencies

7.3.3 Response Cycles

In both cases the Response to the IIS took on the form of a dialectical interchange with circular characteristics. This leads to the statement that

L. The Response to the IIS is the central element of a dialectic behavior cycle between he business and IT people. This cycle is destructive if the Response is Rejection, and positive in the case of Acceptance.

7.3.4 Utility and Control

The derivative concept of Utility is firstly related to the level of rationality in the dialectic interchange between users and IT within the Response Cycle. Not logically dichotomous, Control, i.e. the use of an IIS to enhance levels of central control, nevertheless has a contrary effect:

M. Utility facilitates rational interchange between Users and IT. Control generates political interchange. Through the level of rationality in the dialogue, Utility is also is connected to positive motivation and attitude towards an IIS. Control, on the other hand, exerts an opposite, negative influence on users' motivation: Utility increases the probability of Acceptance whereas Control decreases it.

Since the common core tends to be generated by central management, it is the Response from local users that counts:

N. Utility as perceived by local management determines their Acceptance.
O. Local management resist an IIS that imposes undue[16] levels of central control.

7.3.5 The Role of Design

The axiomatic truth that only good design is acceptable to users found confirmation in both cases:

P. Goodness of design is a prerequisite for Acceptance.

In the context of an IIS, it seems to be the effect of IS=Ops which is at the heart of acceptable design:

Q. IS=Ops as the foundation for design builds Acceptance;
R. IIS design without IS=Ops content initiates and/or perpetuates a Rejection cycle.

7.3.6 IIS Development Skills

The J Lauritzen case added only indirectly by confirming the categories identified in the Co-op case:

---

[16] That is Control that is out of line with the level of control inherent in the prevailing global business strategy.

S. State-of-the Art professionalism is a sine qua non for IIS. The Co-op case demonstrated that sloppy practices, e.g. in the management of an RFP, lead to disaster when they are perpetrated internationally.
T. Participation from users at the local level is essential for ensuring IS=Ops in the design, acceptance and co-operative implementation.

A significant corollary of T is contained in the necessity for internationalism:

U. Knowledge of the international users' local requirements and their business culture is essential for designing and implementing an IIS.

The higher complexity of international business environments also poses specific requirements:

V. The analysis of IIS requires extraordinary conceptual capability.

The contrasting nature of the two cases had added considerable scope and depth to the 2nd Theoretical Framework. This had occurred especially in the areas of *Response*, in clarifying the nature of the Force Field interactions and where the quality of the IIS's functionality is concerned. Table 7.6 below demonstrates this extension in theory from the first to the second framework. The areas in *italics* were expanded from the 'Response and Force Field' in the 1st Theoretical Framework. New theorems introduced in the 2nd framework are shown as shaded.

Table 7.6. Development of the theoretical frameworks between the Co-op and the J Lauritzen cases

Area	1st TF – Co-op	2nd TF – J Lauritzen
Architecture of an IIS	Theorem A. An IIS for a diverse international firm must have a Core/Local Split Theorem B. Nature of the business and its autonomy structure determine the contents of the IIS core Theorem C. The extent of the Local parts of the IIS is more determined by political factors than by rational/logical analysis.	Theorem A. An IIS for a diverse international firm must have a Core of common functionality for all users and Local parts with differing functionality for different users Theorem B. The Nature of the Business determines the Applications Architecture and functionality of the IIS core Theorem C. Functionality and Management of the IIS must be aligned to the Autonomy Structure inherent in the Global Business Strategy Theorem D. Synchronicity determines the nature of the Technology Architecture Theorem E. A Central Core has strong Gravitation
Alignment and Force Fields	Theorem E. The implementation of an IIS that is perceived as an instrument of central control meets conflict from local management (Force Field) Theorem H. Backing by local business management (not just by central executive) is required for design and implementation of the IIS.	Theorem F. Alignment of global business strategy and IT strategy influences the design and implementation of international information systems. Theorem G. Alignment determines Acceptance or Rejection Theorem H. Alignment governs the business effectiveness of the IIS and the degree of organizational learning as a result of its implementation. Theorem I. Alignment determines the nature of the force field between IT and business/users; Theorem J. Alignment determines nature of the conflict resolution in the force field Theorem K. The Politics of the Response depend on Alignment

Area	1st TF – Co-op	2nd TF – J Lauritzen
Response Cycle	Theorem J. Response, i.e. Acceptance and Rejection are determined in Force Field interactions between Users and IT people	Theorem L. Response is the central element of a dialectic behavior cycle between business users and IT people
Utility & Control		Theorem M. IS=Ops and Control motivation determine the nature of the dialectic interchange within the response cycle Theorem N. The acceptability of the 'core' to the local sites depends on the utility of the systems functionality and the perceived degree of central control it will impose Theorem O. The implementation of an IIS that is perceived as an instrument of undue central control meets conflict from local management
Design		Theorem P. 'Goodness of the Design' is a prerequisite for the Acceptance of the IIS Theorem Q. IS=Ops increases the probability for an IIS Design to be accepted by users Theorem R. IIS design without IS=Ops initiates and perpetuates a Rejection cycle
Development Skills for International Information Systems	Theorem D. Decision making authority for the creation and implementation of the IIS must reflect the business authority structure. Theorem F. Creating and implementing an IIS requires international knowledge Theorem G. The analysis preceding IIS design requires an extraordinary high level of conceptual capability Theorem I. State of the art professionalism is required for the design and implementation of an IIS	Theorem S. State of the art professionalism is a pre-requisite for the design and implementation of an IIS Theorem T. Backing by local business management (not just by central executive) is required for design and implementation of the IIS. Theorem U. Creating and implementing an IIS requires international knowledge Theorem V. IIS design analysis requires an extraordinary high level of conceptual capability

7.4 Theoretical Sampling

The first step in this theoretical sampling process is therefore an assessment of what the second case has added to the knowledge. From this flows an evaluation of the saturation status of both the categories discovered so far and the current theoretical framework.

7.4.1 Contribution of the J Lauritzen Case

The J Lauritzen case added a significant amount of 'theoretical properties' (in terms of Glaser et al., 1967) to the categories brought forward from the Co-op case. The case also lead to the discovery of important new categories. These results indicate that the strategy of maximizing differences by choosing a 'contrasting case' was successful. On the other hand, however, some of the differences (e.g. the absence of any sizeable systems development projects at J Lauritzen's) meant that a number of categories are still unsaturated.

7.4.2 Categories' Saturation Levels

A number of categories were assumed 'saturated' after the J Lauritzen case. They include *Lack of IT Sophistication, Business Strategy Migration* and *Tradition of Local Autonomy* from the business domain and *IS Professional Skills, Domestic Mindset* and *IS Initiative* from the Information Technology domain. The *Global Standard IS Design* category was eliminated altogether and replaced with one that emphasizes *Common Core Design.* Five further categories were assessed as close to 'saturation' – where the principle was understood, but the scope still needed investigation. of the 'derivative' categories, especially the relationship between the concepts of *Utility* versus *Control* needs more confirmation. *Synchronicity*, potentially an important design determinant, requires confirmation of its connection – or otherwise – with *I=A=T* and the architecture of the IIS.

7.4.3 Assessment of Theorems

In a way similar to categories, the parts of the theory themselves need to reach a level of 'saturation' and a direction for theoretical sampling for the next case should take such an assessment into account.

Table 7.7 below illustrates the saturation levels of the main theorems that make up the current theoretical framework. Shading from low to high indicates saturation.

The assessment is based on the assumed saturation level of the categories underlying each theorem and on the degree of 'conjecture' inherent in them. Conjecture is defined in its rigorous (mathematical) sense, i.e. a logical deductions from other theorems before it has been proved or disproved. Other factors taken into account are the theorem's plausibility in the context of general knowledge within its substantive domain and the degree to which it is logically anchored in other parts of the theory.

Table 7.7. Assessment of theorems: requirements for further evidence

Th#	Theorems	(low) Level of Saturation (high)
	Architecture of an IIS	
(A)	An IIS for a diverse international firm must have a core/local split	
(B)	The nature of the business determines the applications architecture and functionality of the IIS core	The importance of *operations* is clear, but the Co-op case has only indirect evidence for the role of *control*
(C)	Functionality and management of the IIS must be aligned to the autonomy Structure inherent in the global business strategy	
(D)	Synchronicity determines the nature of the technology architecture (I=A=T)	High potential for a deterministic technology architecture model
(E)	A central core has strong gravitation	
	Alignment, Response and Force Fields	
(F)	Alignment of global business strategy and IT strategy influences the design and implementation of international information systems.	More evidence about the linkage between Alignment and Design would further clarify the role of Design
(G)	Alignment determines acceptance or rejection	
(H)	Alignment governs the business effectiveness of the IIS and the degree of organizational learning as a result of its implementation.	Conjectural theorem: more evidence needed
(I)	Alignment determines the nature of the force field between IT and business/users;	
(J)	Alignment determines nature of the conflict resolution in the force field	
(K)	The politics of the response cycle depend on alignment	More evidence would also benefit (I) and (J)
	The response cycle	
(L)	Response is the central element of a dialectic behavior cycle between business users and IT people	
	Utility and Control	
(M)	IS=Ops and control motivation determine the nature of the dialectic interchange within the response cycle	More (direct) evidence needed on the role of *Control* in the *Rejection* cycle

Th#	Theorems	(low) Level of Saturation (high)
(N)	The acceptability of the 'core' to the local sites depends on the utility of the systems functionality and the perceived degree of central control it will impose	Verification of the postulated 'Trade-off' between *Utility* and *Control* would increase the predictive power of the model
(O)	The implementation of an IIS that is perceived as an instrument of undue central control meets conflict from local management	The linkage between the concept of 'undue' level of *Control*, the *Global Business Strategy* and *Alignment* needs investigating
	The Role of Design	
(P)	IIS design relies on IS=Ops to be accepted by users	
(Q)	IIS design without IS=Ops initiates and perpetuates a rejection cycle	This is still conjecture, extrapolated from indirect evidence in the Co-op case
(R)	'Goodness of the design' is a prerequisite for the acceptance of the IIS	
	IIS Development Skills	
(S)	Creating and implementing an IIS requires international knowledge	
(T)	The analysis preceding IIS design requires an extraordinary high level of conceptual capability	
(U)	Backing by local business management (not just by central executive) is required for design and implementation of the IIS.	Conjecture, like (Q), extrapolated from indirect evidence in the Co-op case
(V)	State of the art professionalism is required for the design and implementation of an IIS	

Assessed extent of 'saturation'

From this assessment, more data seems to be needed for the theorems to do with *Alignment, Synchronicity* and *Utility* versus *Control.* As these were the concepts developed last as 'secondary' constructs, this was not surprising. Altogether, the principles of the theorems in need of further investigation are not in question, but their scope is.

The next case should be able to add to the extent to which the theorems can be generalized across the substantive area. Glaser et al. (1967) recommend a sampling strategy of 'minimizing data and maximizing group differences' so as to 'develop fundamental uniformities of greatest scope' (ibid. p. 58). This means that the next case should have the following qualities:

- It should come from the same – or – similar data class, i.e. an international information systems environment in a multinational firm with wide global reach;
- As a firm, however, it should have different attributes:
  - larger than J Lauritzen;
  - with ongoing information systems' development projects;
  - where information systems are of – more – strategic importance;
  - in an affluent, or at least non-austere economic situation.

PANALPINA, a world-wide firm in the forwarding business was selected as the third case because

- They have offices in 60 countries and a sophisticated portfolio of international information systems;
- They are some 8–10 times the size of J Lauritzen (albeit only two thirds the size of the Co-op);
- They have a number of ongoing developments and a staff of information technology experts that specialize in systems development and maintenance;
- Their information systems are a declared strategic priority;
- They are a profitable and cash-rich concern.

PANALPINA are headquartered in Switzerland and have significant information technology centers in Europe, the US and around the Pacific Rim region.

Chapter 8
Case Three: PANALPINA International Forwarders

The third case is analyzed in this section. Subsequently another update to the theory is carried out to arrive at the 3rd Theoretical Framework, which is then assessed for saturation. The case proved exceedingly fruitful – it yielded nearly three-quarters as many 'raw' categories as did the foundation case. Given the advanced degree of saturation at this stage of the study, however, the larger proportion of these categories confirmed and annotated the properties of existing ones. Nevertheless, the minority of 'new' categories added critical value to the theory so far. For this reason, the case story is told with a sharp focus towards the areas that contribute most to the theory. Similarly, the interpretation will concentrate on the salient aspects of new theoretical contributions. Full details of the case – together with the detailed description of findings, interpretations and theorems – are, again, available from the author on demand.

8.1 Case History: PANALPINA

The traditional freight forwarders market is defined as 'managing the door to door transportation of goods (larger than parcels but smaller than bulk) by reselling transport capacity purchased wholesale'.[1] European companies, mostly of German speaking origin, seem to dominate the global market. The traditional reliance of European business on trade across caountry-borders – and the centuries of experience in it – seems to have given European firms a distinctive advantage in the global market. PANALPINA is one of the largest, as Figure 8.1 shows.

[1] Quoting the Chairman of the Supervisory Board of PANALPINA Austria.

H. Lehmann, *The Dynamics of International Information Systems*,
Integrated Series in Information Systems 23, DOI 10.1007/978-1-4419-5750-4_8,

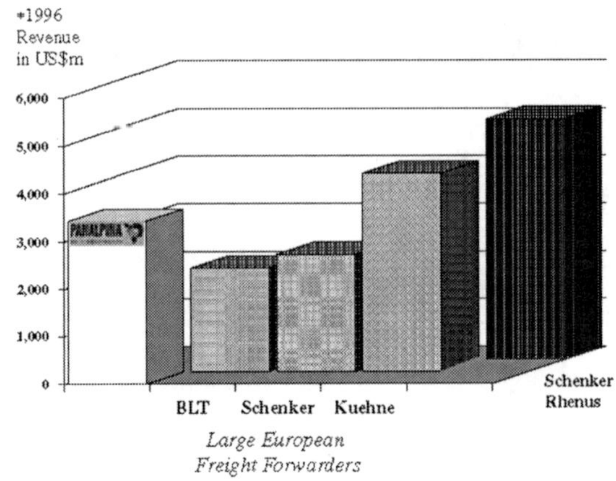

Figure 8.1. Comparing PANALPINA with two other large European freight forwarders – and one integrated logistics firm (Schenker-Rhenus)

The European companies are on the whole significantly larger than their American competitors: Air Express, the largest American freight forwarder, is only about a third of the size of PANALPINA. Figure 8.2 compares PANALPINA with the largest U.S. companies.

The freight forwarding industry was influenced by two events over the last two decades. First, the swing to just-in-time manufacturing since the late 1980s has increased the importance of transport. Secondly, world trade has continued to expand and has accelerated since the 1993 GATT round. Both those developments have meant that the markets for forwarding have grown considerably, bringing with it a large number of profitable opportunities – all of which involve information technology on a global scale.

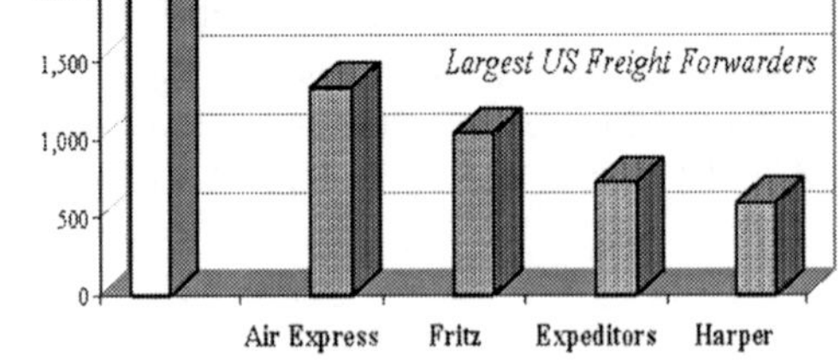

Figure 8.2. Comparison of PANALPINA with the largest US freight forwarders

8.1.1 History of PANALPINA

Walter Schneider, an astute entrepreneur, began to work in the transport industry after the Second World War in Vienna. In 1948 he founded his own trucking company to engage in the trade – fired by Marshall-Plan aid – between Austria and its neighbors across the Alps. In the 1950s he expanded the company through acquisitions and in the 1960s, as he began to acquire international freight forwarders in Switzerland, it became more economical to move to Switzerland too. Since then PANALPINA expanded in rapid succession across the globe by first co-operating with local firms, then entering into joint-ventures before acquiring them outright.

This growth by 'stepwise acquisition' has formed the global management style and philosophy of PANALPINA. Giving considerable freedom to the independent agencies in order to let them build up the business as best as their local knowledge would allow, global control was only impressed onto the subsidiary offices as far as the integration into the world-wide operations dictated. Furthermore, the emphasis on the international nature of the business was building up a solid understanding of working with different business cultures in a positive, effective way. This resulted in a transnational mix of global control over the operations and systems aspects of the business and local autonomy to maximize customer opportunities.

As is customary in Switzerland, PANALPINA is governed by a supervisory board, of which Walter Schneider is still the honorary chairman. The firm is run by the 'Extended Executive Board' of the holding company (shown in Figure 8.3 below). The head of MIS is at an equal level with the executives responsible for the operation in each of the regions. In a recent management move, the (previous) head of MIS moved on to take the head position in France – as the previous head of France takes over the Group Chief Executive role. All executives and the large majority of regional management staff are Swiss.

8.1.2 Business Strategy

PANALPINA has followed the same two-pronged strategy for most of it's fifty year existence: growing geographically and beating the market by working together more effectively than the competition. Information technology has always played a major role in all the main components of this strategy, as

- an accelerator for geographical expansion; it establishes all standard business processes in the key operational areas, shortening the learning curve for new local staff; and
- as a major enabler in the development of the 'niche' markets, complementing the core business competencies required there.

Consequently, information systems are a key competencyIS in the forwarding industry. PANALPINA have recognized this very early on: Walter Schneider was one of the first users of IBM's card based computer equipment in Austria. His view of information systems as a major driver of competitive advantage is still a high priority for the firm today.

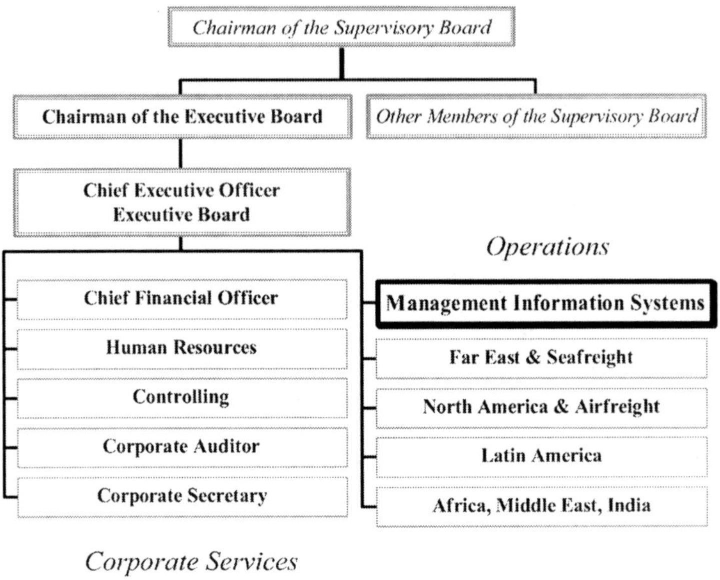

Figure 8.3. PANALPINA organizational structure at executive board level

8.1.3 Nature of the Business

Engaged in the 'Door-to-door delivery of goods', the activities of PANALPINA can be grouped into two interdependent areas:

1. the traditional management of air, sea and overland (road and rail) transport – the 'physical' side of the business; and
2. value added services, which are in the main used to 'feed' the traditional business.

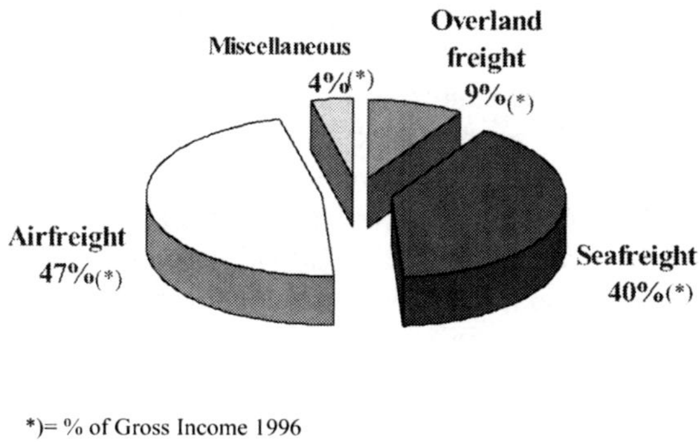

Figure 8.4. Revenue derivation – 'physical' business

The proportions to which PANALPINA's income is derived from the respective areas of its 'physical' business are depicted in Figure 8.4. In terms of gross revenue, about a quarter each comes from Europe, North America and Asia, with the rest of the world sharing the last 25%.

Maintenance of the 'pole position in niche markets' means in essence the development and honing-to-perfection of value added services which generate feeder business for the traditional business activities. The most important one of those is the provision of logistics services for multinational clients.

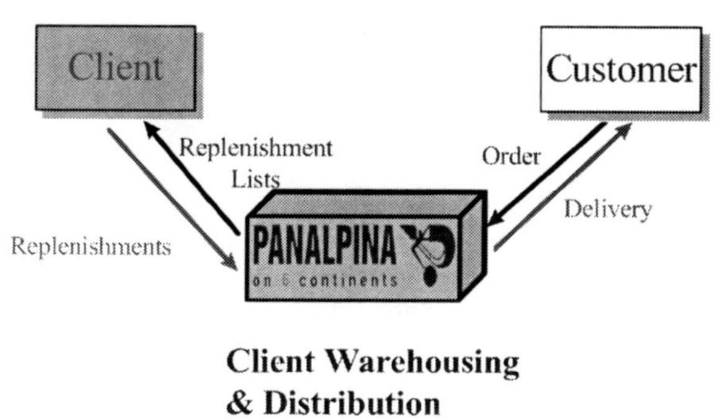

Figure 8.5. PANALPINA's client linkage for inventory management and distribution services

The reason is its future potential: there is a high degree of leverage that can be gained from each client for introducing their own customers – as new PANALPINA clients. It consists in its simplest form in the exclusive delivery of a client's products to their customer's world-wide. A further stage of this service is where PANALPINA is linked into the clients sales and inventory systems and fulfils orders automatically as they arise from the client's customers. A logical extension is the application of this link-up to both ends of the clients value chain, i.e. also automatically picking up consignments from the client's suppliers. As it then becomes more economical for PANALPINA to keep a buffer stock, it is only a short step for them to take over inventory management as an further service. Figure 8.5 above depicts this service.

8.1.4 Information Systems in PANALPINA

Freight forwarding is a business where the effectiveness of operations nearly entirely depends on information and knowledge about consignment details, routing and tracking as well as clients and carrier schedules. Because of this, information systems have been closely mirroring the physical operations very much from the inception of computerization in the mid 1960s.

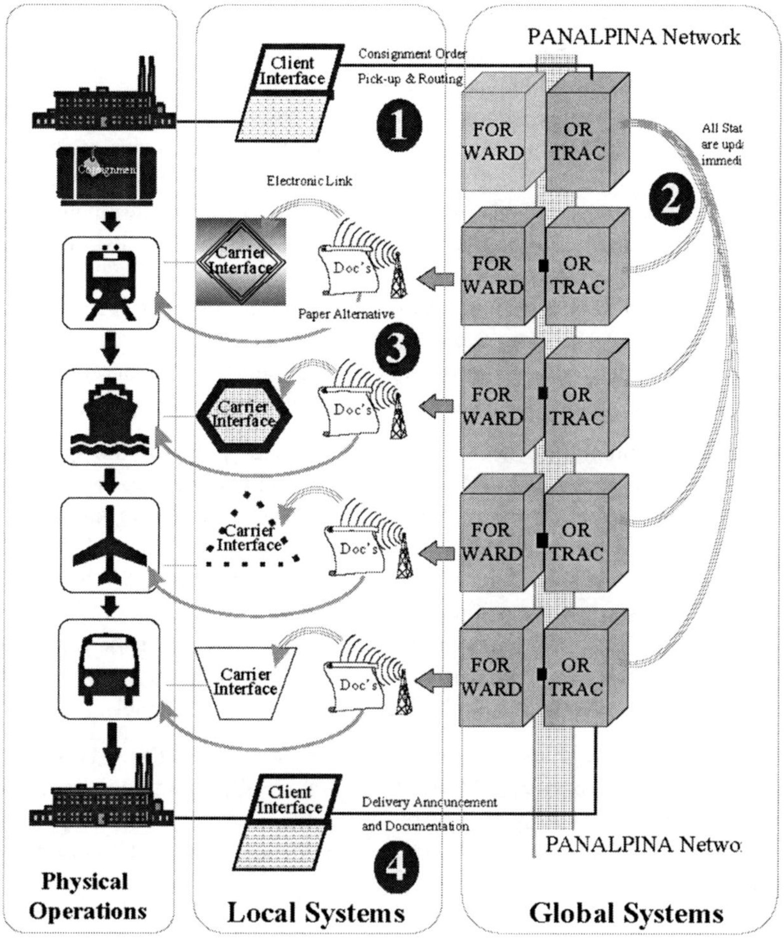

Figure 8.6. Interplay of business operations and information systems

Today information technology is an essential ingredient of the business and considered a key core competency for PANALPINA. Figure 8.6 above illustrates the way in which information systems are integrated into the forwarding operations across the three strategic domains of physical operations, local client interaction and central co-ordination. There are four logical stages (following the black numbers in the figure) in the transactions of PANALPINA with its customers:

1. The client advises PANALPINA that there is a consignment to ship – mostly computer-to-computer electronic linkages or PC front ends; this initiates the physical transport chain. In parallel, the data enters ORTRAC, the main consignment routing and ORder TRACking system;
2. The system establishes a route for the consignment and generates records for all of PANALPINA's branches involved with the consignment. It subsequently updates the databases in all the servers which the respective branches are connected to and establishes linkage for the life of the consignment: from now on every movement and/or transaction connected with the consignment will be updated in all data bases concerned;
3. Now FORWARD, the second major information system comes into play: it generates the necessary documentation for the consignment as it passes through the stations of its route. The documents are then handed forward to the next branch office en route. Based on this, and where applicable:

   - The documentation necessary for whichever physical transport agent is involved is generated and either produced in paper form, or converted into the input format for the respective carrier interface; these carrier interfaces are often local (e.g. third-party information agencies such as TDNI or STAR for specialized air freight and ocean carriers in the U.S.A.) but some (such as airline connections) are international;
   - The third form of documentation which is produced (or the major items of data collated for manual processing) are for local statutory or regulatory authorities, who increasingly deal through on-line channels.

4. Once a reliable estimate is available of the consignment's arrival at its final destination, the respective PANALPINA branch office can advise the receiving client, either system-to-system or by email, fax – or phone. Following this, the physical delivery can be scheduled and the documentation (delivery notes, etc.) is prepared.

This deep integration of the system into the business is critical for PANALPINA for two reasons:

- Firstly, it allows the prediction of delivery times with maximum accuracy – as the physical transport performance is visible instantly all the way to the final destination. This allows PANALPINA in the first instance to take corrective action on its own to bring the consignment back on time. Should the problem still remain, then the client can be forewarned at the earliest possible time;
- Secondly, the in-built early advice of physical transport requirements for the total life of a consignment allows PANALPINA an early and accurate accumulation of capacity needed. In this way the best possible advantage can be taken of volume and pre-booking discounts with carriers. As PANALPINA's profit are made in the difference between rates paid and rates charged, this directly affects the Group's profitability.

Whilst these core systems are in a state of continuous stepwise improvement and upgrading to keep pace with the ever-changing technology, new systems are being built on top of their databases, their real-time capabilities, the interfaces to third-party carriers/hauliers, regulatory authorities/agencies and the client linkage connections with customers. These may be called 'second-generation' systems because they derive their foundations from the basic operational systems, which, in turn, have now become 'utility systems': they feed data and information into the new information systems.

One main area where these 'second-generation' systems are being developed and used to great success is in the Project Management of logistics activities. These systems utilize the consignment database and the real-time capabilities of ORTRAC together with ASB's timetable and schedule data base as well as the linkage with a multitude of carriers. In this way PANALPINA can take over the management and co-ordination of time-critical, often interdependent consignments. Figure 8.7 below illustrates this.

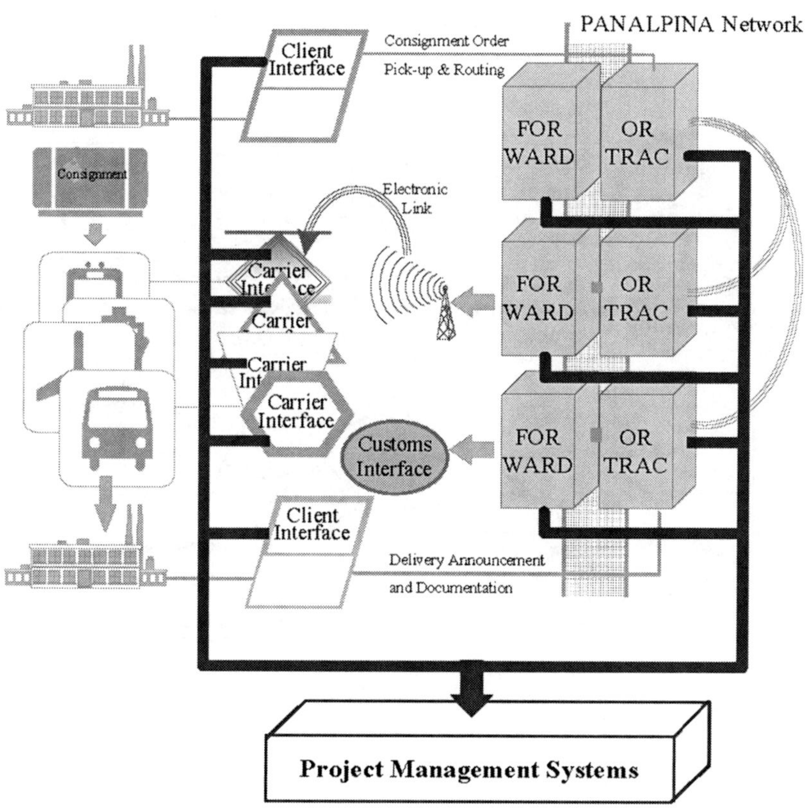

Figure 8.7. Secondary services built around information systems: the example of the project management service

These developments in information technology reflect the movements in the industry as a whole: the main strategic thrust for forwarding companies seems to be the ability to add value to their basic freight hauling capacity. While other companies progress towards this goal by merger and strategic alliances PANALPINA utilizes its information technology competencies to build competitive advantage.

The 'backbone' for all of PANALPINA's information systems and applications is a series of IBM RS/6000 servers, connected with third-party networks, which run ORTRAC and FORWARD. These base systems interface with two further layers of systems:

1. LANs in the local offices, with PCs that also act as terminals for ORTRAC and the FORWARDING system; they, in turn, link to third-party carriers, hauliers and regulatory agencies;
2. Material Handling Systems, which use information technology extensively to automate the flow of goods between customers and PANALPINA.

Figure 8.8 below gives a conceptual view of PANALPINA's main information technology infrastructure.

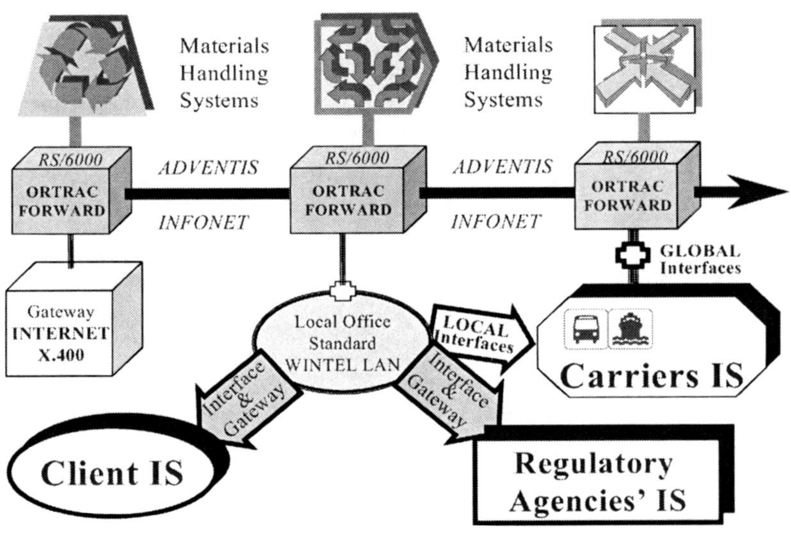

Figure 8.8. PANALPINA's international information technology and systems architecturei

8.1.5 Management of Information Systems

Two aspects of the management of information technology within PANALPINA may be regarded as key factors for the successful management and operation of the information technology portfolio:

- The philosophy, and its resulting strategy and policies, of what should be a common standard for all PANALPINA business units and what should be initiated, designed and managed locally
- The role of 'Panal-Centre' (i.e. the MIS head-office) in the development and implementation of international information technology projects.

8.1.6 The Global Versus Local Philosophy

PANALPINA firmly subscribes to the philosophy of 'Think global, act local'. This means that there is a balance between the autonomy of local operations and global management by 'fiat' from the centre: where business operations dictate a unitary process, the information system used will be a globally standardized one, maintained by Panal-Centre. Other than that, every local or regional office has full freedom to

> ...react to local or even regional needs within [their] sphere of influence...we're doing a lot of local country business and for that we need [that autonomy] .[2]

The approach is based on a deep-seated understanding that it would not be possible to create a system that reflects the totality of all user requirements world-wide:

> We don't want to cover all of PANALPINA world-wide to a 100%. That is just not possible, not even in an international team, which is spread all around the world. We're also forever extending the business into more and more new things, everywhere. It simply can't be done.

This declared absence of any intent to impose systems or business practices from the centre unless there is a rational benefit for the local office is important because it delimits clearly the extent and nature of the 'core' information systems applications. There is furthermore a clear management process to decide what should be a global standard functionality and what should be left to vary with individual, local business requirements.[3] The reaction of the users to the global systems, the way in which they interface with local systems and how they adapt to local requirements on the whole indicates that the approach works. The business people interviewed were very complimentary about the functionality of the information systems and their degree of fit with local requirements. A case in point are the Austrians, who, because of the significantly different nature of their

[2] Quoting PANALPINA's International Development Manager.

[3] As described further on in the following section on *The Management of Projects*.

business,[4] are only marginal users of the global systems – but have extensive and sophisticated local information systems and technology.

There are, however, requirements that are more than local but not – yet – global: not business processes compulsory for everyone, but where a number of local users might benefit. Examples are

- the UK suffers from not being able to customize client linkages (partly because there are very few MIS people supporting a major region), but Austria has an automated interface generator for this purpose ready and working; for similar reasons of resource shortage for developing system-to-system interfaces, Los Angeles limits client linkages and warehousing services to large, multinational accounts;
- The UK has a working EDI interface in place with key clients – at the same time as Panal-Centre[5] had written an add-on for ORTRAC with essentially the same functionality.

Panal-Centre approached the 'commonalization' of local solutions with the acquisition of software for requirements that are common for a number of offices, such as a third-party warehousing system. This was bought and used in Asia originally, and will be offered to any other office that wants to use it – once it can be shown that the operation warrants Panal-Centre support for the installation. This support philosophy underlines the importance of information technology for the business – and the self-image of MIS as an integral part of the Group's operations: nothing less than in-depth support is acceptable. However, like in any other area of PANALPINA, cost-effectiveness is a significant consideration.

8.1.7 The Management of Projects

PANALPINA's information systems development approach reflects the deep integration and strategic significance of information technology. It is characterized by

- continuous, stepwise improvement of information systems rather than big, wholesale replacement projects;
- careful piloting with experienced sections of the business;
- making adjustments and refinements at each phase of a project.

The definition of an information systems project and backing within the organization is the first concrete step towards its realization. Clarity of mandate

---

[4] That is predominantly overland, virtually no sea- and airfreight – a diametrically different business structure of the rest of PANALPINA.

[5] Headquarters of PANALPINA's global information technology support function.

and responsibility of the project sponsor are the main considerations at this stage of the project:

This is not something that someone just thought of along the way somehow, no, we will have spent perhaps two, three months just to clarify the problem in our minds and we would have been working with the Auftraggeber (sponsor) to come to a final job/problem definition.[6]

Once the project has found a sponsor, the other parts of the organizational structure are put into place:

There are two additional committees we have installed: One is the Project Committee, which is at the functional business level and which clarifies functional questions and sanctions functional solutions that is not always easy in an international environment, there always are conflicts. In addition to the functional committee we then have the Clearing Committee, which is essentially the executive level management affected by the project who have the ultimate supervision and who have to give the final blessing to whatever they decide.[6]

Assembling the project team for carrying out the work of defining and specifying the proposed information systems solution is the next step:

What we have done to cover the international character of the projects is to have a project team of about 15 people on average, user representatives from around the world which we have invited to us here in Basle. They then spend about 70% to 80% of their time on the project, although that changes from phase to phase. We also went out and traveled around the world, went to the local branches, presented our point-of-view and got information from them.

This process takes time:

[for the SAP project] we've spent more than two years at a conceptual level, so as to get the whole system absolutely clean from a conceptual perspective, before we even started the realization – and today, I think, we're cashing in on that.

This project organization structure model is depicted in Figure 8.9 below.

[6] The following quotes are from PANALPINA's MIS Director and International Development Manager.

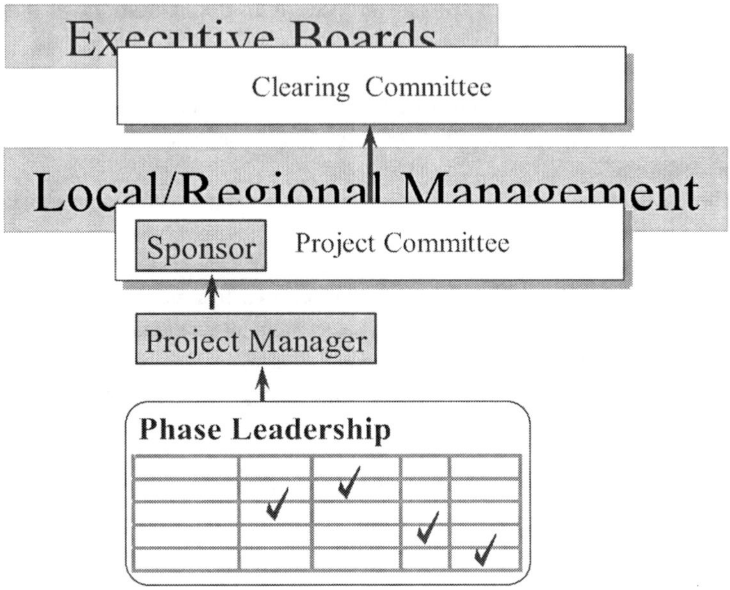

Figure 8.9. The four layers of the typical information systems project in PANALPINA

It is in this phase that conflicts and contradictions are resolved in the 'committee' process:

It was first of all a team forming process [which] the project team underwent themselves, until all the people... speak a common, uniform language and develop a common understanding for the [analysis and requirements specification] techniques we use. And, of course, there are discussions, and they stem from the work of the team itself – it's quite clear that the representative from New York has different needs from the representative in Frankfurt, and in parts their requirements will be contrary. So you try and find a solution acceptable to both sides. And sometimes we went a step further and asked for the heart of the problem: what are the business and operating policies underlying the problem? Does it have to be like that? Can it not be done in any other way? And you try and find an optimal solution. And where that was not possible, we just had to say: OK, we'll do it this way or that way in the core system, the rest is local enhancement, and can you please do that yourselves.

The careful approach to the specification of the business solution is then complemented by an equally participatory development process, lead by the best 'domain' experts at each stage. Any changes to business processes (e.g. to resolve conflicts), however, have to be ratified by the executive level steering committee. Similarly, any changes to the 'core' information system has to be sanctioned by the executive director MIS, to assure that their technical impact is analyzed, understood and accommodated.

Implementation of the new system goes through a series of pilot stages before it is 'rolled-out' to more locations simultaneously – in a series of 'cascades': Panal-Centre in Basle quite often leads the first pilot projects with key people from the regions as integral part of the team. These 'understudies', in turn, would then lead teams from the local offices, teaching local key staff how to provide front-line support for the new system.

Panal-Centre maintain that this proprietary way of project management is a key ingredient to their relative success with making large international information systems an integral part of PANALPINA's business core competence.

8.2 Analysis of the PANALPINA Case

Altogether 15 in-depth interviews with 11 participants were carried out for the PANALPINA case study. They amounted to 31.5 h, nearly evenly split between business and IT people (14.5 – 17 h, respectively). The data was gathered in Basle (Switzerland), the head-office of PANALPINA and in four regional offices around the world: Vienna (Austria), London, Los Angeles and Auckland (New Zealand).

The interviews were transferred[7] onto some 400 pages of transcripts. This interview data was supported by another 800 pages of documentation. The data gathering took place from March to June of 1996.

The analysis of the case begins with the coding of categories and the identification of new ones for the case. Their interactions are considered next. This is then compared with the two previous cases. Theoretical conclusions are then drawn and the 3rd Theoretical Framework is set out. The chapter is structured accordingly.

8.2.1 New Categories

Some 92 categories were coded during the open coding stage. Of these, 65 represented or related closely to categories already existing in the theoretical framework. The other 27 contained new 'discoveries', which were condensed into 8 'new' categories. However, only one of those is an entirely new category. The others are re-formations or significant enhancements of previous categories.

Table 8.1 below summarizes the new core categories.

---

[7] The interviews from Switzerland and Austria (some 13 h) were translated from German during the coding process.

Table 8.1. Core categories with significantly new characteristics in the PANALPINA case

Domain	Core and sub-categories	Status
Business	**Nature of the business** Common resource Economic restrictions **Information intensity of the business** **Strategic products & services**	Confirmed; **SIGNIFICANT** **NEW sub-categories**
Business & information technology interaction	*Management of IT Projects* **Consensus building** **BPR first** **Deep and Broad Project Structure** **Cascade Roll-out;**	*MAJOR NEW* core category; Extends **Global IS Creation**[8] with **systems implementation**, i.e. the IT aspects of cascade Roll-out
	IT/S Architecture Information technology Architecture Information Systems Architecture	**NEW** Core Categories: Split from the previous **IT management** category; **NEW**/extended **sub-category**
	IT/S Management Local IT management Central It management **IT strategy**	
	IS=Ops (IS mirrors business operations) **Strategic unity** **Profit driver** **Secondary information systems**	*Enhanced and re-defined*; **SIGNIFICANT** **NEW** **sub-categories**
Information technology	**Intellectual globalism** **Low: domestic mindset** Multi-domestic mindset **High: international mindset** Cultural differences	**New/extended** core category**,** Defines a continuum with **domestic** and **international mindset** as end-points; **NEW sub-category**
	IIS driving force **IS initiative** No economic justification **Business initiative**	**New/extended** core category**,** Defines a continuum with **IS initiative** and **(new) business Initiative** as end-points;

The main new category in the case is the *Management of IT Projects*,[9] which covers all aspects of developing and implementing information systems. *Consensus Building* is a main characteristic of this category, often achieved with

---

[8] Because the inclusion of *Implementation* now goes outside the 'Design' area, the category's name had been adjusted

[9] In this chapter *New Categories* and *New Sub-categories* are formatted thus.

Business Process Re-Engineering. Once the systems building phase is underway, a *Deep and Broad Project Structure* ensures involvement from all stakeholders at every level and at every major step. In the *Cascade Roll-Out,* key users are trained to take over the management of their own roll-out projects. An existing core category, *IT Management*, had previously contained both *Style* and *Architecture* sub-categories. In the PANALPINA case, however, it became prudent to define the latter into a 'new' *IT/S Architecture* category. In two instances, new categories turned out to be the inverse of existing ones. Subsequently, new categories were created to cover both ends of the respective continua. They are:

- *Intellectual Globalism*, which combines the Co-op's *Domestic Mindset* with its contrast, the *International Mindset* at display in the PANALPINA case;
- **IS Driving Force** combines the Co-op's *IS Initiative* with PANALPINA's ***Business Initiative*** as the driver for information systems projects.

The *IS Mirrors Business Operations (IS=Ops)* category, too, was significantly enhanced. In the PANALPINA case, the *Strategic Unity* of IT and business is often the very core of important global business strategies. *Secondary Systems* open strategic business opportunities using information technology that has primary systems for its input. For this reason, IT is the predominant *Profit Driver* for the firm.

The *Information Technology Intensity of the Business,*[10] a significant – new – aspect of the *Nature of* PANALPINA's *Business,* is the root cause for its strategic importance. It is also the reason why most new *Strategic Products & Services* rely entirely on information systems. Figure 8.10 below shows the information intensity assessment of the main products and services within PANALPINA

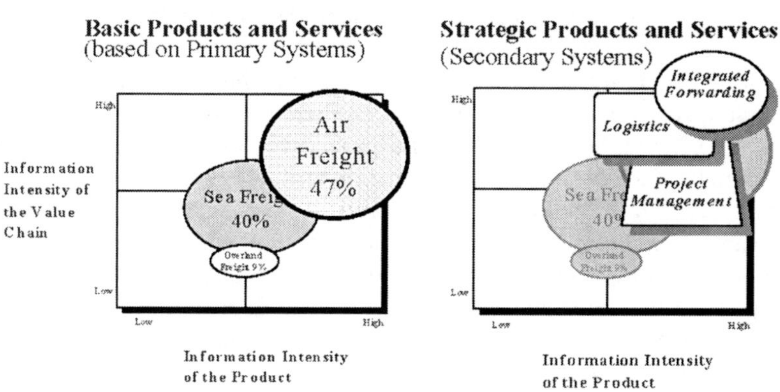

Figure 8.10. Information intensity of PANALPINA's products and services

[10] This follows the concept outlined by Porter & Millar (1985).

8.2.2 Main Interaction Between Categories

As in the J Lauritzen case, there was a reinforcing structure of influences at work. Figure 8.11 below shows this.

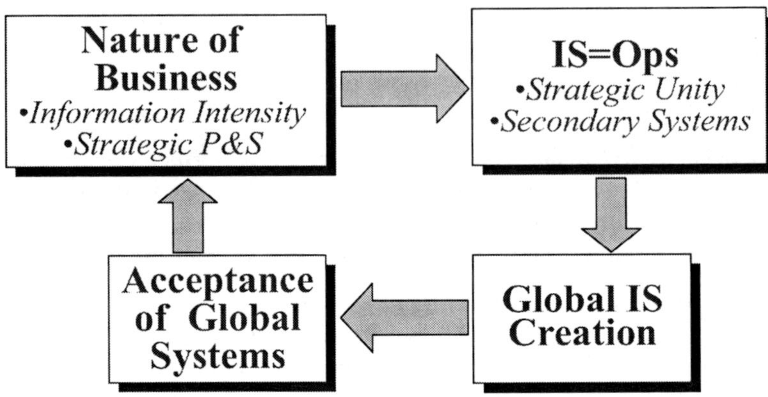

Figure 8.11. Cyclical influence of the 'effecter' categories in the PANALPINA case

The high profile of information technology in the *Nature of the Business* leads to an *IS=Ops* category characterized by a virtual unification of information systems and business which is manifest in products entirely based on information technology. This deep integration enhances the *Global IS Creation*[11] process, which is characterized by close co-operation between users and information technology people throughout all stages of systems building and implementation. As a result, *Acceptance of the Global Information Systems* is never in doubt and the users' positive attitude is a fertile ground for more – and more intense – interaction between business and information technology.

There are five 'conditioning' categories at work, shaping and defining the categories in the cycle. *IS=Ops* and *Strategic Weight of IS* have a mutual effect on each other: information technology is a key driver of PANALPINA's profitability whence it derives its strategic importance. This high Strategic Weight, on the other hand, ensures continued integration of information systems into strategic business initiatives, An equally powerful influence on *IS=Ops* is established by the *Business Initiative* sub-category of *IS Driving Force* . The business' need for maximum return from its IT investments deepens the *IS=Ops* integration. Figure 8.12 below shows the effect of the 'conditioners' and illustrates the interactions between all the main categories at work in the PANALPINA case.

[11] This new category is an extension of *Global IS Design* to include the implementation phase.

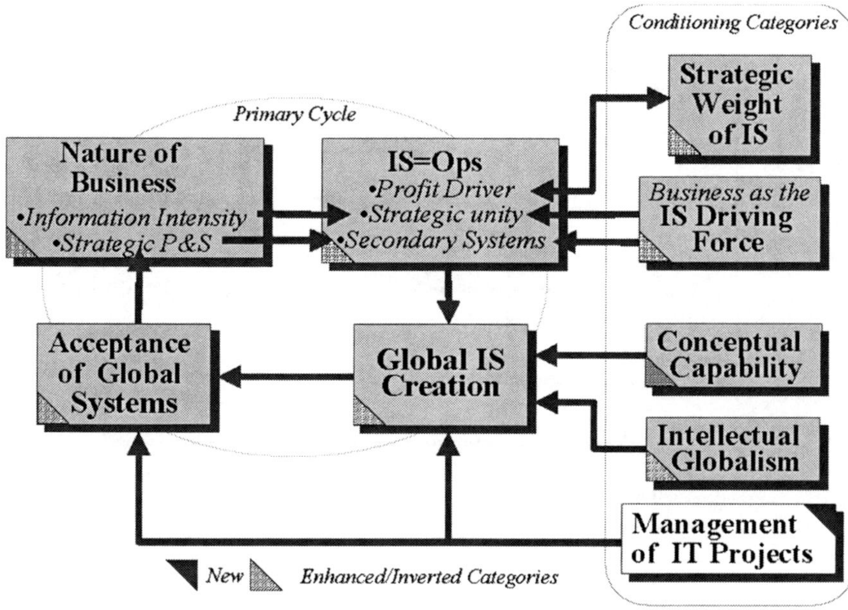

Figure 8.12. Interaction of the major core categories in the PANALPINA case

The strong direct and indirect business influences on the *Global IS Creation* process are further joined by high conceptual *Capability* and a mature *Intellectual Globalism*. The broad involvement of users and the consensus approach to process engineering in the *Management of IT Projects* improve the quality of the *Global IS Creation*. The principle of user implementation management ensures *Acceptance of the Global Information System*.

In J Lauritzen, the interaction between Nature of the Business and IS=Ops was linear, dictated by the needs to manage the *Common Resource*. In PANALPINA, however, this straightforward relationship is replaced by independent, iterative, interaction between the sub-categories of the *Nature of the Business* and *IS=Ops*.

Figure 8.13 below shows this cyclical reinforcement:

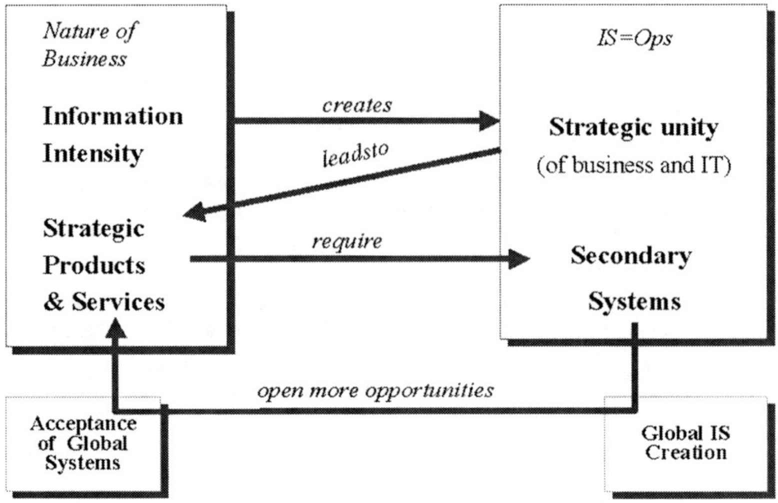

Figure 8.13. Interaction between nature of the business and IS=Ops within the 'role of IT' component of the acceptance cycle

The *Information Intensity* component of the *Nature of the Business* category intensifies the connection between information systems and business operations and created the *Strategic Unity* of both;

This leads to the creation of *Strategic Products & Services* ; their success then encouraged the business to demand even more from IT;

Their using *Secondary Systems* opened yet more opportunities for *Strategic Products* – using more *Secondary Systems,* and so forth.

In essence, thus, the *IS=Ops* category has transcended from where IT merely 'mirrored' operations (in the J Lauritzen case) into a new dialectic of mutually enhancing interchanges of *core competencies*[12] in PANALPINA. These are at the heart of the firm's business strategy and form the foundations for the products and services the firm offers. Figure 8.14 below shows that *Core Competence Interchange*[13] between the business and information technology domains.[14]

---

[12] ...in the sense of Prahalad et al. (1990).

[13] A new derivative category.

[14] This follows a notion first developed in Lehmann (1993, 1994a).

8.2.3 Comparison of the Co-op, J Lauritzen and PANALPINA Cases

The comparison follows the topic groups in the 2nd Theoretical Framework. Only the salient facts, with a relevant theoretical contribution, are discussed here. A detailed comparison is available from the author on demand. Finally, *Management of IT* and its *Projects*, the new topic group from the PANALPINA case, is put into the wider context.

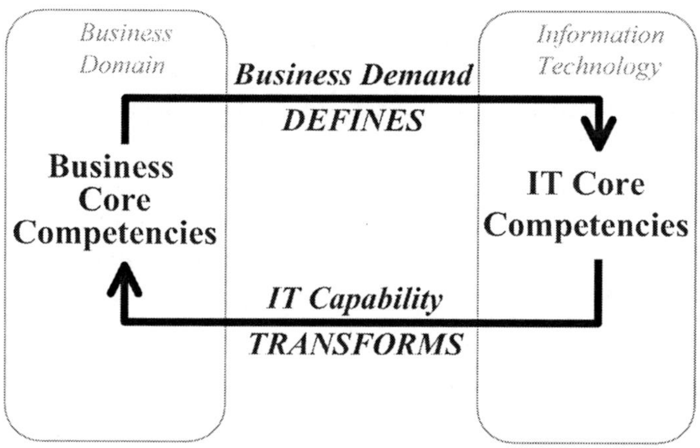

Figure 8.14. Dialectic interchange of business and information technology core competencies

8.2.3.1 Architecture of International Information Systems

The PANALPINA case added a new type of 'local' system to the architecture model. These are information systems used by some, but not all local users and their use is not compulsory for every local office – as the 'core' systems are. This adds a third dimension, of 'Common Local' systems, to the model. 'Core' is now specifically reserved for systems that are compulsory for *all* offices. Local systems not in the common pool are '*Unique* Local' information systems. Furthermore, the PANALPINA case has also shed some more light on the connection between *I=A=T*[15] and *Synchronicity* postulated in the J Lauritzen case, where it was proposed that *I=A=T* (and the information technology architecture it

[15] The paradigmatic assumption that obtaining *equal* *I*nformation content requires *identical* *A*pplication systems, running on the *same* *T*echnology Infrastructure.

typifies) depends on the degree of Synchronicity. PANALPINA has all three $I=A=T$ configurations in its multi-layered architecture:

- The *Common Core* requires $I=A=T$, i.e. full identity of data, systems and technology such as the ORTRAC/FORWARD dyad, which reaches into every office. Simultaneous updates to and access from numerous sites establish high Synchronicity;
- For the *Common Local* systems, however, the requirement is only for '$I=A\neq T$'. For example, the project management systems need a congruence of data/information. For ease of data interchange, they most likely require scalable identity of application systems but the technology platform can vary. Synchronicity exists, but only among some participants in the project management activity.

(W) *Unique Local* information systems (such as local client interfaces) are independent of most other systems. They require data/information likeness to ease interface problems, but otherwise '$I\neq A\neq T$' applies – as there is no Synchronicity requirement.

Overall, the best expression for PANALPINA would be $I{\sim}A{\sim}T$[16], meaning 'the same information *need not* require identical applications or identical technology'. What needs to be identical depends on the degree of Synchronicity inherent in the underlying business operation.

8.2.3.2 Response Cycle

The PANALPINA case confirmed the cyclical nature of *Response.* Specifically, it enhanced the previously established Response model by adding the close dialectic of its *Core Competence Interchange* to the Acceptance cycle. The enhanced *Response* cycle is shown in Figure 8.15 below.

If rejection occurs, the process is not left to uncontrolled political interaction, but is governed by the *Management of IT Projects.* Its broad based, consensus oriented structures and processes substitute 'Political Persuasion' for the antagonistic politics that characterized the Co-op case.

[16] The ~ operator, as in (~*p*) for 'the negation of *p*', was first used in 1910 by Alfred North Whitehead and Bertrand Russell in the first volume of *Principia Mathematica* (Cajori vol. 2, p. 307). However, current formal logic notation has widely replaced ~ with the ¬ symbol. The ~ operator is adopted here to symbolize '*need not* be equal/identical'.

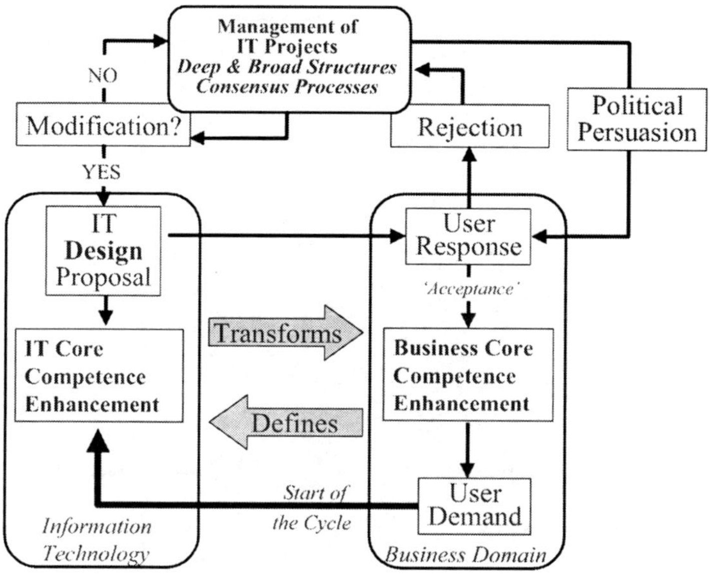

Figure 8.15. The PANALPINA response model incorporates the dialectic of their core competence interchange

Across all three cases, the interaction between the business and IT people is correlated with the depth of IT integration of the information technology function into the business processes of the firm: the deeper the integration, the closer the interaction. This relationship is a new derivative category, named *Closeness of the interaction between Business and IT*, shortened to *B→IT.* The *Management of IT Projects* and *B→IT* have 'methodized' the force field interchanges and systematized them firmly onto a rational level, minimizing antagonistic politics. They take the place of the 'Force Field' interchanges, as Figure 8.16 below demonstrates.

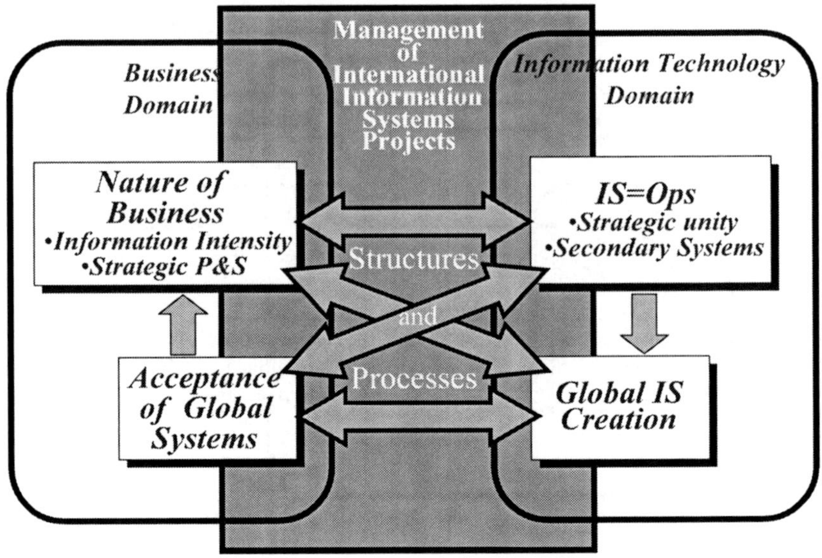

Figure 8.16. Methodization of the force FieldIT between business and information technology domains in the PANALPINA case

8.2.3.3 Utility and Control

PANALPINA, as a *transnational* firm, combines utility and control in the purpose of its information systems. *Strategic Unity,* however, means that the utility-type systems still prevail. Furthermore, the current installation of SAP was necessitated by multinational clients' needs for consolidated accounts for such *Strategic Products and Services* as Logistics and Project Management. Greater control over local management was 'negotiated' in exchange for the increased business introduced by the new products and services.

Adding to J Lauritzen's concept of *undue* control, this seems to indicate that such *undue* control can be tolerated if a utility/control trade-off is negotiated. Figure 8.17 proposes a model of such a relationship between response, utility and control.

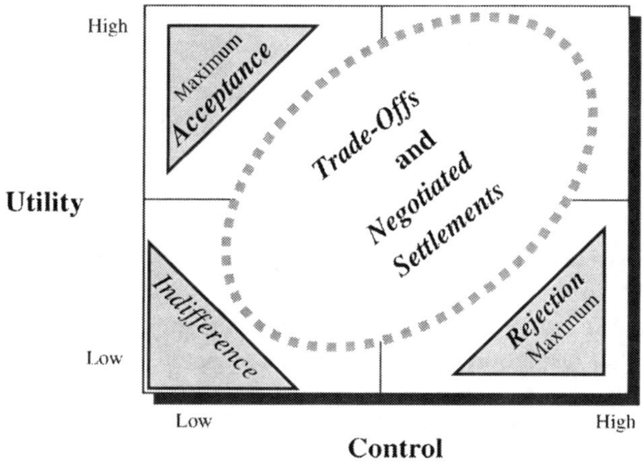

Figure 8.17. Response as a function of utility and control

8.2.3.4 The Role of Design

The *IIS Driving Force* category[17] is an important factor in the users' response to the systems. Comparing the three cases along business versus IT initiative and the resulting position in terms of Acceptance and Rejection elicits a clear picture (Figure 8.18 below):

Acceptable design is thus seen as a function of business users' input – the more the better – and the closeness of their involvement. PANALPINA's Core Competence Interchange works well for all systems, core or local, whereas J Lauritzen's systems are mainly central.

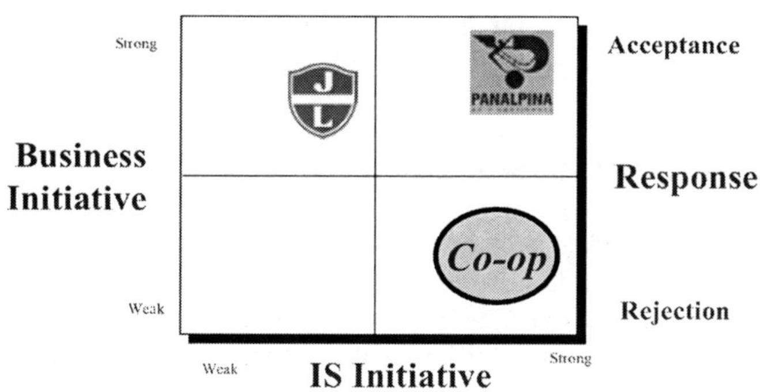

Figure 8.18. International IS drivers and response

17 A new/extended core category that defines a continuum between *IS Initiative* and *Business Initiative* as its end-points.

8.2.3.5 Skills for the Development of International Information Systems

1. Table 8.2 below compares PANALPINA with the Co-op case[18] along each of the 'IS Professional Skills' categories. The comparison yielded four dominant themes:
2. Right Analysis Paradigms such as I~A~T are important;
3. Conceptual Excellence is essential;
4. *Intellectual Globalism* (i.e. combining *International* and *Domestic Mindset*) is required;
5. *Avoidance of Political Conflict*; a new derivative category, this is the systematization of conflict resolution to avoid irrational antagonism.

Table 8.2. Comparing IS professional factors between Co-op and PANALPINA

Category	PANALPINA	Co-op
Analysis	Knowledge-based use of the right analysis tools for international IS	Assumptions were wrong and tools inappropriate
IS professional skills	Experienced alliances with first-tier technology firms	Mediocre professional practices; and outdated technology
Conceptual capability	'Best' domain specialists take 'months to get the conceptual basis right'	Central IT people create simplistic and unworkable solutions;
Intellectual globalism	High – respect, understanding and integration of international cultures	Low – premise that international and domestic environments are equal
International IS drivers	Business orientation and core competence interchange	IT initiated the IIS project to re-establish central HQ dominance
IS by force	Methodisation defuses antagonistic politics and conflicts	Antagonistic politics replace rational means to overcome IIS rejection

PANALPINA's good acceptance record points to a high degree of professionalism as an essential prerequisite for creating systems which users accept and work with.

8.2.3.6 New Topic Group: Information Intensity

There are fundamental differences in the Nature of the Business between the Co-op on the one hand, and J Lauritzen and PANALPINA on the other. Apart from the greater diversity of the Co-op's business over both J Lauritzen and PANALPINA, the three cases also differ in the Information Intensity of their business. Figure 8.19 below shows a comparison of the three cases.

[18] J Lauritzen did have no information systems projects under development.

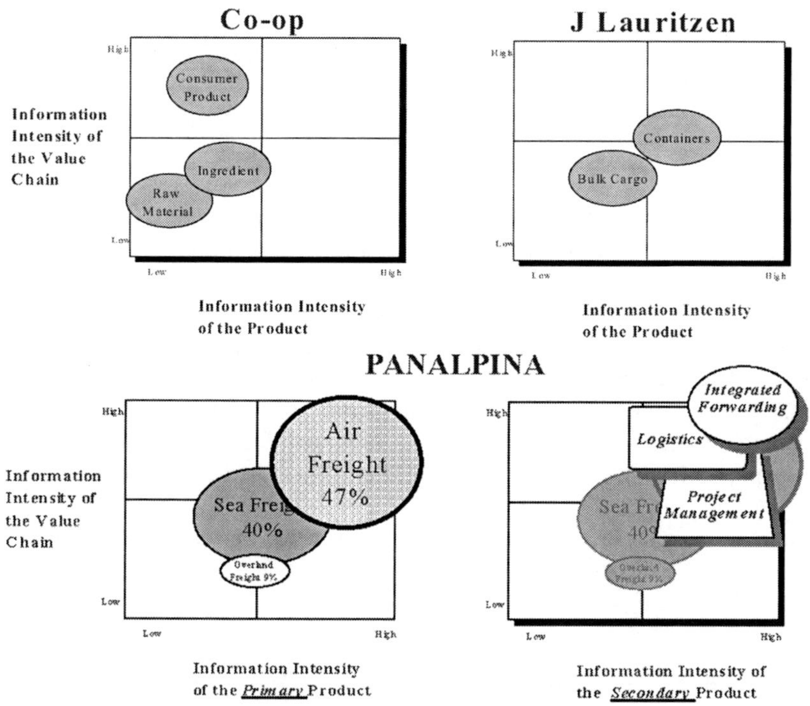

Figure 8.19. Comparative information intensity across all three cases

It seems to be the information intensity of the *product* directs information technology integration towards the IS=Ops category. The information intensity of the *value chain*, on the other hand, may well be linked to an emphasis on local, and perhaps unique information technology applications[19]. Where both combine, IS=Ops transforms into the closer Core Competence Interchange – and may be instrumental for creating PANALPINA's 'common local' systems.

8.2.3.7 New Topic: The Management of Information Technology Projects

Table 8.3 below compares the Management of IT Projects between the Co-op and PANALPINA cases – J Lauritzen did not have any developments ongoing during the case period.

[19] The supermarket interface in the Co-op's UK Consumer Products operation is an example of this.

Table 8.3. Comparison of the management of IT projects across the Co-op and PANALPINA cases

Management aspect	Co-op	PANALPINA
Team participants	Mostly IT	Users and IT
Conflict resolution	Confrontation	Consensus
Structure	IT leads all	Users lead, IT manages
Implementation	IT leads	Users lead

The characteristics of the Management of IT Projects employed by the Co-op follow closely their attitude of *IS Initiative*. The lack of influence granted or input allowed to the business people correlates with their judging the project as unworkable and unjustifiable and ultimately led to the limited success the IIS project enjoyed. User management and consensus, on the other hand, prevail at PANALPINA, where IT is strategic. It is fair to assume that PANALPINA has internal politics like any other large enterprise. Whilst the business objects of information systems may be subject to such politics, PANALPINA's project management, however, carefully excludes them once the systems building process begins.

The new insights in a number of theoretical areas provided a rich foundation for enhancing the theory.

8.3 Enhancing the Theory Further: The 3rd Theoretical Framework

The 2nd Theoretical Framework was evaluated in the light of the theoretical contributions from the PANALPINA case. New theorems were incorporated and the 3rd Theoretical Framework was established in 25 main theorems, supported by 102 theses and postulates. Focusing on the new theoretical insights from the PANALPINA case and from the comparison of all three cases a distinction is made between *primary* theorems, which reflect the discovery of new insights, and *secondary* ones, which confirm, re-formulate or enhance existing theory.

8.3.1 Primary Theoretical Contributions

There are 8 Primary Theorems from 6 topic groups, which were new to the theoretical framework so far. They are discussed in the paragraphs below.

In the area of *Architecture of International Information Systems*, a third element was discovered in the PANALPINA case to add to the architecture model. The updated theorem states that the *generic architecture for IIS has three basic components, namely* Common Core (*compulsory for all Local*), Common Local (*optional for Local*) *and* Unique Local (*specific to one Local*). Figure 8.20 below updates the graphic expression of this theorem and shows the influence of other factors and constructs on the definition of the architecture elements.

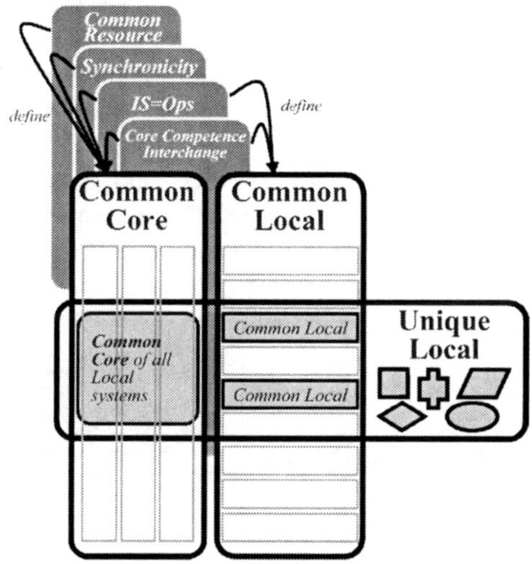

Figure 8.20. Generic structure of an international information system

Strategic Stability, derived from the comparative analysis is a new concept in the *Alignment and Response* group:

- The higher the Strategic Stability the higher the probability of positive (i.e. Acceptance) Response

In the *Response Cycle* area, the PANALPINA case introduces the *Core Competence Interchange,* a closer version of IS=Ops:

- Strategic Unity, which enables the creation of Strategic Products and Services, works through a mutual Core Competence Interchange, where business demands enhance the IT Core Competence, the application of which, in turn, enhances the business Core Competence

Information Intensity, a new sub-category of the *Nature of the Business*, is also derived from the comparison of the three cases; it influences the closeness of business and IT in general, has a link to *Core Competence Interchange* and correlates with the 'Common Local' architecture element. The following theorems set out these relationships:

- Information Intensity is a main contributor to Strategic Unity, which, in turn, is the basis for the development of Strategic Products and Services that require more information technology. These information technology applications themselves in time point out further development opportunities for more Strategic Products and Services.

The following link exists between Information Intensity and the closeness of business and IT:

- Low information intensity is related to weak connections between IS and Operations;
- High information intensity of the value chain leads to IS=Ops;
- High information intensity of both value chain and product is correlated with Core Competence Interchange;
- Increased Information Intensity of Products and Services also increases the occurrence of the 'Common Local' type information technology application in the IIS Architecture. Figure 8.21 below shows this linkage.

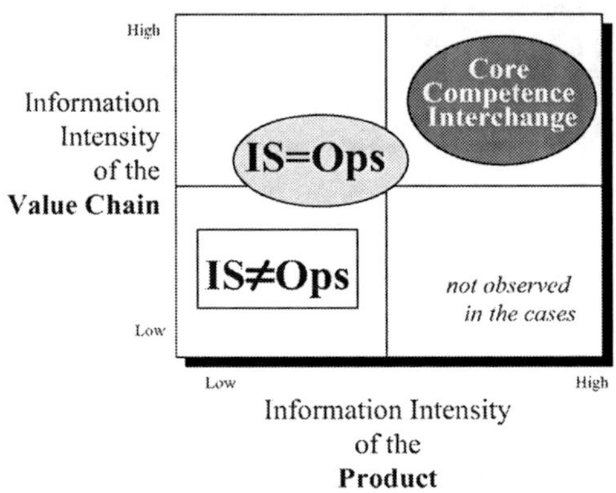

Figure 8.21. Information intensity determines the degree of the closeness of the interaction between business and information technology functions in the enterprise

Management of IT Projects is a new core category which fundamentally influences the nature of users and IT interactions:

- A procedural construct that methodizes Force Field interactions between business and IT in the Response cycle avoids antagonistic politics and fosters users' Acceptance of the Global Information Systems.

This concept of 'methodizing' the user-IT interaction, together with the concept of Core Competence Interchange made it necessary to update the 'Response Cycle' construct, as shown in Figure 8.22 below;

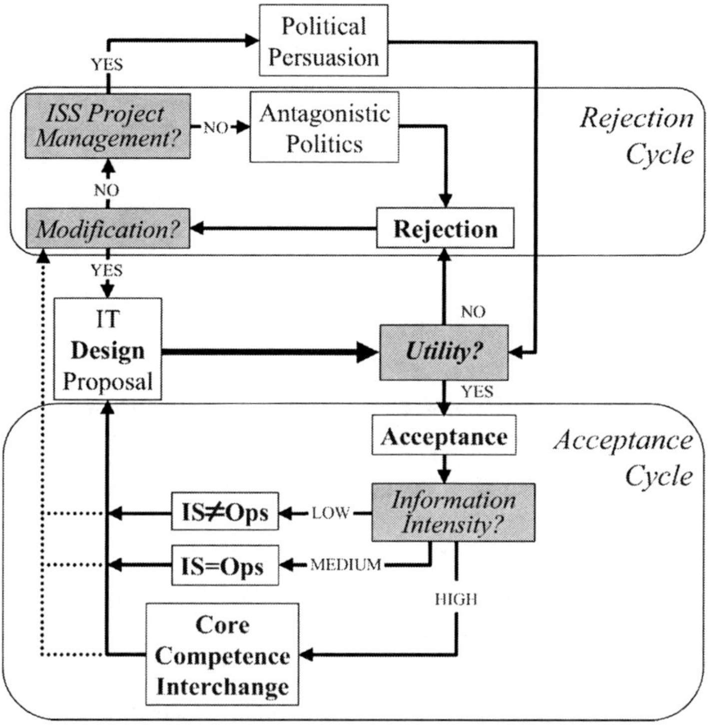

Figure 8.22. Rejection and acceptance cycles in the context of the full *Response* cycle

In the area of *Development Skills* the PANALPINA case brought out the importance of the 'IS Professional Skills' group of categories. The theorem states:

- Employing 'best practice' in information systems development methods is an essential prerequisite for international information systems. Issues of specific relevance for IIS are:
  - Assumptions that local businesses are the same in different locations are incorrect;
  - unity of information, application and technology (I=A=T) is usually not required for global systems;
  - IIS need more conceptual capability than domestic ones; Cosmopolitanism[20] is needed for systems design and user interaction;

[20] This is defined as the understanding, knowledge and respect of foreign cultures, environments and customs.

8.3.2 Secondary Theoretical Contributions

The theoretical input from the PANALPINA case and the ensuing three-way comparative analysis enhanced a number of already established theorems. Three topic groups were involved:

- The I=A=T aspect of the *Architecture of International Information Systems* group, where the inclusion of the PANALPINA findings allowed a more general formulation of the connection between Synchronicity and I=A=T; this now states:
- I~A~T moves from I≠A≠T to I=A=T when Synchronicity increases from low to high

Utility and Control; the 'trade-off' postulate for the link between *Utility*, *Control* and *Response* was firmed into a theorem (see Figure 8.17 above):

- Positive Response rises with the net Utility of an IIS and sinks with the net Control it imposes; wherein 'net' Utility means after any Control elements in a system have been taken into account;
- *IT/S Management*; adding evidence from the PANALPINA case this theorem confirms the 'Gravitation to a 'Central Core' stated in the 2nd Theoretical Framework;
- Where importance of IT for the business is high, direction of IT is placed close to the firm's international control centre.

In conclusion, the PANALPINA case added significant theorems in three areas: firstly it enlarged the architecture model for IIS. Secondly, it clarified and enriched the concepts surrounding the integration of an IIS in the operations of the multinational firm. Lastly, in the form of a project management structure and process it added a means of 'methodizing' the antagonistic politics that potentially surround an IIS. Together, these insights helped to reassess the nature of the *Response* dialectic and the role of *Utility* and *Control* in it.

As Table 8.4 below shows[21], the 3rd Theoretical Framework extended the 2nd one considerably Shaded areas and cells mark the new theoretical contributions after each case.

---

[21] This condensed version is presented instead of the fully detailed theoretical framework itself, which is, however, contained in the companion website – please email Hans.lehmann@vuw.ac.nz for access.

Table 8.4. Theoretical contributions from the three cases (shaded areas show the contribution s added by cases 2 and 3 respectively)

Theory area	1st TF – Co-op	2nd TF – J Lauritzen	3rd TF – PANALPINA
Architecture of an IIS	Theorem A. An IIS for a diverse international firm must have a Core/Local Split Theorem B. Nature of the business and its autonomy structure determine the contents of the IIS core Theorem C. The extent of the Local parts of the IIS is more determined by political factors than by rational/logical analysis.	Theorem A. An IIS for a diverse international firm must have a Core of common functionality for all users and Local parts with differing functionality for different users Theorem B. The Nature of the Business determines the Applications Architecture and functionality of the IIS core Theorem C. Functionality and Management of the IIS must be aligned to the Autonomy Structure inherent in the Global Business Strategy Theorem D. Synchronicity determines the nature of the Technology Architecture Theorem E. A Central Core has strong Gravitation	Theorem A. A generic architecture of International Information Systems for diverse international firms has three parts: Common Core functionality used by all users; Common Local applications, optional for local users; and Unique Local information systems with differing functionality for different users. Theorem B. The Nature of the Business determines the functionality of the Common Core and Common Local applications Theorem C. Synchronicity determines the nature of the Technology Architecture such that I~A~T moves from I≠A≠T towards I=A=T when Synchronicity increases from low to high Theorem D. Functionality of the IIS must be aligned with the Global Business Strategy Theorem E. A Central Core has strong Gravitation
Alignment and force fields	Theorem E. The implementation of an IIS that is perceived as an instrument of central control meets conflict from local management (Force	Theorem F. Alignment of global business strategy and IT strategy influences the design and implementation of international	Theorem F. Alignment of global business strategy and IT strategy influences the design and implementation of international

Theory area	1st TF – Co-op	2nd TF – J Lauritzen	3rd TF – PANALPINA
	Field) Theorem H. Backing by local business management (not just by central executive) is required for design and implementation of the IIS.	information systems. Theorem G. Alignment determines Acceptance or Rejection Theorem H. Alignment governs the business effectiveness of the IIS and the degree of organizational learning as a result of its implementation. Theorem I. Alignment determines the nature of the force field between IT and business/users; Theorem J. Alignment determines nature of the conflict resolution in the force field Theorem K. The Politics of the Response depend on Alignment	information systems. Theorem G. Alignment governs the business effectiveness of the IIS and the degree of contribution to the organization's core competencies. Theorem H. Alignment determines the strength of the conflict potential in the force field between IT and business/users; Theorem I. Alignment determines nature of the conflict resolution in the force field Theorem J. The Politics of the Response depend on Alignment
Response cycle	Theorem J. Response, i.e. Acceptance and Rejection are determined in Force Field interactions between Users and IT people	Theorem L. Response is the central element of a dialectic behavior cycle between business users and IT people	Theorem K. Response is the central element of a dialectic behavior cycle between business users and IT people
Utility & control *New in the 2nd TF*		Theorem M. IS=Ops and Control motivation determine the nature of the dialectic interchange within the response cycle Theorem N. The acceptability of the 'core' to the local sites depends on the utility of the systems functionality and the perceived degree of central control it will impose Theorem O. The implementation of an IIS that is perceived as an	Theorem L. Alignment determines the Response direction (Acceptance or Rejection) Theorem M. The higher the Strategic Stability the higher the probability of positive (i.e. Acceptance) Response Theorem N. Response depends on the utility of the systems functionality and the perceived degree of central control it will impose

Theory area	1st TF – Co-op	2nd TF – J Lauritzen	3rd TF – PANALPINA
		instrument of undue central control meets conflict from local management	Theorem O. Design utility is a prerequisite for the Acceptance of the IIS
Design *New in the 2nd TF*		Theorem P. 'Goodness of the Design' is a prerequisite for the Acceptance of the IIS Theorem Q. IS=Ops increases the probability for an IIS Design to be accepted by users Theorem R. IIS design without IS=Ops initiates and perpetuates a Rejection cycle	Theorem P. Design utility increases with the degree of *B*→*IT* and the level of Development Skills Theorem Q. Acceptance of the IIS design depends on design utility and *B*→*IT* Theorem R. Rejection depends on design utility, *B*→*IT* and the absence or presence of a Management of IIS Projects structure.
Management of IIS *New in the 3rd TF*	Theorem D. Decision making authority for the creation and implementation of the IIS must reflect the business authority structure.	Theorem S. State of the art professionalism is a pre-requisite for the design and implementation of an IIS Theorem T. Backing by local business management (not just by central executive) is required for design and implementation of the IIS.	Theorem S. Management of the IIS must be aligned to the Autonomy Structure inherent in the Global Business Strategy Theorem T. Alignment and Information Intensity determine the nature of the Interaction between the Business and Information Technology functions (*B*→*IT*) in the response cycle Theorem U. *B*→*IT* intensifies with the presence of a Management of IIS Projects structure and the propensity for user/IT consensus in its processes. Theorem V. A procedural construct that methodizes Force Field interactions between business and IT in the Response cycle avoids antagonistic

Theory area	1st TF – Co-op	2nd TF – J Lauritzen	3rd TF – PANALPINA
			politics and fosters users' Acceptance of the Global Information Systems
IIS development skills	Theorem F. Creating and implementing an IIS requires international knowledge Theorem G. The analysis preceding IIS design requires an extraordinary high level of conceptual capability Theorem I. State of the art professionalism is required for the design and implementation of an IIS	Theorem U. Creating and implementing an IIS requires international knowledge Theorem V. The analysis preceding IIS design requires an extraordinary high level of conceptual capability	Theorem W. Applying 'best practice' in information systems development is a pre-requisite for the design and implementation of an IIS Theorem X. Creating and implementing an IIS requires international knowledge Theorem Y. The analysis preceding IIS design requires an extraordinary high level of conceptual capability

Chapter 9
A Substantive Theory of International Information Systems

The system of theorems, propositions and postulates which make up the 3rd theoretical framework represents what Glaser & Strauss (1967) refer to as a 'first theoretical construct', which now needs to undergo a process of 'delimitation' (ibid., p. 109ff). Reducing the 'terminology' and 'densifying the text' in this process aim at increasing the theory's parsimony[1] while at the same time widening its scope.[1] The process is designed to expand a conceptual construct narrowly steeped in three cases into a more general 'substantive theory' with claims of validity for the subject area of international information systems.

The chapter briefly describes the salient reductions arrived at in the delimitation process and then introduces the resulting substantive theory.

9.1 Delimiting the 3rd Theoretical Framework

After the findings from the PANALPINA case had been taken into account, the 3rd theoretical framework consisted of 25 theorems, gathered in five theory areas (TAs), namely:

1. Architecture of an International Information System;
2. Alignment and Force Fields;
3. The Response Cycle;
4. Management of IT;
5. IIS Development Skills.

---

[1] Important 'canons for assessing [the quality of] a theory', as listed by Glaser & Strauss (1967, p. 4–5).

H. Lehmann, *The Dynamics of International Information Systems*,
Integrated Series in Information Systems 23, DOI 10.1007/978-1-4419-5750-4_9,

The 'Architecture' theorems in TA(1) could not be further reduced. On the other hand, the theorems of TA(2), dealing with the *Alignment* of business and information technology strategies, have been eliminated altogether. *Alignment*, itself a multi-dimensional category, is correlated to a number of univariate categories such as *Utility*, *Synchronicity*, *B→IT* and *Information Intensity of the Business*. These underlying, 'first-order' categories thus became direct determinants for such categories as *Response* and effectiveness of the *Global IS Creation*. The two *Alignment* theorems were therefore replaced[2] with these clearer and more explicit first-order relationships.

To enhance the theory's substantive focus on IIS, most of the theorems relating to TA (5) *IIS Development Skills* have been disregarded because they equally apply to any large-scale information system, whether domestic or international. Only two, namely *Conceptual Capability* and *International knowledge* have been included in the final theory. They form a separate topic area to do with the 'rightness' of the functionality of 'Core' and 'Common' systems.

The theorems concerning the users' Response (3), the Force Field in which it is played out (the non-*Alignment* part of 2) and the role of IT Management (4) have all been amalgamated into a 'Stakeholder-Dynamics' topic area. Some theorems related to the *Response* to an IIS and the *Management* of its creation and installation were disregarded as non-specific for IIS.

In this way, the delimitation process reduced the main theory areas from five to three. Two areas describe the 'content' aspects of an IIS and the third deals with the interplay of the actors involved in it:

Area I. *The Generic Architecture of an International Information System*;

Area II. *The Functional Quality of the IIS*;

Area III. *The Dynamics among the Stakeholders of the IIS*.

This 'densifying'[3] resulted in a minimum of redundant variables in these theory areas. The remaining categories are distinct and self-contained. Their relationships have been streamlined, simplified and are now of adequate parsimony.

This new, more focused and altogether much clearer understanding of the theoretical landscape required a certain re-ordering of the ideas and a new, and final, linking together of propositions and their interdependencies.

---

[2] This is termed 'definitional reduction' or 'axiomatisation' by Zetterberg (1965, p. 94ff) and is one method for reducing a set of propositions to their 'axiomatic' format.

[3] Glaser & Strauss (1967, p. 6) term for the delimitation process.

9.2 Shaping the Final Theory

In the following sections the building blocks of the final theory, i.e. the remaining categories and their relationships, are developed and described for each area in turn.

9.2.1 Area I – The Generic Architecture of an International Information System

The notion that any international information system has a generic structure consisting of a small number of distinct elements has been corroborated in all three cases. Both the Co-op and J Lauritzen cases suggested a two-part architecture consisting of a 'Core' of systems used by everybody and a collection of 'Local' systems, only used in certain local sites. The PANALPINA case specified a third type, the 'Common Local' system that is used by more than one local site, but not in use everywhere, as are the 'Core' systems. This distinguished them from the truly 'Local' systems, which were subsequently defined as being unique to just one Local site.

'Core' and 'Common Local' systems were in all three[4] cases created and administered centrally. For this reason, and because they are logically the same type – multi-user[5] applications – it seemed useful to combine them into one part of the information systems architecture, the 'CENTRAL' systems. The 'LOCAL' systems, as unique and substantively different single-user systems, constitute the second generic architecture element.

Figure 9.1 below shows this generic two-dimensional architecture model of an international information system. The individual system configuration (shaded grey) in each individual site within the enterprise comprises

- An implementation of the CENTRAL systems, i.e. globally standardized information systems, usually centrally maintained. These include the 'Core' systems (compulsory for all) and such of the 'Common Local' systems as are in use in the site in question; and
- 'LOCAL' information systems, not in use anywhere else.

[4] The Co-op's 'intent' to develop and administer such systems from HQ is included in the count.

[5] 'User' in this context means 'local user community' i.e. all users in one geographical/organisational business unit.

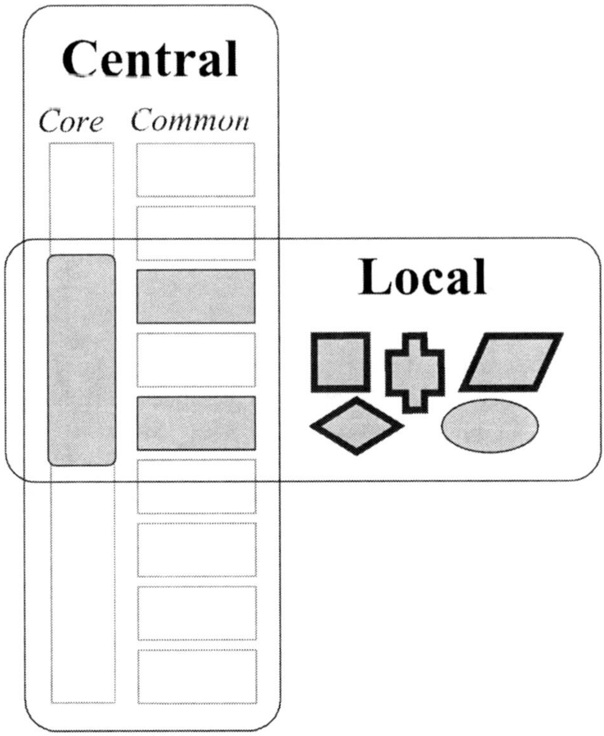

Figure 9.1. The generic architecture model of an international information system

The shape of the individual architecture, especially the weight given to CENTRAL and LOCAL dimensions, is determined by the business' *Synchronicity*, i.e. its need to execute multiple interactions by several participants across geographical boundaries at the same time. This governs the extent to which each of the three systems types are present in each local site.

Synchronicity also governs the *Technology Homogeneity* of the architecture elements i.e. information, application systems and the technical platform[6] (i.e. the degree of *I~A~T*). The higher the need for Synchronicity, the larger the CENTRAL element of the IIS architecture will be and the more homogenous the technology will have to be. On the other hand, international firms with low Synchronicity in their operations can accommodate LOCAL systems with different technology as long as they adhere to sufficient information standards. Table 9.1 below illustrates this relationship in more detail.

[6] This includes computers, communications technology, their operating software and middle-ware.

Table 9.1. The influence of varying degrees of *Synchronicity* on the dominant architecture elements and the resulting homogeneity of the technology structure of an IIS

Degree of synchronicity in business operations	Dominant architecture element	Technology homogeneity (in terms of I~A~T)
High: most major business processes are requiring synchronous interaction between participants in all sites all of the time	CENTRAL: mostly *Core* systems; few, insignificant Local Applications	*I=A=T*; *same* **Application** need to run on *identical* Technology configuration to produce *only one* set of shared Information
Selective: some business processes require synchronous interaction between participants but not in all sites and only some of the time	CENTRAL: *Common Local* systems are as important as *Core* systems; some Local Applications may be strategic;	*I=A≠T*; *same* Application producing *identical* Information in support of identical/similar business operations; can run on *different* Technologies
Low/None: business operations run independent of each other, information exchange is asynchronous, infrequent and often ad-hoc	LOCAL *Applications* are of key importance; compulsory global *Technology Interfaces*;	*I≠A≠T*; *common* global Information standards, adhered to by *different* Applications, running on *different* Technology.

High Synchronicity and the ensuing centrist architectures[7] seem to create a tendency for further increasing the number and scope of CENTRAL information systems. The motives for this are certainly territorial (to extend the influence of the central IT management group) but economical reasons are also present – central systems were often considered cheaper to build and maintain.

9.2.2 Area II – The Functional Quality of the IIS

Of the two types of information systems in this architecture, only the CENTRAL (i.e. 'Core' and 'Common Local') systems are international or global in their distribution. The LOCAL systems, unique by definition, are domestic information systems. However, they will have restrictions imposed on them in the form of data/information standards and/or in the form of technology specifications that stipulate the interfaces with any CENTRAL systems.

The need for CENTRAL systems to support a variety of divergent and perpetually changing business units introduces a degree of complexity in their analysis and design which is often by orders-of-magnitude higher than in domestic systems. To cope with that, the (central) IT people need firstly a higher level of *conceptual* and intellectual *capability*. To be effective, however, further requires this to be grounded in a thorough *knowledge and understanding* of the workings of the firm in its multiple *international settings*. These, however, change

[7] That is architectures with a prevalence of CENTRAL systems: in the J Lauritzen case this is a significant pre-dominance of the 'Core' systems; in the PANALPINA case the – very – dominant 'Core' systems were complemented by a strategy to increase the number of 'Common Local' systems.

continuously, synchronously and in all locations. Maintaining knowledge of this type, too, is orders-of-magnitude more complex than in a domestic context.

9.2.3 Area III – The Dynamics Among the Stakeholders of the IIS

The interactions involved in the creation and implementation of an IIS are iterative and dialectic social processes. They are centered on the users' Acceptance or Rejection of the system. Each response option then leads to further processes with implications on the future attitudes and actions of both users and IT people.

A suitable model for the interactions between the various stakeholders in an international information system is the notion of a *Force Field*[8] that exists between the stakeholders in two distinct groupings:

1. *Users* and *Creators/Implementers* (i.e. the IT people in an enterprise) of the international information systems; because their most likely point of conflict is over what business processes the IIS will support, and how well it will do it, this is termed the *Functional Force Field;*
2. *Central* and *Local* business management and staff; because between them the extent of local autonomy is the most common issue, this was termed the *Territorial Force Field;*

However, *Users* and *Central* and *Local* management and staff are often the same people. For this reason, the two individual Force Fields are defined as sub-regions of an overarching field, named the Global Business and Technology Force Field. Figure 9.2 below illustrates its topology.

---

[8] In terms of Lewin (1938, 1952).

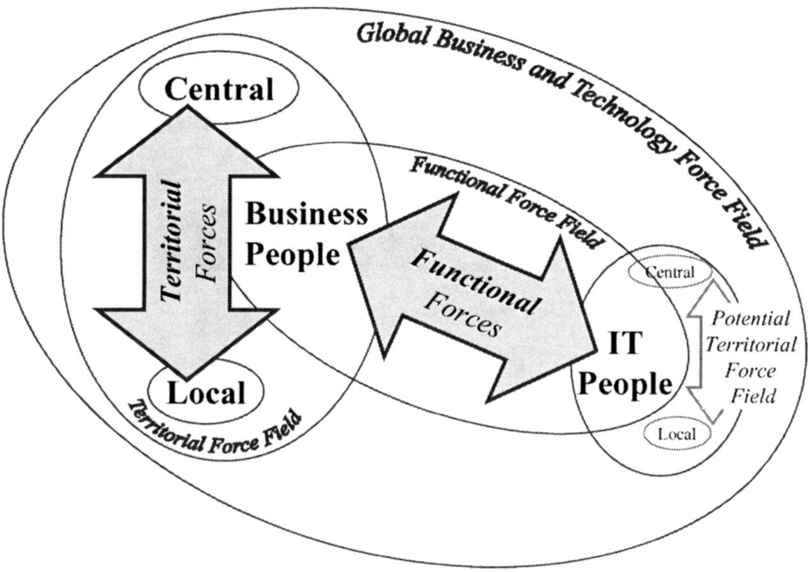

Figure 9.2. The force fields within and between business and information technology people as stakeholders in an international information system

The strength and nature[9] of the force field dynamics are governed by two factors:

1. The degree of *Utility*[10] of the IIS determines whether the interaction between business and IT people will be antagonistic to neutral (low utility) or constructively synergetic (high utility). It influences the strength and nature of the *Functional Force Field*;
2. The degree of *Undue*[11] *Control* (further on referred to simply as *Control*) imposed by the Centre determines the strength of the politics of resistance by Local management, i.e. influences the nature and 'charge' of the *Territorial*

[9] In Lewin's (1938) terms, strength is a combination of the *'Potency'* (ibid., pp. 34, 203ff) of the path the force takes and the positive or negative 'Valence' (ibid., pp. 84ff) of the participants' attitudes. The nature of the force (positive or negative, constructive or destructive, synergetic or diminishing) is further conditioned by the 'Distance' (ibid., pp. 164ff) of their goals and expectations.

[10] That is the extent to which the operational/transactional business processes are supported; as opposed to *Control*, which encompasses all performance assessment management processes supported by the IIS.

[11] That is not in line with the degree of central control/local autonomy inherent in the – accepted – global business strategy.

Force Field. If the IIS is suspected to be an agent of either centre or local management, then the antagonistic politics extend to the IT people, too.

The resultant of the forces at work in these multiple Force Fields forms the *Response* to the IIS, at the centre of the overall dynamics relationships. Response has two main states, positive *Acceptance* or *Rejection*, its negative opposite.

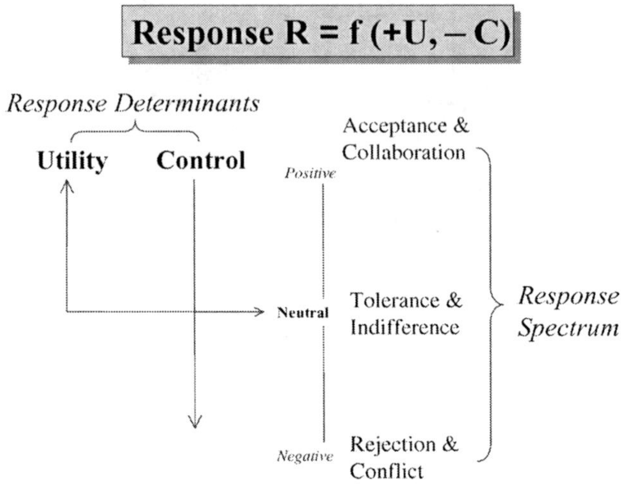

Figure 9.3. Response as a function of utility and undue control

Response can thus be seen as the dependent outcome variable in a model that has *Utility* and *Control* as its independent inputs. Assuming neutrality as the initial state of the user's Response, Utility has an additive effect, i.e. increases positive Acceptance. Control, on the other hand, subtracts from that, decreasing Acceptance and furthering (negative) Rejection. If their combined effects result in net Utility, then the outcome is Acceptance. Otherwise, i.e. when Control outweighs Utility, Rejection results. In both cases, the strength of Acceptance or Rejection seems to reflect by how much Utility outweighs Control or vice versa. Figure 9.3 visualizes this model of Response as a function of Utility and Control.

Glaser & Strauss (1967) suggest, as a first test if the theory 'works', to retell the 'story' using it's terminology and logic. In this sense, the Response model is illustrated on each of the three cases in turn.

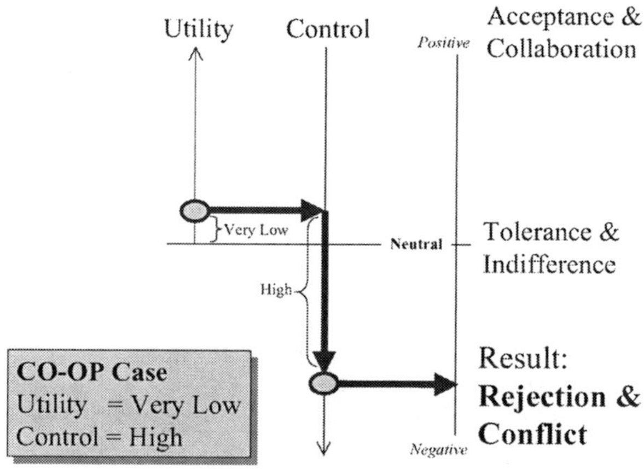

Figure 9.4. The response function in the Co-op's case

In the Co-op's case (Figure 9.4 above), the intended global standard information system was not perceived as having high utility for the local and regional business people. This reflects the IT people's inability to agree on user's requirements and to identify what should be 'Central' and what 'Local' applications. The users suspected that the IIS was a sly attempt to reaffirm strong central control, which was counter to their understanding of the Co-op's global business strategy. Subtracting this high level of 'Undue Control' from the very small amount of perceived Utility resulted overall in negative 'Net Utility'. This caused them to reject the IIS altogether: after a prolonged and bitter political battle the IIS project was terminated.

J Lauritzen have a business with high Synchronicity and this is reflected in an IIS that users perceive as having high Utility (Figure 9.5 below). Head office, not least for economic reasons, also pursues a strong global control strategy. This is not entirely accepted by some local offices – hence the notion of some 'Undue Control' being exerted. The resulting positive 'Net Utility', however, lead to good acceptance of the IIS, which is valued an important business tool for all of J Lauritzen's offices.

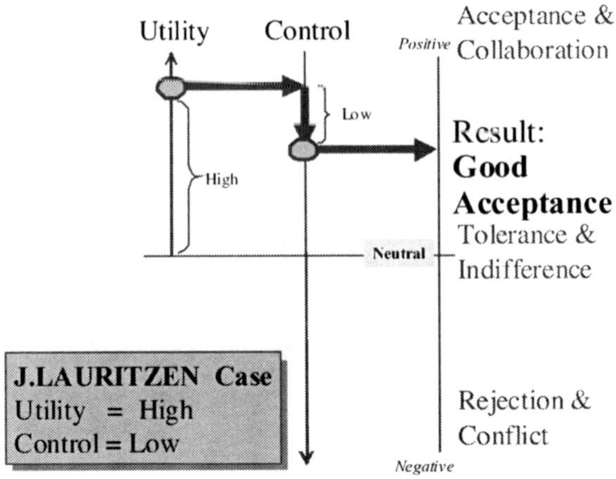

Figure 9.5. The response function in the J Lauritzen case

As Figure 9.6 shows, PANALPINA had integrated their IIS the furthest. In their business, information technology is a strategic part of the business and the perceived Utility of systems is high. Most of their IIS are operational and their creation and implementation follow extensively participatory management processes – often specifically designed to defuse territorial or functional conflict.

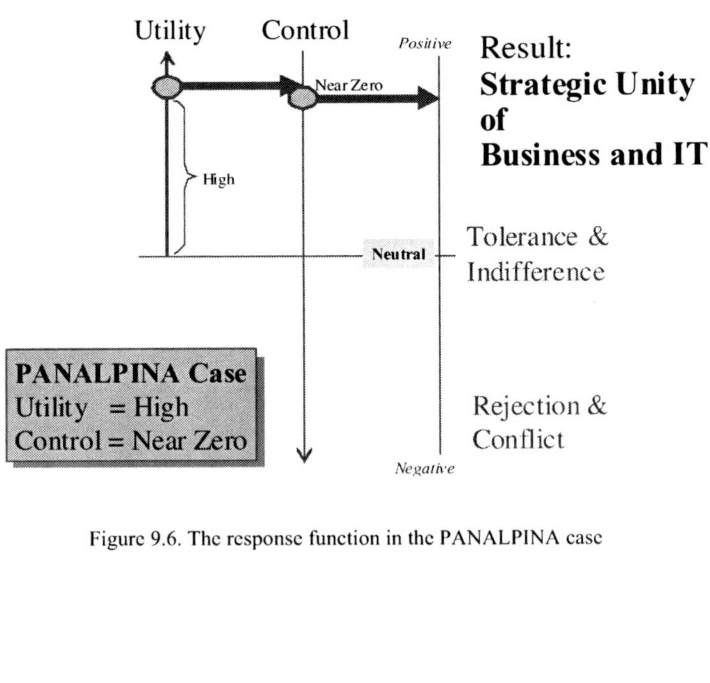

Figure 9.6. The response function in the PANALPINA case

Some of the local and regional offices would like different degrees of autonomy with regard to IIS, but overall there is hardly any discernible perception of 'Undue Control'. Because of the resulting high 'Net Utility', Acceptance of IIS is elevated to the level of strategic unity between business processes and information technology.

A second, significant influence on Response is the *Integration of Business & IT*: The more IT is an integral part of the business, the more likely it is that *IIS Design* with high degrees of *Utility* will be generated.

Integration of Business & IT itself, however, is a correlate of two other categories, namely business/IT affinity, B➔IT, and the Information Intensity of the business.

The axiomatization process focused and sharpened the definition of these categories. Where they were all amalgamated into B➔IT , there is now a distinction between three factors:

- how well this is reflected in the co-operation of the respective business and IT people; this defines B➔IT narrowly as Affinity between the business functions;
- the underlying conceptual closeness of business and information technology: this is its Information Intensity; and
- the actual extent to which IIS are embedded in the firm's strategy and operations, i.e. the Business & IT Integration.

Three levels of *Integration of Business & IT* were observed in the cases. Very little integration, *IS≠Ops*, in the Co-op's case, is accompanied by their business' low Information Intensity. The significant degree to which J Lauritzen's business is driven by information exchange is reflected in their *IS=Ops* category, where information systems are an integral part of global operations. A large part of PANALPINA's business is pure information, creating a **Strategic Unity** between business and information technology. Figure 9.7 below shows the correlative relationship between the three categories.

There is correlation between *B➔IT* and the *Information Intensity* category: *when* information technology is a logical part of the business then closeness of IT and business people will happen more predictably. For similar reasons, *B➔IT* is also correlated to the *International Knowledge* category: affinity with the firm's international (regional and local) business people is conducive to developing knowledge and understanding.

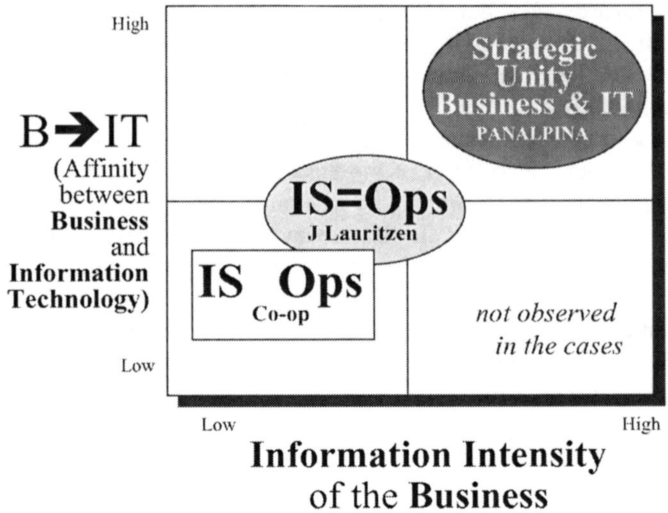

Figure 9.7. Integration of business & IT as a correlate of B→IT and information intensity

Both *Integration of Business & IT* and the *Response* function contribute to a more elaborate theoretical model of the overall dynamics involved in the life cycle of an IIS. The interactions around either Acceptance or Rejection form a cyclical, dialectic interchange between the stakeholders, i.e. business and IT people. A diagrammatic representation of this dynamic interplay of factors in the form of a network of cause-and-effect loops[12] is shown in Figure 9.8. below.

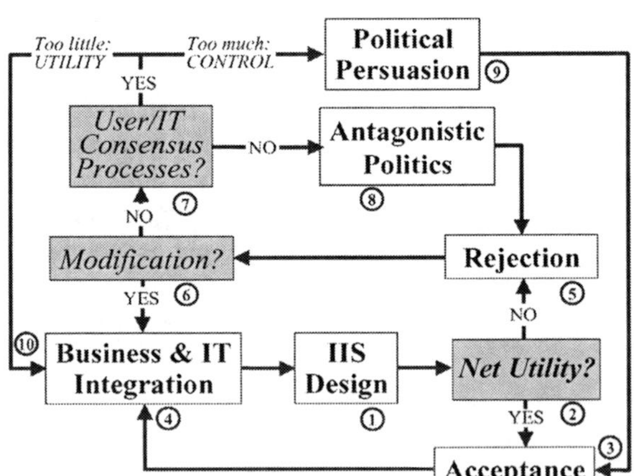

Figure 9.8. The model of stakeholder dynamics surrounding the response to an international information system. (Component numbers correspond to their position in the list below)

[12] After Weick (1979).

The components of the model are described below:

1. The *IIS Design*, i.e. the functionality, structure and architecture of the global information system is at the centre of the model;
2. *Utility* is at the heart of the international system's Functionality: users tend to agree to implement the system where its operational usefulness out-weighs any inherent *Control* elements – otherwise they are reluctant to do so, or refuse the IIS altogether;
3. *Acceptance* of the system and the ensuing user/IT co-operation to install the system increases
4. *Business & IT Integration*, as it embeds the IIS deeper and further into the firms operations and processes; the close working relations and higher IIS integration, in turn, improve the *IIS Design* in terms of the *Utility* of further systems or enhancements, thus increasing the probability of their Acceptance – a virtuous circle of positive reinforcement, the *Acceptance Cycle* on the path around *2*, *3*, *4*, *1*;
5. on the other hand, *Rejection* of the IIS by the users would sometimes lead to
6. *Modifications* by the IT people in an attempt to increase *Utility*; where modifications are not undertaken, the impasse between user rejection and IT's refusal to modify the IIS design must be resolved in a different way;
7. a formal *User/IT consensus Process*, capable of building seems best suited for this;
8. if none exists, however, then an exchange of *Antagonistic Politics* and in-fighting between business and IT results. In the absence of such a mediating facility, users and IT carry on their adversarial political exchange until either one side prevails or an ad-hoc conciliation is carried out. This is the negative dialectic of the *Rejection Cycle* on the path around *1*, *2*, *5*, *6*. A formal *User/IT Consensus Processes*, however, resolves impasses and sets up a forum to facilitate negotiated solutions. Depending on the reason for Rejection, the processes follows one of two pathways:
9. *Political persuasion* (as opposed to 'antagonistic politics') is applied where a perception of too much Control obstructs users' Acceptance;
10. Lack of Utility is tackled by directing users and IT people towards a *co-operative re-specification* of the system (enhancements). The resulting closeness of business and IT is conducive to increasing the *Integration of Business and IT*, increasing the potential for higher **Utility** and with it the probability of *Acceptance*. Channeling efforts towards constructive dialogue in this way establishes a *Conflict By-Pass Cycle*– following the path around *6*, *7* and then either *7*, *9* or *7*, *10*.

The working of the overall model of stakeholder dynamics can be demonstrated on the specific paths through the model that the three cases took.

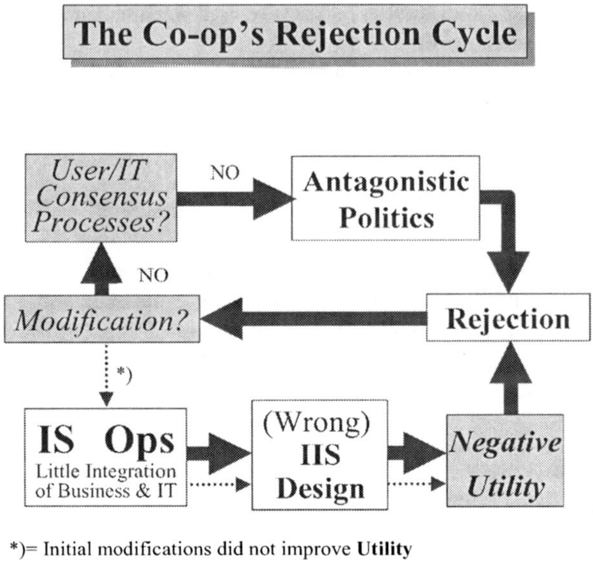

Figure 9.9. Stakeholder dynamics in the Co-op

Although there were differing degrees of IT integration into the various regional and local businesses, the Co-op started out their IIS project with minimal integration between business and the central IS department (Figure 9.9). The low Information Intensity inherent in most of the Co-op's business, in addition to the lack of user input resulted in the design of a rigid, globally standard system. The IIS was rejected by business as firstly dysfunctional and, secondly, because it was perceived as a disguised effort to re-impose central control over a business with a strong tradition of local autonomy. Further modification efforts were also rejected because they, too, failed to close the gap between regional/local management and the IT people.

Following that, the IT people embarked on a series of political campaigns, to which the business people answered in kind. Because there was no means of enforcing a co-operative solution, the antagonistic politics from both sides soon established a cycle of rejection, political reaction, renewed rejection and so on. The creation of the system was severely handicapped by this and implementation was made impossible in all but one, insignificant pilot site. Eventually the business side's rejection prevailed and the IIS project was abandoned altogether.

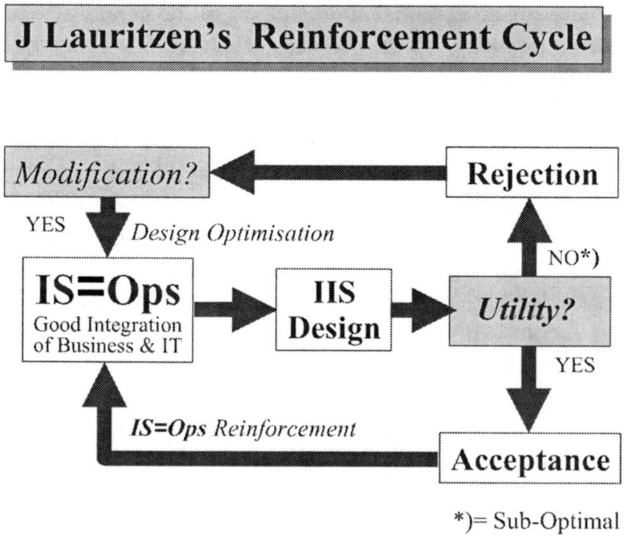

Figure 9.10. The cycle of acceptance and design optimization in the J Lauritzen case

J Lauritzen's way of addressing international information system issues is significantly different (Figure 9.10). In part, this is because the role of information technology in their business is different: although the overall business's Information Intensity is only in the medium range, information systems are an essential part of the firm's operations. Because the centrist nature of the business is accepted by all, information systems are not seen as means of exerting control. Furthermore, the operational focus meant that ever from the first information system built, users and IT people had worked in unison and created systems of the 'right' functionality for the business. The affinity with the users also meant that sub-optimal system parts (i.e. not enough Utility) were corrected or modified as a matter of course in dialogue with the business people involved. The Utility resulting from this co-operative building process ensured ready Acceptance of the systems from the business. This in itself increased further the integration of international information systems into J Lauritzen's global business. Higher integration meant design closer to the 'right' functionality to optimize Utility in supporting the business operations – establishing a self-fulfilling cycle Acceptance and in-built design optimization.

PANALPINA takes the degree of integration of systems one step further still. Their business consists of two distinct parts: the physical movement of consignments and the management of these physical activities. Having outsourced most of the physical side to alliance partners, PANALPINA concentrates mainly on the management aspects of the business – nearly all management of data, information and knowledge. Information technology and systems are therefore an essential strategic part of the business. Further increasing the Information Intensity of its business, PANALPINA moved into a second generation of information use with products and services derived directly from their first generation IIS.[13] These 'primary' technologies are large CENTRAL systems and networks of the 'Core' type, which every local office has to have as part of its basic operational environment. Most of the secondary products are implemented on 'Common' systems, used wherever the product or service in question is offered. A number of LOCAL systems complement these global systems. These are, furthermore, an integral part of PANALPINA's business strategy of establishing, at the local level, close electronic links with all their customers to secure a pivotal position within their customers' efforts at supply chain management (Figure 9.11).

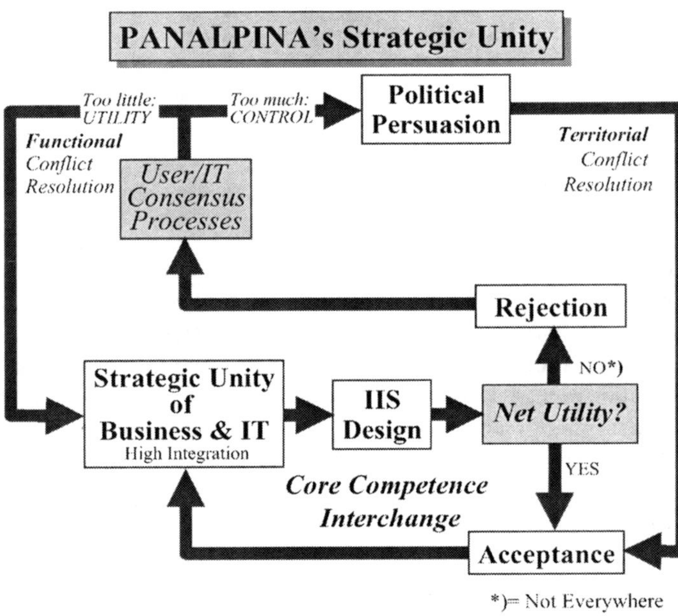

Figure 9.11. The core competence interchange cycle and the conflict avoidance cycle employed by PANALPINA

Balancing the global control over CENTRAL systems with controlling the optimal freedom needed for adapting LOCAL systems to the exact needs of individual customers has required sophisticated methods of managing IIS projects. The strategic unity of IT and business has elevated the Acceptance cycle

[13] *Logistics Management, Contract Warehousing, Project Management* and the 'Integrated Forwarding' concept are examples of such 'secondary' products.

experienced in the J Lauritzen case to a continuous improvement process at the strategic level. This exchanges core competence between business and IT: business guides IT to new technology areas and IT points business to new opportunities arisen from the mastery of such new information technology.

Compared to the other cases the use of information technology is more intense in PANALPINA. Subsequently, IT interaction with the business, particularly as regions and local offices enjoy a large degree of operational autonomy, is also more complex and convoluted. For this reason, Utility, especially for the 'Core' systems is a multi-facetted category and one that is often at dispute between individual local offices and/or the central IT team. The strategic position of IT, however, means that such conflicts could not be allowed to hold up IIS development or endanger the essential co-operation between local offices if systems and technology are to be rolled out to the business timetable. For this reason, PANALPINA developed a system of project management structures and processes that are expressly designed to achieve consensus among all stakeholders by avoiding, defusing or deflecting destructive conflict. Special teams resolve functional problems by delving deeper into the users' disputes and the power structure designed into each IIS project's organizational hierarchy is used to solve political discord by persuasion.

9.3 Formulating the Substantive Theory of International Information Systems

The following sections firstly set out the scope of the theory and give an overview of how its different parts fit together. In the main part, the theory is set out in propositional format, i.e. as an ordered set of theorems, theses and postulates.

9.3.1 Scope and Overview of the Theory

The nature of the theory as a 'substantive' theory requires the definition of the scope and substantive limits of the theory. The *Substantive Theory of International Information Systems* is defined as applying to:

The information systems supporting the operations of enterprises which carry out similar business activities or business functions in highly diverse environments commonly found across country boundaries.

This follows the original[14] definition of international information systems as systems supporting the business of the 'International Operator', i.e. a firm with high Business Focus and whose operations span territories with high

[14] see Chapter 1 – Introduction.

Environmental Diversity. The three cases fit this definition, as Figure 9.12 below shows.

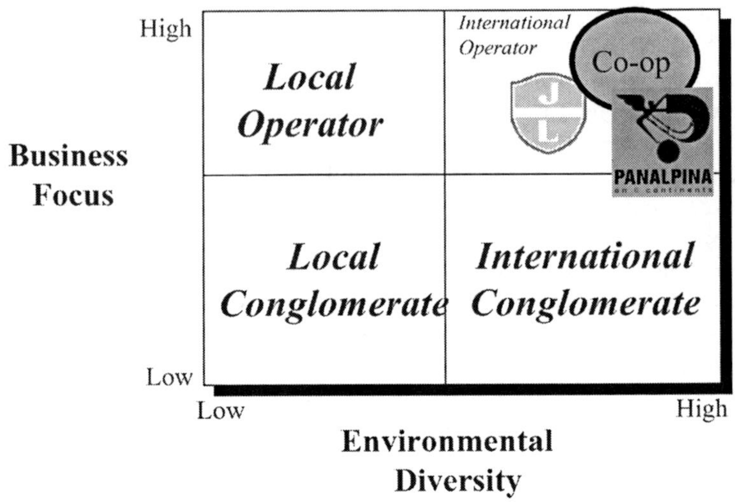

Figure 9.12. Classification of the three cases according to business focus and environmental diversity

The overall theory derived from the grounded study of the three cases shows the factors influencing the Acceptance or Rejection of an International Information System by its stakeholders. Two prerequisite theory elements determine the content of the IIS. They are contained in the theorems of

- Area I, which explains what governs the structure and architecture of an IIS; and
- Area II, which sets out what influences the quality of its functional content.

In Area III, the stakeholder dynamics part of the theory is supported by three groups of theorems which

1. Define the environment in which the dynamics of the stakeholder interactions take place.
2. Set out the variable-relationship that determine users' response to the IIS; and
3. Describe the two main correlates influencing the degree of Integration between business and IT;

The structure components and their relationships within the theory are illustrated in Figure 9.13 below.

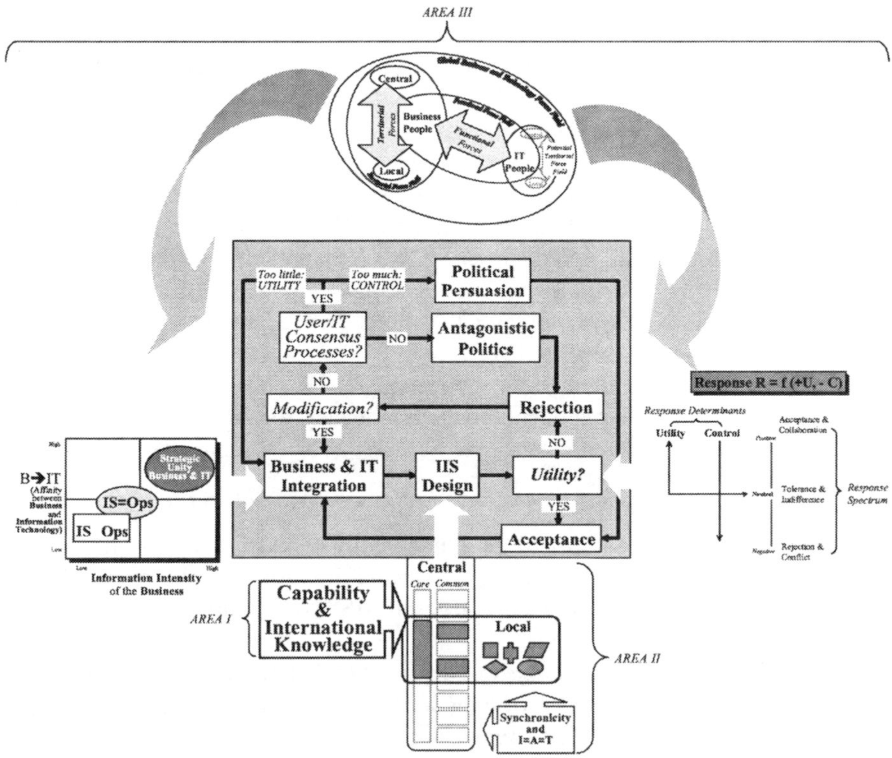

Figure 9.13. The substantive theory of international information system – overview of the interaction between Areas I, II and III, including subsidiary theories in Area III

9.3.2 Propositional Notation of the Substantive Theory

The substantive theory can be formulated in proposition format[15] as follows:

AREA I.	*Structure (Architecture) of an International Information System*
Theorem A.	An International Information System has two principal parts, namely *CENTRAL* and *LOCAL* information systems and technology.
Thesis A.1.	*CENTRAL* systems are either '*Core*' systems (compulsory for all users) or '*Common*' systems, which a number of users can share. They are built, implemented and maintained through a centralized IT function.

[15] This means in terms of theorems, theses and postulates; for their definition see the last paragraphs on p. 197

Thesis A.2. *LOCAL* systems are unique for each individual location and are managed locally.

Theorem B. The degree of *Synchronicity* inherent in the business operations influences the shape of the IIS's architecture in the following way:

Thesis B.1. It determines which systems are '*Core*' and/or can be '*Common*' or '*Local*'; the higher the Synchronicity the more weight is given to the CENTRAL architecture elements.

Thesis B.2. It predisposes the *Homogeneity of the Technology Architecture* (in terms of I~A~T); the higher the Synchronicity the more the Technology Architecture tends towards *I=A=T*.

Thesis B.3. 'Centrist Architectures', i.e. with a large CENTRAL component, create a tendency for increasing this CENTRAL component ever further.

AREA II. *Functional Quality of an International Information System*

Theorem C. *Quality* of the functionality of an IIS depends on two factors:

Thesis C.1. Extraordinary *Conceptual Capability* is required for the analysis and design; IIS pose more and more complex problems.

Thesis C.2. *Knowledge and Understanding* of the workings of the firm in its *International settings*; determines the quality of the IIS's detailed operational functionality.

AREA III. *The Dynamics of the Response Processes among the Stakeholders of an International Information System*

Theorem D. Business and IT people act as antagonists in dialectical interaction within a Force Field. The following theorems describe the relationships between the factors that influence the strength[16] (neutral/indifferent to forceful) and nature[16] (positive or negative) of these interactions.

Theorem E. *Response* depends on *Utility* and the level of *Undue Control*:

Thesis E.1. Design *with (Net) Utility* leads to *Acceptance*;

Thesis E.2. Design *without (Net) Utility* leads to *Rejection*;

Thesis E.3. *Utility* and *Undue Control* interact upon *Response* in the following way:

Postulate E.3.(a). *Utility adds* to *positive Response*, i.e. *Acceptance*.

Postulate E.3.(b). *Undue Control subtracts* from the *Utility* toward *negative Response*, i.e. *Rejection*.

Postulate E.3.(c). *Net Utility* is the *sum* of *Utility* minus *Control*.

---

[16] The equivalent terms in Lewin's field theory terminology are set out in footnote 10 on p. 177

Theorem F. *Acceptance* increases the propensity for *Business & IT Integration*.

Theorem G. *Business & IT Integration* depends on the *Affinity* between Business and IT (B➔IT) and the *Information Intensity* of the business.

Theorem H. The *higher B➔IT* the *higher* the *Business & IT Integration*.

Theorem I. The *higher Information Intensity* the *higher Business & IT Integration.*

Theorem J. The relationships set out in Thesis E.1 and 0 define the self-reinforcing *Acceptance Cycle.*

Theorem K. The reaction of IT to *Rejection* can take two forms:

Thesis K.1. A rejected IIS can be modified in co-operation with the business people: the higher the *Business & IT Integration* achieved during the modification process, the higher the *Utility* of the resulting, modified design.

Thesis K.2. IT refuses to modify and seeks Acceptance of the IIS through *Antagonistic Politics*; this, in turn, may lead to renewed *Rejection.*

Theorem L. The relationships set out in Thesis E.2 and Thesis K.2 define the self-reinforcing *Rejection Cycle*.

Theorem M. If there is a process that facilitates *Business/IT Consensus*, then antagonistic politics can be avoided; this can be effected in one of two ways:

Thesis M.1. Too much *Control* can be dealt with by *Political Persuasion* in negotiations with the right intermediary. This would lower the level of (perceived) Undue Control, would thus increase the net Utility of the IIS proposal and thus increase the likelihood of its Acceptance;

Thesis M.2. Too little *Utility* can be remedied by establishing business/IT co-operation to (re)define the IIS' functionality.; Thesis K.1 applies: the higher the business integration of the modification process, the higher the Utility of the resulting IIS (modification) design.

Theorem N. The relationships set out in Thesis M.1 and Thesis M.2 define the *Conflict By-Pass Cycle.*

Chapter 10
Discussion of the Theory and its Implications for Research and Practice

In the following sections, the substantive theory introduced in the previous chapter will be discussed in the context of other information systems research. Next, its strength and weaknesses will be set out. Finally, implications of the proposed theory for practitioners are set out.

10.1 Salient Themes of the Theory: Previous and Future Research

The substantive theory rests on a number of fundamental themes to do with the nature, structure and quality of international information systems and how they are accepted – or not – by the user community. The salient themes are discussed below.

An IIS has a generic architecture consisting of a Central and Local elements (Theorem A)

The conjecture that there are some structure and/or architecture principles that hold true for most or all global applications of information technology have been discussed in the literature for some time.

The need for variation in international systems to accommodate differing local circumstances has been established early on by Buss (1982), when he found that using 'common' systems across different countries can be fraught with difficulty. In the same year Keen et al. (1982) first articulated a paradigm of a 'common core' of information systems applications with 'local' alterations. There has been little further development of this over the next decade and Ives et al. (1991) concluded that 'the literature offers little guidance for...local versus common applications'. However, the idea that a common structure should link together the

H. Lehmann, *The Dynamics of International Information Systems*,
Integrated Series in Information Systems 23, DOI 10.1007/978-1-4419-5750-4_10,

divergent local elements of a global system had been taken up by Keen's (1991) requirement for a 'transnational platform' to carry the 'transnational information technology capability' required for a firms global operations.

A number of researchers have found that the architecture of international systems seems directly influenced by the strategy and structure of the international firms which use them (King et al., 1993, 1999; Sankar et al., 1993; Kosynski et al., 1993; Butler Cox, 1991; Jarvenpaa et al., 1994). In this way, 'Global',[1] firms would have centralized IIS architectures,[2] 'Inter/Multinationals' might have various forms of distributed information technology structures, whereas 'Transnational' firms would have a 'networked' or 'integrated' architecture. The generic architectures for central systems and distributed computing are well understood. However, definitions of what constitutes the 'networked/integrated' architecture suitable for the 'Transnational' firm, are diffuse and vague.

Both Kosynski et al. (1993) and Sankar et al. (1993) include only hardware and 'middleware' elements in their interpretation of information technology architecture. However, Butler Cox (1991) also include application systems in their definition of systems architecture. This is in line with Earl (1989) who argues that if the architecture in question should have relevance to the development of business systems, then *all* the elements which make up such business systems need to be included in it. Also, information technology infrastructure, in the sense that Weill (1992, 1993) and Weill et al. (1994, 1995, 1998) and Broadbent et al. (1997, 1999) have over the years refined it, does include – at least the common parts of – application systems.

Roche (1992a) added an explicit element of process support to his model of 'pairing' information technology with the business processes they support. He also touched on the notion of common versus local systems by introducing 'Global Core Systems' which are then supplemented in local sites with 'Regional Co-ordinated' systems and 'Local Option Systems'. The proposed classification defines both Global and Regional systems into one class of CENTRAL systems, which can be either compulsory for all or optional for anyone, anywhere. LOCAL systems are unique for each site.

The proposed Central/Local architecture model furthermore extends its scope to include the different discrete architecture models for IIS, i.e. central, replicated[3] decentralized or distributed, networked or integrated, etc. It can accommodate them all:

- *Centralized* and *Replicated* architectures have a 'Local' content of (near) zero;
- *Decentralized* architectures have a 'Central' content of (near) zero;

---

[1] In the Bartlett & Ghoshal (1982) definition of Global Business Strategy.

[2] Butler Cox (1991) and Laudon & Laudon (1997) add a 'replicated' version to the centralized architectures, to which Laudon & Laudon allocate a 'Franchiser' Global Business Strategy.

[3] That is a number of identical *central* information systems in local sites for, e.g. a *Franchiser* global strategy, as defined by Laudon et al. (1997).

- *Networked/Integrated* architectures balance a varying ratio of 'Central' (including 'Core' and 'Common' systems) to 'Local' systems for each location.

An important implication for the practitioner of this architecture model is that IIS can be designed and implemented in parallel. This ameliorates one of the cardinal problems in IIS implementation, the fact that technology cycles are increasingly becoming shorter than implementation cycles.

Synchronicity determines the composition and homogeneity of an IIS (Theorem B)

Butler Cox (1991) found that for 90% of IIS developers agreement on common user requirements was the major hurdle for IIS development. The – new – notion of *Synchronicity* provides an objective yardstick for those business processes in need of 'Common' systems, or, where they are needed for all users, 'Core' system for all global sites.

The application areas defined by Synchronicity, in turn, define the nature of the technology infrastructure, specifically the degree of its *Homogeneity*. That this subject is of importance for IIS design decisions was shown by Tractinsky et al. (1995) where a technical considerations factor contributed about four times as high as other factors in global systems design considerations.

A new discovery in this research is the fact that global information systems do not always need a globally standard technology configuration – this was termed the I=A=T fallacy. Instead, empirical evidence points to a linear dependency between the level of Synchronicity and the required degree of Homogeneity of local technology configurations (expressed as *I~A~T*, where '~' is a symbol for 'need not be equal/identical').

These concepts provide a useful aid to practitioners in delimiting the – often impossible – task of specifying all user requirements across an international firm in order to find the lowest common denominator as the 'core' for the required technology infrastructure.

Future research is, however, needed to solidify the theses contained in Theorem B. As a consequence of the theoretical sampling process, which deliberately introduced juxtaposition, the three cases are somewhat polarized with respect to the Synchronicity of their business processes. The Co-op's operations were found to be mostly asynchronous. Thereafter, in order to sharpen the emerging concept of 'Synchronicity', the next two cases were chosen to contrast sharply with the Co-op's case. A relatively high degree of Synchronicity was found in both. This stems from the fact that the nature of their businesses is similar: they both provide a physical service, which forms the backbone of their international operations. The usefulness of the *Synchronicity* and *I~A~T* categories in assisting architecture and design decision should be further investigated with cases of international firms of a different business nature. As IIS designers take advantage of the Internet and systems and technology architectures become more web-centric, there will be more and more complex options for technology configurations. The importance of a simplified decision framework based on the nature of the participating businesses therefore increases commensurately.

The Response Processes take place in a Force Field
(Theorem D)

Lewin (1938, 1952) models social interactions as the interplay of 'forces' in a 'field', using physical science notations of vectors and topology. Whereas his original vision of a 'general field theory' of human behavior has, in the main, not been followed by social science, the basic model has been used extensively to describe and analyze social change. Business research areas include strategic management (Thomas, 1985; Strebel et al., 1994; Ajimal, 1985), marketing (e.g. Hurt, 1998), human resources management (Elsass et al., 1994), organizational development (Brager et al., 1992) and management accounting (Grundy, 1997). In the information systems field 'Force Field Analysis' is used in the main as a project management technique in systems engineering (see e.g., Nicholas, 1989, 1990, pp. 417–420). Within the context of building information systems, Couger et al. (1989) suggested it as a catalyst to foster design creativity. This is, however, the first time that the concept has been used for theory building in the field of International Information Systems.

The Stakeholder Dynamics around Acceptance and Rejection are circular processes
(Subsuming Theorems I to L)

The chain of events where Acceptance increases Business & IT Integration, which then increases the Utility of the IIS Design, which, in turn, increases Acceptance – and so on[4] – is a causal loop with special qualities. Change in one variable triggers change – in the same direction – throughout the chain, starting a self-reinforcing circle. Weick (1979, p. 72)[5] terms this a deviation-amplifying loop. Rejection,[6] in reciprocal causation with Antagonistic Politics, follows the same pattern: Less politics diminish rejection and vice versa. In such a system, there is no controlling variable: once a circular movement starts, it continues until either the system ceases to exist or until some fundamental change occurs. The Co-op's termination of the IIS project after a series of iterations through the 'vicious circle' is proof of this.

The Conflict By-Pass Cycle[7] is the third major loop in the chain of stakeholder dynamics processes. In contrast to the Acceptance and Rejection cycle, however,

[4] Thesis E.1 and Theorem F form the self-reinforcing *Acceptance Cycle*.

[5] He follows previous psychological research (e.g. Maruyama's 'morphogenesis', 1968, or Bateson's 'regenerative loops', 1972).

[6] Thesis E.2 and Thesis I.2 form the *Rejection Cycle*.

[7] Thesis K.1 and Thesis K.2 form the *Conflict By-Pass Cycle*.

this is a deviation-counteracting loop (after Weick, 1979, pp. 74ff). The interjection of a Business/IT Consensus mechanism between reverses the original reciprocal causation between Antagonistic Politics and Rejection: The more Consensus, the less Antagonistic Politics, the less Rejection, the more Consensus. The existence of such a Consensus mechanism therefore controls and balances the Rejection cycle. In Force Field terms the Consensus variable is an equilibrium inducing force (Lewin, 1952, p. 202).

The concept of organizational and behavioral variables engaging in self-reinforcing, spiral movements has been used in a variety of diverse business research fields. Examples are from

- the strategic management field (Lindsley et al., 1995) to investigate the relationship between efficacy and performance;
- its use in economics (Herrscher et al., 1990) as a possible contributor to hyperinflation; and as
- a factor in the predictive quality of expert systems (Montazemi et al., 1990).

Causal path models are also applied in information systems research (e.g. Byrd et al., 1997; Gregory, 1993; Joshi, 1992; Lederer et al., 1992) where they are frequently quantified with structural equation modeling techniques (such as by, e.g. Sabherwal, 1999; Lederer et al., 1999; Karahanna et al., 1999; Chin et al., 1995; Anderson, 1989).

IIS Design with high Utility requires superior Knowledge of the relevant international environments and high Conceptual Capability
(Theorem C)

The theory of 'bounded rationality' (after Simon, 1961) is a useful framework to interpret this theorem in the particular context of IIS design. The essence of Simon's proposition is that the ability of individuals is usually limited to coping with their 'close' environment (Simon, 1956). This is borne out by the limitations imposed by the 'domestic mindset' in the Co-op's case and to some extent reflected in the 'multi-domestic mindset' in the J Lauritzen case. The role of a 'domestic mindset' as a major 'bounding' factor is also confirmed in Tractinsky et al.'s (1995) study of factors at work in the design decisions for international information systems. Designers devoid of international experience tend to restrict themselves to the technical dimension of IIS and disregard the cultural and political issues[8] instrumental in the local acceptance of global systems.

Conceptual ability, as the substrate of technical skills for building IIS, was also markedly different in the three cases. In terms of Carnegie Mellon's 'Capability Maturity Model' (Paulk et al., 1994), for example, the Co-op would rate at the 'Initial' Level and J Lauritzen one level up, at the 'Repeatable' Level. PANALPINA operate at yet a higher level. With discrete processes in place, they

[8] For example attempting to determine the I~A~T configuration without resorting to Synchronicity issues, as the Co-op did.

certainly fall into the 'Defined' level (3). However, their not – yet –clear enough emphasis on quality assessment processes precludes them from fitting fully into the 'Managed' level (4).

There is a link between the concepts of *Utility*, the *Business/It Consensus* processes and the *Synchronicity* requirements of the business operations, which should be the focus of future research. Further clarification of the relationships between those three concepts would be important. For example, in the current model *Utility* is the single most important determinant of user acceptance. If it could be derived from the degree of *Synchronicity* and/or from the nature of the *Business/IT Consensus* process, then the rationality of the process for choosing common or local application systems should increase significantly. The related lowering of the political energy going into this question would make IIS design more predictable – and much less risky.

The triangular relationship between Information Intensity, B➔IT and Business & IT Integration
(Theorem G)

If the *Affinity between Users and IT (B➔IT)* is accepted as similar to the concept of User-Participation (which includes also User Involvement and User Attitude, in the sense of Barke et al. (1994) below); and if *Business & IT Integration* were accepted as one manifestation of User Satisfaction, then there is a large body of literature confirming that – in general – increased engagement of users in the information systems generating process is often positively correlated with higher 'system success'.

Whilst earlier studies, such as Hirschheim's in 1985, look at user participation as a univariate concept, later studies have found that it is a multi-facetted phenomenon (Barke et al., 1994, confirmed by Hunton et al., 1997; Hwang et al., 1999). McKeen et al. (1994) furthermore discovered complex interactions between determining and conditioning variables: The configuration of 'participation' variables[9] and their effect on 'user satisfaction' was found to be influenced by the complexity of the (business) task and/or the complexity of the system itself.

The finding that Business & IT Integration also depends on Information Intensity[10] seems to align with McKeen's findings. The assumption that increased Information Intensity would have an augmenting effect on task and system's complexity seems certainly a plausible one – in which case Information Intensity may be regarded as a substitute for the 'complexity' variables in McKeen's model.

---

[9] These are: User Influence, User-Developer Communication and User Participation.

[10] Porter et al. (1985) introduced the concept of Information Intensity.

Information Intensity could thus be viewed as an indicator of the firm's Business & IT Integration *potential*, requiring *B*➔*IT* as a catalyst to achieve it. On the other hand, it could well be a fair conjecture that *B*➔*IT* (however close) without sufficient Information Intensity would not lead to any higher degree of Business & IT Integration – nor would it need to. Both those assumptions should be followed up in future research to firm our understanding of the relationship between these three variables.

There could also be a possible connection between *Synchronicity*, *B*➔*IT* and *Information Intensity* of the business: higher *Synchronicity* could well increase *B*➔*IT*, with the strength of the correlation being modulated by the degree of *Information Intensity* in the underlying business.

The Role of the Business/IT Consensus Process
(Theorem K)

The process by which business and IT consensus is achieved and maintained is firstly instrumental in avoiding conflict by providing the *Conflict By-Pass Cycle*, aimed at either increasing Net-Utility or at engineering Acceptance by Political Persuasion.

Simon (1961) points out that, since the limits of rationality for the decision-making environment of an individual (group) are 'given' by an organization, the same organization can also provide the means to widen them.[11] In this sense, the Business/IT Consensus Process could also function as a 'rationality extending' vehicle:[12]

- Increasing Utility through enforced co-operation of users and IT widens the range of possible options for both parties, i.e. it facilitates the move away from the 'close' – and perhaps entrenched – positions of the main antagonists.
- 'Political Persuasion' can be interpreted as a version of the communications vehicle Simon stipulates as necessary for any 'un-bounding' of rationality. Where such communication reinforces the Global Business Strategy, i.e. the 'decisions above the operational level' in Simon's terms (ibid., p. 243) it not only can initiate a discussion about 'Undue Control' conflicts, but it can also provide a space for their resolution.

The second major role of the Business/IT Consensus Process is in the assurance of up-to-date knowledge of the relevant international environment. Knowledge in the context of IIS needs special considerations. The business and IT environments at each individual location across a global organization change continuously, simultaneously and each at their own pace and direction. This means that the complexity of keeping an up-to-date 'knowledge-base' grows in exponential proportions to the extent of the firm's global network. It increases further with the

---

[11] Simon (1961) pp. 123–219 *passim.*

[12] Ibid., pp. 240ff.

degree of autonomy granted to their local operations. Ensuring that accurate, relevant and up-to-date international knowledge is in place requires a formal environment, adapted to the size and business of the international firm. For smaller firms such as J Lauritzen this can be achieved structurally by centralizing IIS expertise and know-how. PANALPINA, spread over a large number of local offices, however, does not maintain international knowledge on an ongoing basis – this may well be too complex. Instead, relevant knowledge is established on an ad-hoc basis, by assembling a team of the 'best' international business and/or technology experts for each project in hand. The team also functions as the main actor and forum for the Business/IT Consensus Process.

Further research should be devoted to investigating and clarifying the dual role of the Business/IT Consensus process, i.e. as a

1. structural development aid to increase the Utility of the IIS design whilst at the same time facilitating the avoidance, bypass or defusing of any user/IS conflict; and as a
2. procedural incarnation of the firm's 'knowledge-base', as well as a way to manage it's complexity.

A greater number of cases where such a process exists should be analyzed as to the extent to which each of the two roles is present and what the factors are that make it effective (or not). Related to that, the degree of complexity of 'knowledge bases' about the – continually changing – operations of multinational companies should be investigated with a view as to whether it is possible to manage it on an ongoing basis.

10.2 Methodology Notes for Future Research

The use of Grounded Theory methodology for the analysis of large cases in this research project was very successful for eliciting concepts and for the knitting together of the substantive theory. Nevertheless, future researchers may want to refine the method further. Such refinements might address the following issues and experiences:

- The method of open coding generates an enormous wealth of data, the more so the richer the case 'story' is in drama and historic detail. The downside of this 'embarrassment of riches' is that a large amount of concepts are seemingly common for all or any information systems, whether large or small, domestic or international;
- Separating the 'any-system' concepts and categories from those specifically relevant to IIS relies substantially on the experience of the researcher;
- This reliance poses a risk to the quality of the resulting theory in two ways:
  - Lack of objectivity – the individual researcher's bias will determine the shape of the theory;

- Incompleteness – concepts which lie outside the individual researcher's experience may not be discovered, may be ignored if they are or may be wrongly categorized, e.g. an any-system concept allocated to an IIS theorem or vice versa.

In this study, it was possible to counteract these 'any-systems' effects by applying a two-stage approach to theory development:

- In the first instance, after every case the categories discovered in that case were brought into the common pool of all concepts and relationships so far. From there, the theoretical framework was updated and the parameters for theoretical sampling for the next case were set. These updates were carried out until the level of the main concepts' theoretical saturation allowed the formulation of a first substantive theory.
- At that point, the theoretical framework was 'densified', i.e. all redundant concepts/relations were eliminated. This included the identification of 'any-system' theorems and their exclusion from the final grounded theory of *international* information systems.

This may, however, be unwieldy for more cases – the worse so, if they all are of great richness, which is, on the other hand, highly desirable. Refinement of the method in future research needs to resolve this conundrum.

10.3 Strengths and Weaknesses of the Theory: Implications for Future Research

In the context of Information Systems and Social Science, there are many definitions of 'theory'. As set out before, the theory definition adapted for use in this study is Whetten's (1989) four component framework, i.e. a theory consists of

1. *factors*, which are linked in
2. *relationships* that the theory
3. *explains* within its
4. boundaries

Just as there are many theory definitions, there is a plethora of opinion what the criteria of a good theory could be. Weick (1995a), supported by DiMaggio (1995), demands that, overall, a 'good theory explains, predicts and delights'. In this spirit, seven criteria for assessing the quality of the theory developed in this study were distilled from previous research.

Table 10.1. overleaf summarizes these goodness criteria and profiles them according to the contributions from the literature.

Table 10.1. Criteria for assessing the quality of a theory – over view of selected literature

	Glaser, Strauss (1967)	Mayhew (1981)	Pfeffer (1982)	Weick (1989)	Whetten (1989)	Bacharach (1989)	Osigweh, Yg (1989)
Clarity	✓	✓	✓	✓ Plausible*		✓	✓ Theoretical and empirical concepts
Parsimony	✓	✓	✓		✓	✓	✓ Denotation and connotation
Logical coherence	✓	✓	✓	✓ Believable	✓	✓	
Scope	✓				✓	✓	✓ Concept stretching
Integration	✓				✓		
Data Fit & falsifiability	✓			✓ Real		✓ Construct validity	
Utility ('works' in Glaser et al. terms)	✓			✓ Interesting		✓ Explanatory and predictive potential	

* Author specific terminology.

In the following paragraphs the theory will be evaluated and discussed in the light of each of these assessment criteria.

Clarity

Most of the concepts, constructs and variables used in the theory are widely understood and used in the information systems field. Their relationships are expressed in terms of causality, mostly uni-directional but some circular. However, the emphasis of the research was mainly to maximize the scope of the theory. From this perspective, construct clarity was a secondary concern. For this reason, some of the major constructs such as Acceptance, Rejection, Utility and Control are only very broadly defined. This reduced clarity does not seem to affect the validity of the constructs: theoretical sampling (i.e. adding more, and more detailed, descriptions) has resulted in sufficient 'convergent' validity (in Bacharach's (1989) terms). Identifying the constructs over three different cases also establishes an adequate level of 'discriminant' validity (Bacharach, 1989) for them to be able to be used in the relationships set out by the final substantive theory.

Future research, by focusing more narrowly on theoretical samples of different cases and different business structures, should aim at maximizing the concept clarity of a small set of constructs at a time.

Parsimony

This requirement of expressing the theory with the least number of constructs, variables and relationships can itself be expresses as the ratio of the number of 'initial' theory elements to their sum total in the final form.

The rate at which categories were added across the three cases and the way in which this contributed to the growth of the theoretical frameworks stipulated at the end of each case is shown in Table 10.2 below.

Table 10.2. Growth in the number of categories and theory statements across the three cases

	Co-op	J Lauritzen	Panalpina	
	New categories added			Total categories
Raw categories	133	33	27	**193**
Substantive categories	27	8	8	**43**
Core categories	13	4	1	**18**
	Theoretical frameworks (TFW)			Final theory
	1st TFW	*2nd TFW*	*3rd TFW*	
Theorems	9	22	25	**12**
Theses	25	87	102	**23**

In the Grounded Theory methodology two ratios would be relevant as a measure of such 'conceptual redundancy':

1. Comparing initially coded categories with the 'core categories' as the result of secondary, theoretical coding; across all cases, 193 primal categories were coded, resulting in 18 core categories. Although there is no guidance in the literature as to what a desirable ration should be, it seems plausible that a reduction of more than ten-to-one may well indicate a low level of category redundancy;
2. Initially, theoretical statements were added to the preliminary 'theoretical framework' whenever a new or additional relationship emerged. At the end of the third case, the 3rd Theoretical Framework consisted of some 25 theorems, supported by 102 detailed theses and postulates. The subsequent process of 'densification', as prescribed by Glaser et al. (1967), reduced the final theory to just 12 theorems, supported by 23 theses. Again, there are no quantitative criteria in the literature, but such a compression ratio of 2 to 1 and 5 to 1 respectively seems satisfactory.

The theory has been expressed in natural language, which in itself is more redundant than, say, mathematical notation. Future research should investigate to which extent it would be possible to densify the theory further by expressing it in the terms of *qualitative mathematics*[13] or by using formal logic notation. Especially the 'process theory', setting out the stakeholder dynamics, could well lend itself favorably for such a more rigorous formulation.

Logical Coherence

Distinguishing 'process' theory from 'variance' theory, Markus et al. (1988) identify 'Logical Structure' as one of three dimensions of causal structure ('Causal Agency' and 'Level of Analysis' are the others). Both are present in this theory: the dynamics of the stakeholders' interaction form a process theory, whereas the theorems describing and defining the variables involved in these dynamics form a variance theory. The individual theorems are largely logically independent but complement one another. Where applicable, they are also syllogistically sound, i.e. concluding theorems are supported by sufficient presuppositions.

Scope

As a 'substantive' theory, the model claims validity for a specific class of multinational companies, namely those with similar operations in a multitude of different countries around the world. The three cases are different in size and the

[13] Researchers into qualitative reasoning (in the artificial intelligence field) such as Forbus (1997) use this term.

nature of their business is different to a sufficient degree to presume that generalizability beyond their immediate confines is given.

A weakness of the theory is, however, that it is based on a type of technology architecture that is now being eroded and superseded. All three cases follow the 'distributed' information technology paradigm, where a network of independent computers at each local site carries out all the processing. The only allowable exceptions are where CENTRAL information systems are run directly from a head-office computer (such as in J Lauritzen) or are duplicated over several of them (such as in PANALPINA). The emerging 'web-centric' architecture paradigm for global information technology applications, on the other hand, only distinguishes between server and client applications, irrespective of where either is positioned – organizationally or geographically. As this paradigm takes hold throughout multinational firms over the next few years, the theory will need to be adapted accordingly. The part most directly affected will be the 'Technology' part of the theorems relating to I~A~T.

Integration

As shown throughout the discussion above, the theory fits well into a number of frameworks well established, predominantly in the social sciences, but also in information systems research. This goes with the organizational, rather than pure technical, character of the theory.

This good fit, however, can also be an apparent weakness. The fit, particularly with some established 'canons' of information systems development, may be seemingly too good and the theory statements may be considered 'obvious', or just common sense. But as Weick (1989, p. 526) points out, this obviousness may well be 'a clue to significance as well as a clue to triviality'. An example is the stated importance of conceptual capability and knowledge: these requirements may be 'obvious', but their resolution in the context of multinational information systems is all but trivial. Moreover, their high rank as failure factors strongly underlines their significance.

Data Fit and Falsifiability

Reflection of the data by the theory is a given by virtue of the Grounded Theory methodology with which it was developed. The major component of falsifiability, i.e. clarity of the concepts and constructs, is present, if qualified by the wide definition boundaries of some of the concepts.[14] Broad definitions, together with the inherently qualitative nature of some of the variables and concepts, make the establishment of metrics often somewhat strenuous. Measurement, however, is an important prerequisite in the traditional way to falsify models. To overcome this difficulty, Weick (1989) offers the concept of

[14] As outlined above under the 'Clarity' heading.

the *'demonstrable plausibility'* of theories as an indicator of their construct validity to overcome this weakness.

Utility

Glaser et al. (1967) establish this quality of a theory by testing if it 'works', i.e. if it can be used to explain and predict what 'goes on' in a story. A convenient test is the re-telling of the story in the words and concepts of the theory and to see whether this adds to the story. This test was carried out a number of times during theory development:

- The cyclical model of Reaction/Rejection was developed by re-telling the Co-op's case;
- The 'Response Cycles' part of the theorems describing the stakeholder dynamics was further enhanced by re-telling both of the other cases with respect to this particular aspect;
- Similarly, the Utility/Control influence on Acceptance/Rejection was validated – and refined – by re-telling all three cases.

As a mid-range theory, however, it only 'works' within the confines of its substantive context. Future research needs to extend this.

10.4 Implications for the Practitioner

Whilst the learned literature on IIS failures is still very sparse, there are some strong anecdotal pointers. In a survey of major users and builders of IIS, Butler Cox (1991) found that

- 90% of IIS developers have difficulties with the definition of Core versus Local systems;
- Three out of four projects fail to co-ordinate the development effort adequately; and
- One in two fails to engender ownership of the new IIS in the global firm's local people.

Obstacles like these could explain why only 8% of a large sample of European multinational companies managed to implement international systems satisfactorily (KPMG, 1993).

The substantive theory developed in this research has established a number of relationships with direct implications for the practitioners' problems in organizing and managing International Information Systems. The following paragraphs set out the main ramifications for the practical work with IIS.

Assessment of the Synchronicity requirements of the global operations will help identify the application areas that are candidates for Core or Common systems and give a first indication of their Utility. This allows a specification of the CENTRAL systems architecture – from which the LOCAL application systems and technology can be defined by complement. For example, if such an assessment had been carried out in the Co-op's case, it would have identified the asynchronous nature of their operations from the outset. This, in turn, would have clearly indicated that there was no need for a globally standardized information systems and technology.

The CENTRAL architecture contains the structure and inter-relationships of 'Core' and 'Common' applications, ranked by their Utility and the degree that they are required for Synchronicity reasons. Together with the requirements of the largest/most important LOCAL sites, this architecture will then serve as the basis for defining the I~A~T structure of the IIS. With the Co-op's asynchronous operations, i.e. without any Synchronicity to support, there was no Utility in a global system. On that basis, the Co-op should have set out a predominantly distributed I~A~T structure: an *information* standard would have sufficed as there was no need for the same application systems or the same technical platform at all local sites. At a later phase in the implementation of their 'Transnational' strategy perhaps a migration to I=A~T (i.e. using common software) in the area of demand forecasting (to streamline production planning) might have become useful. The attempted, full I=A=T architecture, however, was never needed.

Setting up, as PANALPINA does, a broadly based development team for the design, building and implementation of the IIS with specific emphasis on making the 'best' business experts taking on leadership positions will have two benefits:

- It will avoid a predominance of the domestic mindset and provide the vehicle for obtaining the most up-to-date knowledge – further assuring the Utility of the IIS;
- It will be a forum for the settling of differences and for tat reason its structure has been set up to include executive representation to provide closure in the resolution of conflicts.

The application blueprint defined by Synchronicity and in the I~A~T analyses then provides the means for locating and defining the areas of high conceptual complexity in the design. These can be convoluted data structure issues such as the Co-op's Universal Product Code problem. Or they can be scope-of-knowledge problems, i.e. elements of knowledge that had not been put together and analyzed in their entirety before. The Unified Account Structure project in the Co-op's – misguided – quest for one, global general ledger falls into this category.

The resulting map of high-complexity areas then allows the establishment of task groups specifically skilled, experienced or trained to tackle each of them individually. These groups would either be recruited from the panel of 'best' experts assembled for the development team (see above) or acquired from external sources for problems new to the firm.

The applications architecture is furthermore needed for another important preparatory analysis, the identification of conflict potential due to local cultural diversity/differences. Including the respective local exponents into design and implementation teams with 'central' people should diffuse most possible antagonism. The areas where this fails, however, are then already clearly defined and will be highlighted as candidates for political persuasion.

Reducing the global scope of the IIS to the 'Core' and/or 'Common' applications and their technical architecture allows the local areas to get on with information technology planning for their LOCAL system independently from the centre. The only restrictions placed upon them are the requirements of the CENTRAL systems. As these are by definition the ones with high Utility for the local people, their Acceptance is assured.

An overarching benefit for the practitioner is that the activities suggested by the theory lend themselves to be formulated as a step-by-step methodology. Such a set of guidelines would have a number of advantages. Firstly, it provides an objective means of defining the central/local application split. This objectivity may well eliminate political arguments about it altogether. Furthermore, the development team structure is geared not only to supply sufficient skills and knowledge, but also to provide a forum to resolve cultural and/or political conflict. The broadly based structure also helps to engender ownership of the IIS.

Finally, it allows the parallel building and implementation of the various IIS elements. 'Core' elements would have to be built by a centrally managed team (with multi-local participation). 'Common' elements could be created by teams representing the respective stakeholders and under their control – possibly in parallel to each other. 'LOCAL' information technology would be implemented by each local group independently and entirely to their own timetable – parallel with each other and the central/common teams.

This simultaneity should ameliorate the time squeeze conundrum experienced by the more mature transnational companies, such as PANALPINA. They found that technology changes faster than a new system can be implemented sequentially throughout the global firm: by the time their X.400 email project was fully installed, the Internet and TCP/IP based email had already made it obsolete.

Chapter 11
Conclusion

Nearly thirty years ago Buss (1982) first observed that international information systems are different from domestic ones. Further research has addressed numerous aspects of global applications of information technology – but the question of why these systems are different and how they could be dealt with more successfully had not yet been answered. This research has contributed to bringing clarity into this field. It has resulted in a theory about international information systems that explains

their specific nature and architecture,
what affects the way in which they are built; and
why their users will accept or reject them.

In this, the research has met its purpose, which was to create a theoretical foundation for guiding the creation of information systems for multinational companies.

The first of the two research questions stated at the outset of the project aimed at finding out what is specific about the nature, structure and characteristics of International Information Systems. In response, the theory defines a *generic architecture* for international information systems, consisting of two parts, namely

- A 'Central' part contains 'core' systems, mandatory for *all* business units, and 'common' systems, shared by an undefined number of sites;
- 'Local' systems are unique for their site and managed locally.

The systems configuration at each individual site is a mixture of 'Central' and 'Local' technology elements. Two factors shape this architecture and determine the 'mixture':

1. *Synchronicity*, the degree to which processes and operations at various global sites require online, same-time use of identical data and information. This determines what should be the 'Central' applications – and what can be left 'Local';
2. *I~A~T*, which postulates that the same Information (I) from different sites does not need to come from the same Application systems (I~A); neither do identical

H. Lehmann, *The Dynamics of International Information Systems*,
Integrated Series in Information Systems 23, DOI 10.1007/978-1-4419-5750-4_11,

applications require identical Technology[1] (I~A~T). Synchronicity governs the configuration of I, A and T as a determinant of the technical architecture of the IIS.

Where information systems are important, the split between systems under 'Central' control and those within 'Local' discretion can become an adversarial, often acrimonious and predominantly political issue, which can have disastrous consequences for the enterprise. The insights provided by *Synchronicity* and *I~A~T* can be used to de-politicize this critical decision process by putting it onto a – more – rational basis.

Nevertheless, the existence of an ever present 'Force Field', on which these antagonistic politics are acted out, is an essential construct in the theory of international information systems. IIS add the discord between the centre and regional management to the natural[2] tension between Users and IT people, which *quadruples*[3] the conflict zones active in these systems. This provides the key to why so many IIS projects suffer from seemingly interminable – and often lethal – political infighting.[4] The two related variables that influence the intensity of the Force Field interactions are:

- *Utility* of the system's functionality lowers the conflict potential all around: nobody argues where technology makes work easier, more profitable or helps win more new business; on the other hand,
- using the IIS to increase central *Control* intensifies local management's resistance against invasion of their 'turf'.

The theory shows how the probability of *Acceptance* or *Rejection* of an international information system depends on the net-balance of these opposing forces. It thus creates a clear, simple and practical mechanism for lowering the heat of political antagonism by – once again – providing the means of rational exchange between the actors.

At a more sophisticated level, *User/IT Consensus Processes* are shown as the ultimate instruments for neutering damaging faction politics. By assembling all stakeholders they marshal and maximize the knowledge about the global operation that the IIS supports. This makes *User/IT Consensus Processes* doubly effective: the deep knowledge they generate maximizes the *Utility* of the resulting system, whilst the stakeholder forum de-fuses any 'Control' conflict with rational dialogue or amicable persuasion.

The second research question in this research project was

---

[1] The definition of 'Technology' in the I~A~T context is restricted to hardware and middleware (e.g. operating and communications software) so as to distinguish it from Application software.

[2] That is occurring in any type of information system, whether international or domestic.

[3] Conflict is possible between Central Users and Central IS people as well as Local IS people; Local Users face the same adversaries.

[4] See the previously mentioned anthologies and monographs on large information systems failure, i.e. Glass (1992, 1998), Flowers (1996), Yourdon (1997), Collins et al. (1999).

'What is the nature and interaction of the specific factors that shape an international information systems such that it is acceptable to its users?'

The insights gained into the variables that govern the nature and acceptance of an IIS together with the detailed understanding of the causal dependencies between them discharge this research question in its entirety. Moreover, most of the theory can be directly translated into a practical methodology for designing, building and implementing international information systems. In that sense the theory not only 'works' because it explains and predicts the processes observed in the cases, but it also allows the construction of practitioner guidelines to make the building of these systems more efficient, less risky and therefore more effective.

Many parts of the theory, however, are still in an 'approximate' state, to use Weick's (1995b) terms. They point to several future research projects, concerned with refining concepts, constructs and their relationships as well as further adapting and improving the very methodology used. The usefulness of the theory stemming from this research should thus be taken as no more than a lead to begin work on its replacement – with a wider, more detailed and more up-to-date one. Or, in the words of one of history's more successful leaders[5]:

> "Now this is not the end. It is not even the beginning of the end. But it is, perhaps, the end of the beginning."

[5] Winston Churchill, in a BBC Radiobroadcast, November 10, 1942.

References

Ajimal, K. S. 1985. Force field analysis – A framework for strategic thinking. *Long Range Planning*, 18(5), 55–60.

Alavi, M., Carlson, P. 1992. A review of MIS research and disciplinary development. *Journal of Management Information Systems*, 8(4), 45–62.

Alavi, M., Young, G., 1992. Information technologies in international enterprise: An organizing framework. In: Palvia, S., Palvia, P., Zigli, R. (eds.), *The Global Issues of Information Technology Management*. Idea Group Publishing, Harrisburg, PA, 495–516.

Anderson, E. E. 1989. The implementation of information systems for workers: A structural equation model. *Information Management*, 16(4), 171–186.

Applegate, L. M., McFarlan, F. W., McKenney, J. L., 1996. *Corporate Information Systems Management, Text and Cases*. 4th edition. Irwin, Chicago, IL, 684–691, Chapter 12.

Apte, U. M. Mason, R. O. 1995. Global disaggregation of information-intensive services. *Management Science*, 41(7), 1250–1262.

Atkinson, G. J. 1996. *A study of perception of individual participants of a client group undertaking a series of meetings supported by a group support system*. Unpublished Doctoral Thesis at the Curtin University of Technology, Perth, WA, Australia, 15–307.

Bacharach, S. B. 1989. Organizational theories: Some criteria for evaluation. *Academy of Management Review*, 14(4), 496–515.

Barke, H., Hartwick, J. 1994. Measuring user participation, user involvement and user attitude. *MIS Quarterly*, 18(1), 59–82.

Barsoux, J.-L. 1992. Following the leaders. *International Management*, 47(7), 40–41.

Bartlett, C. A., Ghoshal, S. 1989. *Managing Across Borders: The Transnational Solution*. Harvard Business School Press, Boston, MA, Chapters 2–5.

Bateson, G. 1972. *Steps to an Ecology of Mind: Collected Essays in Anthropology, Psychiatry, Evolution, and Epistemology*. Chandler Publishing Co., San Francisco, CA, 68ff.

Benbasat, I., Goldstein, D. K., Mead, M. 1987. The case research strategy in studies of information systems, *MIS Quarterly*, September, 369–386.

Benney, M., Hughes, E. 1956. Of sociology and the interview: Editorial preface. *American Journal of Sociology*, 62, 137–142.

Brager, G., Holloway, S. 1992. Assessing prospects for organizational change: The uses of force field analysis. *Administration in Social Work*, 16(3,4), 15–28.

Broadbent, M., Weill, P. 1997. Management by maxim: How business and IT managers can create IT infrastructures. *Sloan Management Review*, 38(3), 77–92.

Burn, J. M., Cheung, H. K. 1996. Information systems resource structure and management in multinational organizations. In: Palvia, P. C., Palvia, S. C., Roche, E. M. (eds.), *Global Information Technology and Systems Management – Key issues and Trends*. Ivy League Publishing Ltd, Marietta, GA, 293–324.

Buss, M. D. J. 1982. Managing international information systems. *Harvard Business Review*, Sep/Oct 60(5), 153–162.

Butler Cox plc. 1991. Globalization: The information technology challenge. *Amdahl Executive Institute Research Report*, London, Chapters 3, 5, 6.

Byrd, T A., Marshall, T E. 1997. Relating information technology investment to organizational performance: A causal model analysis. *Omega*, 25(1), 43–56.

Carney, T. F. 1990. *Collaborative inquiry methodology*. University of Windsor, Division for Instructional Development, Windsor, ON, Canada, 78ff.

Cavaye, A., Mantelaers, P., van de Berg, W., Zuurmond, A. 1998. Towards guidelines for development and management of transnational information systems. *The Australian Journal of Information Systems*, 5(2), 34–58.

Chin, W. W., Newsted, P. R. 1995 The importance of specification in causal modeling: The case of end-user computing satisfaction. *Information Systems Research*, 6(1), 73–81.

H. Lehmann, *The Dynamics of International Information Systems*,
Integrated Series in Information Systems 23, DOI 10.1007/978-1-4419-5750-4,

Christmann, T. 1998. Developing a global information vision. *Information Systems Management*, 15(4), 46–54.

Chua, W. F. 1986. Radical developments in accounting thought. *The Accounting Review*, 61, 601–632.

Collins, R. W., Kirsch, L. 1999. *Crossing Boundaries: The Deployment of Global IT Solutions*. Practice-Driven Research in IT Management Series™, Cincinnati, OH, Chapters 4, 5.

Couger, J. D., Higgins, L. F., McIntyre, S. C. 1993 (Un)structured creativity in information systems organizations. *MIS Quarterly*, 17(4), 375–397.

Cummings, M. L., Guynes, J. L. 1994. Information system activities in transnational corporations: A comparison of U.S. and non-U.S. subsidiaries. *Journal of Global Information Management*, 2(1), 12–26.

Deans, C. P., Karwan, K. R. (eds.). 1994. *Global Information Systems and Technology: Focus on the Organization and Its Functional Areas*. Idea Group Publishing, Harrisburg, PA, Chapters 3, 5–8.

Deans, P. C., Jurison, J., 1996. *Information Technology in a Global Business Environment – Readings and Cases*. Chapers 5–7. Boyd & Fraser, New York.

Denzin, N. K., Lincoln, Y. S., 1994. Introduction. In: Denzin, N. K., Lincoln, Y. S. (eds.), *Handbook of Qualitative Research*. Sage Publications, Thousand Oaks, CA, 1–18.

Denzin, N. K. 1994 The art and politics of interpretation. In: Denzin, N. K., Lincoln, Y. S. (eds.), *Handbook of Qualitative Research*. Sage Publications, Thousand Oaks, CA, 500–515.

DiMaggio, P. J. 1995. Comments on 'what theory is *not*'. *Administrative Science Quarterly*, 40, 391–397.

Donovan, A., Laudan, L., Laudan, R. 1988. Testing theories of scientific change. In: *Scrutinising Science – Empirical Studies of Scientific Change*. Kluwer Academic Publishers, Dordrecht, 148–166.

Doz, Y. L. 1980. Management in multinational companies. *Sloan Management Review*, 21(2), 114–137.

Dubin, R. 1969. *Theory Building*. The Free Press, New York, Chapters 3, 5.

Earl, M. J. 1989. *Management Strategies for Information Technology*. Prentice-Hall, London, Chapters 6–8.

Earl, M. J., Feeny, D. F. 1996. Information systems in global business: Evidence from European multinationals. In: Thomas, N., O'Neal, D., Kelly, J. (eds.), *Strategic Renaissance and Business Transformation*. John Wiley & Sons, Chichester, 183–210.

Ehrlich, E. M. 1989. Information Technology, Global Linkage, and U.S. competitiveness. *Vital Speeches*, 55(24), 755–759.

Ein-Dor, P., Segev, E., Orgad, M., 1993. The effect of national culture on IS: Implications for international information systems. *Journal of Global Information Management*, 1(1), 33–44.

Eisenhardt, K. M. 1989. Building theories from case study research. *Academy of Management Review*, 14(4), 532–550.

Elsass, P. M., Veiga, J. F. 1994. Acculturation in acquired organizations: A force-field perspective. *Human Relations*, 47(4), 431–453.

Fernandez, W. D., Lehmann, H. P. 2005. Achieving Rigour And Relevance In Information Systems Studies – Using grounded theory to investigate organsational cases. *Grounded Theory Review*, 5(1), 23–40.

Feyerabend, P. K. 1988. *Against method*. Verso, New York, 31

Flowers, S. 1996. *Software Failure: Management Failure*. John Wiley & Sons, New York, Chapters 3, 4–8, 9.

Fontana, A., Frey, J. H. 1994. Interviewing: The art of science. In: Denzin, N. K., Lincoln, Y. S. (eds.), *Handbook of Qualitative Research*. Sage Publications, Thousand Oaks, CA, 361–376

Forbus, K. D. 1997. Qualitative mathematics. In: *Building and Using Large Common Sense Knowledge Bases*, http://www.teknowledge.com/HPKB/meetings/EastCoastKickoff/Forbus/index.htm, Slide 8.

Freese, L. 1980. Formal theorizing. *Annual Review of Sociology*, 6, 187–212.

Gadamer, H.-G. 1976. The historicity of understanding. In: P. Connerton (ed.), *Critical Sociology, Selected Readings*. Penguin Books Ltd, Harmondsworth, 117–133.

Galliers, R. D. 1991. Choosing information systems research approaches: A revised taxonomy. In: Nissen, H. E., Klein, H. K. Hirschheim, R. (eds.), *Information Systems Research: Contemporary Approaches and Emergent Traditions*. Elsevier Science Publishers (North-Holland), Amsterdam, 327–345.

Galliers, R. D., Land, F. F. 1987. Choosing appropriate information systems research methodologies. *Communications of the ACM*, 30(11), 900–902.

Gallupe, R. B., Tan, F. B. 1999. A research manifesto for global information management. *Journal of Global Information Management*, 7(3), 5–18.

Gibson, R. 1994. Information technology planning and architectures for networked global organizations. In: Palvia, P. C., Palvia, S. C., Roche E. M. (eds.), 1996: *Global Information Technology and Systems Management*. Ivy League Publishing, Nashua, NH, 276–292.

Glaser, B. G. (ed.). 1995. *Grounded Theory: A Reader*. Vols. I and II. Sociology Press, Mill Valley, CA, Chapters 3, 5, 7–14.

Glaser, B. G. 1978. *Theoretical Sensitivity*. Sociology Press, Mill Valley, CA, Chapters 3, 4–7.

Glaser, B. G. 1992. *Emergence vs. Forcing: Basics of Grounded Theory Analysis*. Sociology Press, Mill Valley, CA, Chapters 1, 2, 5, 8, 11.

Glaser, B. G. 1996. Edited Transcript of the Proceedings of a Grounded Theory Workshop conducted by Dr. Barney Glaser in Christchurch, New Zealand, 8–10 May 1996. Unpublished Proceedings, 23.

Glaser, B. G., Strauss, A. L. 1970. Case histories and case studies. (Reprinted from: Glaser, B. G., Strauss, A. L. *Anguish*. Sociology Press, Mill Valley, CA, 1970.) In: Glaser, B. G. (ed.), *More Grounded Theory Methodology: A Reader*. Sociology Press, Mill Valley, CA, 233–245.

Glaser, B. G., Strauss, A. L. 1967. *The Discovery of Grounded Theory*. Aldine Publishing Company, Hawthorne, NY, Chapters 2–12.

Glass, R. L. 1992. *The Universal Elixir and Other Computing Projects Which Failed*. Computing Trends, Bloomington, IN, Chapters 5, 6, 9.

Glass, R. L. 1998. *Software Runaways*. Prentice Hall PTR, Upper Saddler River, NJ, Chapter 3.

Goodman, S. E., Green, J. D. 1992. Computing in the Middle East. *Communications of the ACM*, 35(8), 21–25.

Gordon, S. 1994. Global interconnectivity: Doing business by satellite. *Telecommunications (International Edition)* 28/5, 67–68.

Gregory, F. 1993. Cause, effect, efficiency and soft systems models. *Journal of the Operational Research Society*, 44(4), 333–344.

Grover, V., Segars, A H. 1996. The relationship between organizational characteristics and information system structure: An international survey. *International Journal of Information Management*, 16(1), 9–25.

Grundy, T. 1997. Management accounting for strategic performance. *Management Accounting-London*, 75(11), 63–64.

Guba, E. G., Lincoln, Y. S. 1994. Competing paradigms in qualitative research. In: Denzin, N. K., Lincoln, Y. S., (eds.), *Handbook of Qualitative Research*. Sage Publications, Thousand Oaks, CA, 105–117.

Haig, B. D. 1996. Grounded theory as scientific method. In: *Philosophy of Education 1995*. University of Illinois Press, Urbana, IL, 281–290.

Hamelink, C. J. 1984. *Transnational Data Flows in the Information Age*. Studentlitteratur AB, Lund, Sweden. Chapter 4.

Heitzman, J. 1990. Information systems and development in the third world. *Information Processing and Management*, 26(4), 489–502.

Herrscher, E. G., Herrscher, R. M. 1990. Systemic aspects of hyperinflation in Argentina. *Human Systems Management*, 9(2), 89–105.

Hirschheim, R. A. 1985. User experience with and assessment of participative systems design. *MIS Quarterly*, 9(4), 295–304.

Hsu, C. Bouziane, M., Rattner, L., Yee, L. 1991. Information resources management in heterogeneous, distributed environments: A metadatabase approach. *IEEE Transactions on Software Engineering*, 17(6), 604–625.

Hunton, J. E., Beeler, J. D. 1997. Effects of user participation in systems development: A longitudinal field experiment. *MIS Quarterly*, 21(4), 359–388.

Hurt, F. 1998. Implementing great new ideas through the use of force-field analysis. *Direct Marketing*, 61(1), 54–56.

Husserl, E. 1970. *Logical investigations*, and Husserl, E. 1982. *Ideas pertaining to a pure phenomenology and to a phenomenological philosophy*, cited in Klein, H. K., Myers, M. D. 1999. A set of principles for conducting and evaluating interpretive field studies in information systems. *MIS Quarterly*, 23(1), 67–94.

Hwang, M. I., Thorn, R. G. 1999. The effect of user engagement on system success: A meta-analytical integration of research findings. *Information Management*, 35(4), 229–236.

Ives, B., Jarvenpaa, S. L. 1991. Applications of global information technology: Key issues for management, *MIS Quarterly*, March, 15(1), 33–49.

Ives, B., Jarvenpaa, S. L. 1994. MSAS Cargo International: Global freight management. In: Jelass, T., Ciborra, C. (eds.), *Strategic Information Systems: A European Perspective*. John Wiley and Sons, New York, 230–259.

Ives, B., Jarvenpaa, S. L. 1992. Air Products and Chemicals, Inc: Planning for global information systems. *International Information Systems*, April, 78–99.

Jarvenpaa, S. L. 1988. The Importance of laboratory experimentation in IS research. *Communications of the ACM*, 31, (12), 1502–1504.

Jarvenpaa, S. L., Ives, B. 1993. Organizing for global competition: The fit of information technology. *Decision Sciences*, 24, 547–580.

Jarvenpaa, S. L., Ives, B. 1994. Organizational fit and flexibility: IT design principles for a globally competing firm. *Research in Strategic Management and Information Technology*, 1, 8–39.

Jones, C. 1994. *Assessment and Control of Software Risks*. Yourdon Press, Prentice-Hall, Upper Saddle River, NJ, 29.

Josephson, J. R., Tanner, M. C. 1994. Conceptual analysis of abduction. In: Josephson, J. R., Josephson, S. G. (eds.), *Abductive Inference*. Cambridge University Press, Cambridge, 5–30.

Joshi, K., 1992 A causal path model of the overall user attitudes toward the MIS function: The case of user information satisfaction. *Information Management*, 22(2), 77–88.

Karahanna, E., Straub, D. W. 1999. The psychological origins of perceived usefulness and ease-of-use. *Information Management*, 35(4), 237–250.

Keen, P. G. W. 1992. Planning globally: Practical strategies for information technology strategies in the transnational firm. In: Palvia, S., Palvia, P., Zigli, R. (eds.), *The Global Issues of Information Technology Management*, Idea Group Publishing, Harrisburg, PA, 575–607.

Keen, P. G. W., Bronsema, G. S., Auboff, S. 1982. Implementing common systems: One organization's experience. *Systems, Objectives and Solutions*, (2), 125–142.

Keen, P. G. W. 1991. *Shaping the Future: Business Design through Information Technology*. Harvard Business School Press, Cambridge, MA, Chapters 4, 6.

Kelley, N. 1980. Checkpoints for international data systems. *Infosystems*, 8, 44–48.

Keohane, R. O., Nye, J. S. Jr. 1972. *Transnational Relations and World Politics*. Harvard Business School Press, Cambridge, MA, 34.

King, W. R., Sethi, V. 1993. Developing transnational information systems: A case study. *OMEGA International Journal of Management Science*, 21(1), 53–59.

King, W. R., Sethi, V. 1999. An empirical assessment of the organization of transnational information systems. *Journal of Management Information Systems*, 15(4), 7–28.

King, W. R., Sethi, V. 1992. A framework for transnational systems. In: Palvia, S., Palvia, P., Zigli, R. (eds.), *The Global Issues of Information Technology Management*, Idea Group Publishing, Harrisburg, PA, 214–248.

Klein, H. K., Myers, M. D. 1999. A set of principles for conducting and evaluating interpretive field studies in information systems. *MIS Quarterly*, 21(1), 67–94.

Kneitel, A. M. 1980. Evolving and implementing a worldwide management information system (IMS/MIS). *MIS Quarterly*, 4(3), 31–40

Kobielus, J. 1992. Privacy issues loom as global net hurdle: Part I. *Network World*, 9(3), 27–51.

Konsynski, B. R., Karimi, J. 1993. On the Design of Global Information Systems, in Bradley, S. P., Hausman, J. A., Nolan, R. L. (eds.), *Globalization, Technology, and Competition: The Fusion of Computers and Telecommunications in the 1990s*, Harvard Business School Press, Boston, MA, 81–108.

KPMG Peat Marwick. 1993. Pan-European business systems, London. *KPMG Management Consulting Private Research Report*, Brussels, 3–45.

Kroenke, D., Hatch, R. 1994. *Management Information Systems.* McGraw-Hill, New York, 21–28.

Kuhn, T. S. 1970. *The Structure of Scientific Revolutions.* University of Chicago Press, Chicago, Chapters 3, 4.

LaPlante, A. 1991. Global information officers entering IS picture. *Computerworld*, 25, 33, 70.

Laudon, K. C., Laudon, J. P. 1995, 1997, 1999. *Essentials of Management Information Systems Organization and Technology*. 1st, 2nd and 3rd editions. Prentice Hall, Upper Saddle River, NJ, 454–491 (3rd edition).

LeCompte, M. D., Preissle, J. 1992. Toward an ethnology of student life in schools and classrooms: Synthesizing the qualitative research tradition. In: LeCompte, M. D., Millroy, W. L., Preissle, J. (eds.), *The Handbook of Qualitative Research in Education*. Academic Press, New York (Cited in: Denzin & Lincoln, 1994), 30–31.

Lederer, A. L. Sethi, V. 1992. Root causes of strategic information systems planning implementation problems. *Journal of Management Information Systems*, 9(1), 25–45.

Lederer, A. L. Prasad, J. 1998. A causal model for software cost estimating error. *IEEE Transactions on Software Engineering*, 24(2), 137–148.

Lee, A. S. 1989a. A scientific methodology for MIS case studies. *MIS Quarterly*, 13(1), 32–50.

Lee, A. S. 1989b. Case studies as natural experiments. *Human Relations*, 42(2), 117–137.

Lee, A. S. 1991. Integrating positivist and interpretive approaches to organizational research. *Organization Science*, 2(4), 342–365.

Lehmann, H. P. 1993 Core competence and learning alliances. *Journal for Information Technology*, 8, 217–225, Chapman and Hall, London.

Lehmann, H. P. 1994a. Coupling core competencies – Wiring information technology into the business. In: Hawryszkiewycz, I. T., Underwood, B. A., Glasson, B. C., Weber, R. A. (eds.), *Business Process Re-engineering: Information Systems Opportunities and Challenges*, North-Holland, Oxford, 377–386.

Lehmann, H. P. 1994b. Between heterarchies and serendipity – Exploring the development of international information systems. *Proceedings of the Second European Conference on Information Systems,* Breukelen, Netherlands, 463–485.

Lehmann, H. P. 1995. Reducing the risk of global information systems development – An exploratory study. *Proceedings of the Academy of International Business – US West Region Conference at Thunderbird,* Glendale, Arizona, 26–27 May 1995, Section F2.2, 4.1–4.16.

Lehmann, H. P. 1996a. Towards a specific architecture for international information systems: An exploratory study. *The Journal of International Information Management*, Spring, 5(1), 15–34.

Lehmann, H. P. 1996b. Towards a common architecture paradigm for the global application of information systems. In Glasson, B. C., Vogel, D. R., Bots, P. W. and Nunamaker, J. F. (eds.), *Information Systems and Technology in the International Office Of The Future*, 199–218, Chapman and Hall, London.

Lehmann, H. P. 2000. The fatal politics of multinational information systems: A case study. *Journal of Information Technology Cases & Applications*, 2(3), 40–64, New York.

Lehmann, H. P. 2001. Using grounded theory with technology cases: Distilling critical theory from a multinational information systems development project. *Journal of Global Information Technology Management*, 4, (1), 45–60, Memphis, TN.
Lehmann, H. P. 2003. An object oriented architecture model for international information systems? An exploratory study. *Journal of Global Information Management*, 11(3), 1–18, London.
Lehmann, H. P. 2004. The Australasian produce co-operative: A global information systems project. *Communications of the AIS (CAIS)*, 13, Article 17 March, 2004; as the paper is intended for use as a teaching case, the submission also includes, *The APCO Case – Instructor Materials*, comprising MS PowerPoint presentation (31 Slides) of the case history and analysis; and *Case Teaching Note*; both formatted as web-downloadable documents.
Lehmann, H. P. 2006. European International Freight Forwarders – Information as a strategic product, *Journal of Cases on Information Technology*, 8(1), 63–78.
Lehmann, H. P., Gallupe, R. B. 2005. Information systems for multinational enterprises – Some factors at work in their design and implementation, *Journal of International Management*, 11(4), 28–49.
Lewin, K. 1938. *The Conceptual Representation and the Measurement of Psychological Forces*. Vol. I, No. 4 of the series: Contributions to Psychological Theory. Duke University Press, Durham, NC, Chapters 5, 7–9.
Lewin, K., 1952. *Field Theory in Social Science: Selected Theoretical Papers*. Cartwright, D. (ed.), Tavistock, London, Chapters 5, 8.
Lewis, I. M. 1985. *Social Anthropology in Perspective*. Cambridge University Press, Cambridge, 380ff.
Lincoln, Y. S., Guba, E. G. 1985. *Naturalistic Inquiry*. Sage, Beverly Hills, CA, Chapters 1, 2.
Lindsley, D. H., Brass, D. J., Thomas, J. B. 1995. Efficacy-performance spirals: A multilevel perspective. *Academy of Management Review*, 20(3), 645–678.
Lofland, J., Lofland, L. H. 1995. Analyzing social settings: A guide to qualitative observation and analysis. Wadsworth, New York, Chapters 3, 5, 8.
Maisonrouge, J. G., 1981. Regulation of international information flows. *The Information Society*, 1(1), 17–30.
Mandell, S. L., Grub, P. D. 1979. Survey of multinational corporate computer-based information systems. *European Journal of Operational Research*, 5, 359–367.
Markus, M. L., Robey, D. 1988. Information technology and organizational change: Causal structure in theory and research. *Management Science*, 34(5), 583–598.
Martin, P. Y., Turner, B. A. 1986. Grounded theory and organizational research. *The Journal of Applied Behavioral Science*, 22(2), 141–157.
Maruyama, M. 1968. The second cybernetics: Deviation-amplifying mutual causal processes. In: Buckley, W. (ed.), *Modern Systems Research for the Behavioral Scientist: A Sourcebook*, Aldine, Chicago, IL, 297–313.
Mayhew, B. H. 1981. Structuralism versus Individualism: Part II, ideological and other obfuscations. *Social Forces*. 59, 627–648.
McKeen, J. D., Guimaraes, T., Wetherbe, J. C. 1994. The relationship between user participation and user satisfaction: An investigation of four contingency factors. *MIS Quarterly*, 18(4), 427–451.
Merton, R. K. 1968. *Social Theory and Social Structure*. The Free Press, New York, Chapters 2, 3.
Miles, M. B., Huberman, A. M. 1994. *Qualitative Data Analysis: An Expanded Sourcebook*. 2nd edition. Sage Publications, Thousand Oaks, CA, Chapters 1, 3–5, 7.
Montazemi, A. R. Chan, L. 1990. An analysis of the structure of expert knowledge. *European Journal of Operational Research*. 45(2,3), 275–292.
Moore, S. 1984. Information managers must face the international communication web. *Data Management*, 3, 30–32.
Morgan, G., Smircich, L. 1980 The case for qualitative research. *Academy of Management Review*, 5(4), 491–500.

Myers, M. D. 1997. *Qualitative Research in Information Systems.* 'Living work' first published May 1997 in MISQ Discovery at http://www.misq.org/misqd961/isworld/ Section: *Introduction.*

Nelson, C., Treichler, P. A., Grossberg, L. 1992. Cultural studies. In: Grossberg, L., Nelson, C., Treichler, P. A. (eds.), *Cultural Studies*. Routledge, New York, 1–16.

Nelson, K. G. 1996. Global information systems quality: Key issues and challenges. *Journal of Global Information Management*, 4(4), 4–14.

Neo, B. S. 1991. Information technology and global competition: A framework for analysis. *Information and Management (Netherlands)*, 20(3), 151–160.

Nicholas, J. M. 1989. Successful project management: A force-field analysis. *Journal of Systems Management*, 40(1), 24–30, 36.

Nicholas, J. M. 1990. *Managing Business and Engineering Projects: Concepts and Implementation*. 1st edition. Prentice Hall Inc, London, Chapter 3.

O'Brien, J. A. 1998. *Introduction to Information Systems: An Internetworked Enterprise Perspective*. Irwin McGraw-Hill, Boston, MA, Chapter 8.

Orlikowski, W. J. 1993. CASE tools as organizational change: Investigating incremental and radical changes in systems development. *MIS Quarterly*, September, 17(3), 309–337.

Orlikowski, W. J., Baroudi, J. J. 1991. Studying information technology in organizations. *Information Systems Research*, March, 2(1), 1–28.

Orlikowski, W. J. 1995. *Organizational change around groupware.* Working Paper CCS 186, Massachusetts Institute of Technology.

Osigweh, C. A. B. 1989. Concept fallibility in organizational science. *Academy of Management Review*, 14(4), 579–594.

Palframan, D. 1991. The great software sort-out. *Management Today*, 86.

Palvia, P. C. 1998. Global information technology research: Past, present and future. *Journal of Global Information Technology Management*, 1(2), 12–32.

Palvia, P. C. 1995. Global management support systems: A new frontier. *Journal of Global Information Management*, 3(1), 3–4.

Passino, J. H. Jr. 1990. Harnessing the potential of information technology for support of the new global organization. *Human Resource Management*, 29(1), 69–76.

Paulk, M. C., Weber, C. V., Curtis, W., Chrissis, M. B. 1994. *The Capability Maturity Model: Guidelines for Improving the Software Process*. Addison Wesley Longman Inc., Reading, MA, Chapter 1.

Peppard, J. 1999. Information management in the global enterprise: An organizing framework. *European Journal of Information Systems*, 8(2), 77–94.

Pettigrew, A. M. 1985 Contextualist research and the study of organizational change processes. In: Mumford, E., Hirschheim, R., Fitzgerald, G., Wood-Harper, A. T. (eds.), *Research Methods in Information Systems*. Proceedings of the IFIP WG 8.2 Colloquium, Manchester Business School, 1–3 September 1984. Amsterdam, North Holland, 53–78.

Pettigrew, A. M. 1990. Longitudinal field research on change: Theory and practice. *Organization Science*, 1(3), 267–292.

Pfeffer, J. 1982. *Organizations and Organizational Theory.* Ballinger Publishing Company, Cambridge, MA, Chapters 2, 3.

Popper, K. R. 1935. *Logik der Forschung.* 1. Auflage, Tübingen, Chapter 3.

Popper, W. J. 1990. In pursuit of foreign affairs. *Computerworld*, 24, 19, 96.

Porter, M. E., Millar, V. E. 1985. How information gives you competitive advantage. *Harvard Business Review*, January/February, 76–95, Harvard Business School Publishing, Cambridge, MANAGEMENT.

Prahalad, C. K., Doz, Y. L. 1987. *The Multinational Mission: Balancing Local Demands and Global Vision.* The Free Press, New York, Chapter 12.

Prahalad, C. K., Hamel, G. 1990. The core competence of the corporation. *Harvard Business Review*, January/February, 55–78, Harvard Business School Publishing, Cambridge, MANAGEMENT.

Reck, R. M. 1989. The shock of going global. *Datamation*, 1 August, 67–69.

Robey, D., Rodriquez-Diaz, A. 1989. The Organizational and cultural context of systems implementation: Case experience from Latin America. *Information and Management (Netherlands)*, 17(4), 229–239.

Roche, E. M. 1992a. Managing systems development in multinational corporations: Practical lessons from 7 case studies. In: Palvia, S., Palvia, P., Zigli, R. (eds.), *The Global Issues of Information Technology Management*, Idea Group Publishing, Harrisburg, PA, 630–354.

Roche, E. M. 1992b. *Managing Information Technology in Multinational Corporations*. Macmillan, New York, Chapters 5, 8.

Roche, E. M., 1996. The multinational enterprise in an age of the internet and electronic commerce. In: Palvia, P. C., Palvia, S. C., Roche, E. M. (eds.), *Global Information Technology and Systems Management – Key Issues and Trends*. Ivy League Publishing Ltd, Nashua, NH, 424–440.

Sabherwal, R. 1999. The relationship between information system planning sophistication and information system success: An empirical assessment. *Decision Sciences*, 30(1), 137–167.

Sankar, C., Apte, U., Palvia, P. 1993. Global information architectures: Alternatives and trade-offs. *International Journal of Information Management*, 13, 84–93.

Saraswat, S. P., Gorgone, J. T. 1991. Multinational issues in information technology: A perspective from less developed countries. *Information and Management*, 21(2), 111–121.

Sauvant, K. P. 1986. *International Transactions in Services: The Politics of Transborder Data Flows*. Westview Press, Boulder, CO, Chapters 1–3.

Schutz, A. 1967. *Collected Papers*, Vol. 1, Natanson, M., (ed.), Martinus Nijhoff, The Hague, 59; cited in: Schwandt, T. A. 1994. Constructivist, interpretivist approaches to human inquiry. In: Denzin, N. K., Lincoln, Y. S. (eds.), *Handbook of Qualitative Research.* Sage Publications, Thousand Oaks, CA, 118–137.

Schwandt, T. A. 1994. Constructivist, interpretivist approaches to human inquiry. In: Denzin, N. K., Lincoln, Y. S. (eds.), *Handbook of Qualitative Research.* Sage Publications, Thousand Oaks, CA, 118–137.

Selig, G. J. 1982. *Strategic Planning for Information Resource Management: A Multinational Perspective*. UMI Press, Ann Arbor, MI, Chapter 1.

Selye, H. 1964. *From Dream to Discovery – On Being a Scientist.* McGraw-Hill, New York, Chapter 14.

Sethi, V., Olson, J. E. 1993 An integrating framework for information technology issues in a transnational environment. In *Global Issues in Information Technology*, Idea Publishers, Harrisburg, PA, 227–253.

Simon, H. A., 1961. *Administrative Behavior: A Study of Decision-Making Processes in Administrative Organization*. 2nd edition. The Macmillan Company, New York, Chapter 3.

Simon, S. J., 1996. An informational perspective on the effectiveness of headquarters-subsidiary relationships: Issues of control and co-ordination. In: Palvia, P. C., Palvia, S. C., Roche, E. M. (eds.), *Global Information Technology and Systems Management – Key issues and Trends,* Ivy League Publishing Ltd, Nashua, NH, 249–275.

Stake, R. E. 1994. Case studies. In: Denzin, N. K., Lincoln, Y. S. (eds.), *Handbook of Qualitative Research.* Sage Publications, Thousand Oaks, CA, 236–247.

Stern, P. N. 1994. Grounded theory methodology: Its uses and processes. In: Glaser, B. G. (ed.), *More Grounded Theory Methodology: A Reader*. Sociology Press, Mill Valley, CA, 102–123.

Strauss, A. L. 1987. *Qualitative Analysis for Social Scientists*. Cambridge University Press, New York, Chapters 2–5.

Strauss, A., Corbin, J. 1990. *Basics of Qualitative Research – Grounded Theory Procedures and Techniques*. Sage Publications, London, Chapters 2–9.

Strauss, A., Corbin, J. 1994. Grounded theory methodology: An overview. In: Denzin, N. K., Lincoln, Y. S. (eds.), *Handbook of Qualitative Research.* Sage Publications, Thousand Oaks, CA, 273–285

Strebel, P., Valikangas, L. 1994. Organizational change processes in a force field. *International Review of Strategic Management*, 5, 233–262.

Sutherland, J. W. 1975. *Systems: Analysis, Administration and Architecture.* Van Nostrand, New York, Chapters 4, 6.

Sutton, R. I., Staw, B. M. 1995. What theory is not. *Administrative Science Quarterly*, 40, 371–384.

Targowski, A. S., 1996. *Global Information Infrastructure – The Birth, Vision and Architecture.* Idea Group Publishing, London, Chapters 1, 4.

Thomas, J. 1985. Force field analysis: A new way to evaluate your strategy. *Long Range Planning*, 18(6), 54–59.

Thompson, J. M., Faigle, T. W., Short, J. E. 1987. Competing through information technology: We are the world. *Information Strategy,* 3(4), 32–38.

Tractinsky, N., Jarvenpaa, S. L. 1995. Information systems design decisions in a global versus domestic context. *MIS Quarterly*, 19(4), 507–534.

Turner, B. A. 1983. The use of grounded theory for the qualitative analysis of organizational behavior. *Journal of Management Studies*, 20(3), 333–348.

Van den Berg, W., Mantelaers, P. 1999. Information systems across organizational and national boundaries: An analysis of development problems. *Journal of Global Information Technology Management*, 2(2), 32–65.

Wartofsky, M. W. 1968. *Conceptual Foundations of Scientific Thought*. Macmillan, New York, 26–28.

Weber, M. 1947. *The Theory of Social and Economic Organizations.* Oxford University Press, New York, Chapter 1, 67.

Weick, K. E. 1989. Theory construction as disciplined imagination. *Academy of Management Review*, 14(4), 516–531.

Weick, K. E. 1995a. What theory is not, theorizing is. *Administrative Science Quarterly*, 40, 385–390.

Weick, K. E. 1995b. 'Theory'. In: Nicholson, N. (ed.) and Schuler, R., Van de Ven, A. (Advisory eds.), *The Blackwell Encyclopedic Dictionary of Organizational Behavior*. Oxford Blackwell Business, Cambridge, MA, 563–565.

Weick, K. E. 1979. *The Social Psychology of Organizing.* Addison Wesley, Reading, MA, Chapters 3–5.

Weill, P. 1992. The role and value of information technology infrastructure: Some empirical observations. *Working Paper No. 8, University of Melbourne*, Melbourne, July 1992.

Weill, P., Broadbent, M. 1994. Infrastructure goes industry specific. *MIS Quarterly*, July, 35–39.

Weill, P., Broadbent, M. 1998. *Leveraging the New Infrastructure: How Market Leaders Capitalize on Information Technology*. Harvard Business School, Boston, MA, Chapters 3, 5.

Weill, P. 1993. The role and value of information technology infrastructure: Some empirical observations. In: Banker, R., Kauffman, R., Mahmood, M. A. (eds.), *Strategic Information Technology Management: Perspectives on Organizational Growth and Competitive Advantage.* Idea Group Publishing, Middleton, PA, 188–210.

Weill, P., Broadbent, M., St. Clair, D. 1994. Information technology value and the role of information technology infrastructure investments. In: Luftman, J. (ed.), *Strategic Alignment*, Oxford University Press, Oxford, 55–83.

Weill, P., Broadbent, M., Butler, C., Soh, C. 1995. Firm-wide information technology infrastructure investment and services. *Proceedings of the 16th International Conference on Information Systems*, Amsterdam, 181–202.

Weinstein, D., Weinstein, M. A. 1991. Georg Simmel: Sociological flaneur bricoleur. *Theory, Culture & Society*, 8, 151–168.

Whetten, D. A. 1989. What constitutes a theoretical contribution? *Academy of Management Review*, 14(4), 490–495.

Wolf, A. 1922. *Essentials of Scientific Method.* George Allen & Unwin Ltd, London, 48–55, 63ff.

Yin, R. K. 1989. *Case Study Research: Design and Methods*. Sage Publications, Newbury Park, CA, Chapters 2–9.

Yoong, S. P. 1996. *A grounded theory of reflective facilitation: Making the transition from traditional to GSS facilitation*. Unpublished Doctoral Thesis at the Victoria University of Wellington, New Zealand, 10–295.

Yourdon, E., 1997. *Death March: The Complete Software Developer's Guide to Surviving Mission Impossible Projects*. Prentice Hall PTR, Upper Saddler River, NJ, Chapter 5.

Zetterberg, H. L. 1965. *On Theory and Verification in Sociology*. The Bedminster Press, New York, Chapters 3, 6–8.

Ziman, J. 1984. *An Introduction to Science Studies*. Cambridge University Press, Cambridge, Chapter 1.

Zinatelli, N., Cavaye, A. 1994. Case study research in information systems: Strategies for success and pitfalls to avoid. *New Zealand Journal of Information Systems*, 5(1), 33–57.

Index

K

L

M

N

O

P

Q

R

S

T

U

V

Lightning Source UK Ltd.
Milton Keynes UK
UKOW04n1511170414

230178UK00007B/75/P